A New Scotland

'The push for Scottish devolution came with a well-respected agenda for political reform. What would be the equivalent agenda for Scottish independence? This book provides an impressive list of ways to connect constitutional change to social justice reform.'
—**Paul Cairney, Professor of Politics and Public Policy, University of Stirling**

'An important contribution to the debate about the state of our society. It comes against a backdrop of rising social and economic inequality, class division and poverty impacting on too many of our fellow citizens.'
—**Neil Findlay, former councillor in West Lothian and Labour MSP**

'A refreshing and challenging antidote to the stale arguments currently dominating Scottish politics. It roots debate firmly in the search for equality, fairness and sustainability with an impressive array of contributors, ideas and critiques.'
—**James Mitchell, Professor of Public Policy, University of Edinburgh**

A New Scotland

Building an Equal, Fair and Sustainable Society

Edited by Gregor Gall

First published 2022 by Pluto Press
New Wing, Somerset House, Strand, London WC2R 1LA

www.plutobooks.com

British Library Cataloguing in Publication Data
A catalogue record for this book is available from the British Library

ISBN   978 0 7453 4507 9   Hardback
ISBN   978 0 7453 4506 2   Paperback
ISBN   978 0 7453 4510 9   PDF
ISBN   978 0 7453 4508 6   EPUB

This book is printed on paper suitable for recycling and made from fully managed and sustained forest sources. Logging, pulping and manufacturing processes are expected to conform to the environmental standards of the country of origin.

Typeset by Stanford DTP Services, Northampton, England

Simultaneously printed in the United Kingdom and United States of America

To Bob Thomson, for ensuring – without fear, favour or any financial recompense – that the Jimmy Reid Foundation, the progenitor of this collection, has survived and prospered since its launch in 2011.

Contents

List of Figures   x

Acknowledgements   xi

About the Jimmy Reid Foundation (JRF)   xii

Foreword   xiii
Rozanne Foyer

Introduction: Social Justice in Scotland   1
Gregor Gall

PART I: KEY ISSUES

1. The Structural Development of Poverty and
   Inequality   11
   Carlo Morelli and Gerry Mooney

2. Towards Climate Justice   23
   Mary Church, Niamh McNulty and Eurig Scandrett

3. Neo-liberalism and Scotland   35
   George Kerevan

4. Economic Democracy and Public Participation   47
   Andrew Cumbers and Robert McMaster

5. Re-thinking Public Ownership for an Independent
   Scotland   60
   Alex de Ruyter and Geoff Whittam

6. Can Democracy Go Hand-in-hand with
   Efficiency?   72
   David Erdal and John Bratton

PART II: POLICY AREAS

7. Towards an Effective Right to Housing in Scotland 85
   Regina Serpa and Emma Saunders

8. Creating a Healthier Scotland 97
   Iain Ferguson and Gerry McCartney

9. Improving Learning: Education after the Pandemic 109
   Brian Boyd, Larry Flanagan, Henry Maitles and Mary Senior

10. Income, Wealth and Inequality in Scotland 121
    Mike Danson and Francis Stuart

11. Fiscal Policy in Scotland: Under Devolution and Under Independence 136
    Jim Cuthbert

12. Governing Scotland 148
    Robin McAlpine, James Henderson and Claire Bynner

13. Decent Work in Scotland – a Charter for Change 160
    Jane Carolan, Ruth Dukes and Eleanor Kirk

14. Alienation and Exclusion to Empowerment and Inclusion? Human Rights in Scotland 171
    Carole Ewart, Janis McDonald and Sean Whittaker

15. Towards Gender Justice: Enhancing Participation, Reimagining Economics and Ending Gender-based Violence 183
    Kirsty Alexander and Jenny Morrison

16. Race and Migration in Scotland 195
    Gareth Mulvey, Talat Ahmed and Colin Clark

17. Land Ownership and Community Development 207
    Mike Danson and Craig Dalzell

18. Confounding the Capitalist Car-centric Culture 219
*Caitlin Doyle Cottrill, Ellie Harrison and
David Spaven*

PART III: POLITICAL PRACTICE

19. Leisure and Culture 235
Kathryn A. Burnett and Douglas Chalmers

20. Radical Scotland 246
Rory Scothorne and Ewan Gibbs

21. Social Democracy and Labourism 258
Alex Law and Kenny MacAskill

22. 'The People's Parliament', Political Classes and
'the Missing Scotland' 270
Gerry Hassan and Hannah Graham

23. Community Campaigns – the Power to Change 282
*Willie Sullivan, Lynn Henderson, Linda Somerville
and Ruth Lightbody*

24. Constitutional Conundrums: Is There Still a
Third Way? 294
Michael Keating

Afterword: From National to Local 305
Dave Watson

Contributors' Biographies 313
Index 325

Figures

1.1 Income growth by income percentiles, 1988–2008   19
4.1 Economic Democracy Index: rankings by OECD
     member state, 2017   52
4.2 The relationship between the EDI and poverty   54
4.3 The relationship between the EDI and inequality   54
5.1 Private and social benefits of consumption of merit
     goods   64
10.1 Share of total wealth in each 2% wealth band, and
     share of total household income in each 2% income
     band, Scotland, 2016–2018   122
10.2 The labour share, unadjusted for mixed income   124
10.3 Union membership and top 1% share of income
     in the UK   124
10.4 Number of industrial stoppages (UK) and income
     inequality (GB)   125

Acknowledgements

Thanks are due to all the authors for contributing to this collection, given it merely added to their workloads during the demanding period of the pandemic. Particular thanks are due to Mike Danson for his help in the initial stages of preparing this project. Although the professional-managerial class comes in for criticism in this collection, it should be noted that not all its members are culpable. Certainly, those contributing to this collection as academics, practitioners and policy analysts are also activists of different sorts, and it is their commitment to this activism to achieve radical social change that not only marks them out as being different, but also being willing to contribute to the collection.

About the Jimmy Reid Foundation (JRF)

The JRF (https://reidfoundation.scot/) is a registered charity (SC051331) which seeks through the advancement of education to raise critical understanding and analytical and intellectual skills among the general public on key contemporary issues in Scottish society through conducting structured and well-balanced research and writing, based upon evidence, analysis and reasoning. It is concerned with not only diagnosis through critique, but also prognosis, in terms of proffering an array of progressive options for ameliorating economic, environmental, human rights and social issues. The JRF is pleased to work with Pluto Press in this regard.

Foreword

Rozanne Foyer

I was delighted to be invited to write the Foreword to this book on building a fairer Scotland, because on first sight of the chapters and names of the contributors, I could already see that it was going to be a stimulating read. Having now read its contents, it did not disappoint. But that is not to say it was an easy or a light read, because it is a challenging collection. I would not recommend attempting to read it straight through, because your head may well explode with the sheer breadth and volume of the issues it explores and the facts, figures and ideas it contains! Rather, this book should be viewed as a comprehensive, wide-ranging collection of very well evidenced and argued, often standalone, essays covering all essential aspects of Scotland's society, democracy and economy. It requires a slow and deliberate approach and should be dipped into, reading the chapters one by one and ensuring time to process, react to and mull over the content. Each of the chapters in their own ways are challenging, they are educational, and they demand your complete concentration and consideration.

The chapters are delivered by an impressive range of progressive academics, economists, policy-makers, campaigners and trade unionists who have a high degree of experience in their respective fields and seek not only to identify the key problems we face, but to set out solutions that can put Scotland firmly on the road to rebuilding a fairer economy and society. Many of the 24 chapters are written in a collaborative way by more than one author, which gives a real sense of a collective endeavour, bringing their expertise together to develop and promote a shared vision. This book represents a huge combined effort by nearly 60 contributors who know their various subject areas very well indeed.

One of the fundamental themes running through almost all of the chapters is the need, if we are to make any substantive and manifest progress towards a genuinely fairer society, for us to address and eliminate the all-encompassing, institutionalised neo-liberal strictures. This is because they underpin and adversely influence almost all aspects of our economic systems, laws, democratic structures, fiscal arrangements and public services, making a change in approach in any one area a deeply difficult prospect without a wholesale reappraisal of direction.

For example, in Chapter 11 looking at fiscal policy under devolution and any future independence, Jim Cuthbert lays out in detail how the current UK taxation system and fiscal settlement has been designed to disable socially progressive government and actively encourage a neo-liberal approach to running our economy. On the constitutional question, there are a variety of views and opinions within these pages, but the one I most concur with is where George Kerevan states in Chapter 3: 'Independent or not, Scotland and its people will have to escape the siren embrace of neo-liberalism if they are to prosper.'

Similarly, in Chapter 8 on creating a healthier Scotland, Iain Ferguson and Gerry McCartney conclude that much-needed reforms in health and social care are 'unlikely to be realised unless we are able to create a powerful grassroots movement which insists that our health and social well-being should take precedence over the interests and priorities of neo-liberal capitalism'. And in Chapter 9 on improving education and learning after the pandemic, Bryan Boyd, Larry Flanagan, Henry Maitles and Mary Senior assert that 'the neo-liberal model of education provision should be effectively eliminated' and that early years to universities education should be seen as public and societal goods.

There are also some stark facts on display about the gravity of the state we are in when it comes to the growing inequality that exists in Scotland. For example, in Chapter 10 Mike Danson and Francis Stuart observe that 'Scotland's two richest families now have as much wealth as the poorest 20% of the population.' Meanwhile, in Chapter 6 David Erdal and John Bratton assert that the financialisation of our economy has fuelled income inequality, noting that 'in 1998–2020, typical FTSE 100 chief executive pay rose from 48 to 120 times a typical full-time worker's pay'.

In Chapter 15 on gender, Kirsty Alexander and Jenny Morrison argue that tackling gender inequality is not simply about women breaking the 'glass ceiling' and being in key decision-making roles, but also about our addressing the 'sticky floor' and the serious structural pay inequalities affecting those roles traditionally seen as women's work. Meanwhile, in Chapter 16 Gareth Mulvey, Talat Ahmed and Colin Clark address Scotland's historical amnesia when it comes to racism and owning up to its role in imperialism and the slave trade, concluding that a more progressive Scotland can only be realised if neo-liberalism is countered.

Other key themes running through these pages include the need for increased democracy at community level, in our institutions, in our economy and our workplaces, alongside new models of public sector and municipal ownership. Another is the need for serious investment in our public services and a rebalancing of our economy through taxing the rich. A further one is the need to enforce the 'Fair Work' agenda, transforming it from rhetoric to reality, starting by fully using the powers Scotland already has as well as extending sectoral bargaining across key areas.

As head of the Scottish Trades Union Congress, which is highly engaged in arguing for a 'People's Recovery' for Scotland, there was much within these chapters to agree with, and they were stuffed full of useful information that I will undoubtedly deploy going forward. For me, this book is a 'must read' as well as an ongoing resource. It is for anyone in Scotland's campaigning and policy development field who is interested in exploring the steps required to shift Scotland onto a different track, towards a fairer, a more equal and a more socially just society. It may not contain all the answers, but it is definitely asking the right questions, and I hope it will get you thinking about exactly how we can make the changes Scotland so desperately needs.

Introduction:
Social Justice in Scotland

Gregor Gall

Where stands social justice in Scotland two decades into the new millennium? In the summer of 2021, data were released on the ever-rising tide of deaths from drug use in Scotland. These were followed by statistics on death from alcohol abuse. Alongside them stood figures on educational attainment. All three showed clear patterns of social inequality in Scotland – not just class inequality, but also inequality within a class. In other words, the most deprived areas showed considerably higher mortality rates and considerably lower attainment rates. To these can be added a study later in the summer of 2021 on the preponderance of betting shops and their location in areas of greatest deprivation. Here, Glasgow had the second highest concentration in Britain. Issues of growing food and fuel poverty merely add to this litany. The pandemic is only likely to have accentuated these trends. Meanwhile, the 'Who Runs Scotland?' investigation by The Ferret in 2021[1] revealed further evidence of the other side of the inequality equation, namely the wealth and influence of the ruling class and its linked lieutenants, often encased within the professional-managerial class (PMC). Scotland continues to be a rich country by global standards: it is a wealthy country full of poor people, where poverty constitutes much more than wealth and income. Both sides of the equation exist despite,

1   https://theferret.scot/tag/who-runs-scotland/.

some would argue, significant efforts by successive Scottish Governments since devolution to achieve social justice. Some others would go further and suggest they also exist to a significant degree exist *because* of the actions of successive Scottish Governments. Put another way, and contrary to pronounced policies, Scottish Governments have chosen not to act to challenge the vested interests creating and perpetuating social inequality, or have even co-operated in their perpetuation.

So inequality still scars society in Scotland after more than 20 years of devolution, whether gauged by the likes of wealth, life expectancy or educational attainment. Devolution, therefore, has not provided the shield some expected and hoped for against a right-wing, neo-liberal Westminster agenda. Sometimes, this has been attributed to the limited nature of the devolved settlement, and sometimes, as alluded to above, to the choices made by the dominant, left-of-centre, mainstream parties at Holyrood. To this, we could add that some believe – from the right as well as left – that those expectations, for other reasons, were unrealistic. Three key issues arise from these few words of introduction so far. The first concerns social justice, the second the embedded political system in Scotland, and the third the prospects for future change.

All mainstream left-of-centre political parties (Greens, Labour, SNP) in Scotland subscribe to the political ideal of social justice, best epitomised by the pursuit of a 'fairness' agenda. This is part of the problem because, conceptually, there is such elasticity to social justice and its subsidiary, 'fairness'. Indeed, one can convincingly make the case that the domination of the social equality discourse in Scotland means that not even the Conservatives openly advocate social inequality, as Thatcher did, to be their driver of prosperity and freedom. The result is that political debate is stupefied where radicalism is both practically deflected and rhetorically accommodated by this dominant discourse. And all this takes place during the epoch of neo-liberalism. Social democracy in Scotland has been pushed back to a shrunken continuing core by neo-liberalism. Often, the extremely limited new state intervention is to salvage enterprises from the ravages of capitalist market forces, rather than pro-actively taking control of strategic sectors for public benefit. Other than the Scottish Greens and a short-lived period for Scottish Labour (under Richard Leonard's leadership), social democracy barely exists as a political ideal. The SNP claims on its website to be 'Centre left and social democratic', but neo-liberalism in its various guises (like the 'social liberalism' of the SNP) has captured and colonised the public and private institutions of economic, political and social governance in Scotland, where intentions inform processes and processes inform outcomes.

For some, all this points the way to independence rather than enhanced devolution, especially as the 'British road' to social democracy (under the Corbyn project) has ebbed away. But if the case for independence is to be a strong one in terms of achieving social equality, it must be predicated on breaking from these conventions and constraints in order to convincingly answer the questions: independence *from* what and *from* whom, and independence *for* what and *for* whom? It would be somewhat myopically naïve to expect the SNP, given its record in office as well as its policy pronouncements on the future of Scotland, to be the party which will make this break. Equally, the same argument can be made about Scottish Labour, should it return to anything approaching political dominance under enhanced devolution. This leaves the issue of the Scottish Greens. As a small party, it is nowhere near being in contention to be a major player (even on environmental issues), and it remains to be seen what will come of its formal pact with the SNP. This brief consideration bluntly lays out the challenges to securing the required radical outcomes to manifestly reduce social inequality on the path to achieving social equality itself.

For social justice to become useful and meaningful, the principles of distributive justice must become dominant. These span elements of economic, social, environmental and political justice, and encompass norms of equity, equality and egalitarianism as well as the components of power, resources, need, costs and responsibility. More concretely, distributive justice is based upon stipulating qualitative and quantitative aspects of outcomes in terms of setting maximum relativities between social intersections of class, gender, age, race etc. Here, equality of access replaces the spurious notion of equality of opportunity so that equalities of outcome can be achieved, where just distribution over time then becomes less dependent upon greatest benefit necessarily being given to the least advantaged, as there is both levelling up and down.

Therefore, the idea of pre-distribution is highly pertinent (see Chapter 9). It is an idea some may recall from the brief time when then Labour leader Ed Miliband flirted with it in 2012. As with many other ideas, there are varying conceptions of it. Some take the form of corporate social responsibility or liberal notions of a singular national interest. By contrast, the more substantive – and radical – versions believe the state should take steps to prevent inequalities occurring in the first place, rather than seeking to ameliorate them after they have occurred via tax and benefits, as happens with policies of redistribution. Such radical conceptualisations could range from social democracy to even socialism. In any case, ownership of the means of production, distribution and exchange as well as other sources of wealth and income would be vastly widened out (see, for example, Chapters 6 and 17). Modern social democracy is ordinarily defined as the state substantially intervening in the processes and outcomes of the market in order to amend and ameliorate capitalism's consequences, as was the case after the Second World War with the likes of nationalisation of key sectors, price controls (e.g., food, rent), free further and higher education, and mass public house building. This, then, does not involve abolishing the market. A pre-distribution version of social democracy would see far greater emphasis put upon controlling the processes by which capitalism functions so that less *post facto* intervention is needed. Examples might be maximum wages (where the maximum ratio between wages is 1:4) or minimum incomes to reduce wage inequality. The former was a policy idea briefly rekindled during the global financial crisis, especially in the financial services sector because of the state bailouts, but, alas, without much impact. The latter is no longer such a seemingly outlandish idea after the experience of furlough, where the state paid for and guaranteed a minimum income to millions (see also Chapter 10 on Citizens' Basic Income). Levelling up for some would be achieved by levelling down for others. There is, then, a clear and forceful logic to pre-distribution rather than post-redistribution. That said, the challenges in achieving it are potentially even greater because it poses a starker challenge to the vested interests of capitalists and capitalism – if for no other reason than there is less scope for tax avoidance and tax evasion under pre-distribution. Unfortunately, Miliband's version was essentially about saying to voters and vested interests that reversing the austerity following the global financial crisis was not possible, so a rather vague commitment was given to alternative means. Even this did not make it into Labour's 2015 general election manifesto.

The significance of pre-distribution not only lies in rethinking the traditional left reformist and social democratic demands for wealth and power redistribution, because it is also has three other significant characteristics. First, to go beyond merely suggesting the alternative to the liberal market economy (LME), is the co-ordinated market economy (CME). Much centre-left thought has been trapped within the 'varieties of capitalism' thinking following the publication of Hall and Soskice's *Varieties of Capitalism: The Institutional Foundations of Comparative Advantage* (2001), where the political lesson being proffered is that German, Japanese and Swedish forms of CME capitalism are preferable to those of neo-liberalism, namely Australian and Anglo-American LME capitalism – and for reasons of efficiency of wealth generation and equity of wealth distribution. Such CMEs are not even examples of modern social democracy. Second, to advocate 'nudging' is not enough. Another seminal book has been Thaler and Sunstein's *Nudge: Improving Decisions About Health, Wealth, and Happiness* (2008). Emanating from behavioural economics, nudges are informational signals, both direct and indirect, in a market system which can, by changing the architecture of choice, influence behaviour and decision-making processes. Nudges are not based upon education, legislation or enforcement. Nudges can be useful, but they are not up to the scale of the task at hand, take as a given the pre-existing power structures of the current system, and are primarily directed at individuals. Third, 'radical' is an oft used term, but pre-distribution is manifestly radical, in that it both focuses upon the roots of the situation (as per the original Latin meaning) and proposes fundamental – even if not revolutionary – change.

Although not intended as an afterthought, but more as a heuristic device, the current challenges for creating distributive justice are extended and deepened when one adds another critical part to the equation, namely environmental justice. Environmental justice features similar problems of definitional elasticity, and discourse domination by mainstream parties, and the same economic forces which produced the social inequality producing the imminent environmental catastrophe. While simply stating 'climate change requires system change', 'there are no jobs on a dead planet', and that the rich can better protect themselves from the climate emergency has political purchase, this does not take us very far in generating the necessarily great needed changes. Yet we cannot avoid recognising that ideals are the foundation for producing progressive – radical – social change. The ideals are relatively easy to set out and reproduce in policy terms. But they are necessary without being sufficient. The perennial problem for all radicals is how to generate the social forces capable of enforcing and achieving their ideals' implementation in the face of hostility and indifference from opposing forces. Ideals alone, no matter how inspirational, comprehensive or convincing, will not move the masses into action unless they reflect and represent their immediate material interests. This conundrum can only be worked out in practice, albeit studies of past campaigns and ongoing social movements are useful guides. Hence, this edited collection returns to the ideational issues.

So this collection is intended as a singular primer covering the essential issues in achieving social justice in Scotland in its widest sense. This means the collection seeks to provide an introduction to the fundamental issues, concepts and theories where any particular chapter will allow readers to then have the ability to further explore issues and thus deepen their critical understanding. As Rozanne Foyer highlights in her Foreword, the different chapters can be dipped in and out if the reader chooses not to read them sequentially and in one sitting. That said, the links of each chapter to others are highlighted in order to emphasise the concrete connections between them and that the sum of the collection is greater than its parts. More specifically, the core of this collection is centred around asking four questions: What's wrong with the current situation? Why is the current situation like this? What are the progressive, radical alternatives? And how can the alternatives be realised?

The chapters aid the answering of these questions in different ways. Part I provides foundational macro-perspective chapters which cover thematic concerns of neo-liberalism, capitalism, social democracy and socialism. These are followed in Part II by chapters specifically considering issues of application and practice. Part III comprises contextual chapters which draw the preceding threads together to examine the bases of points of departure. Put more pointedly, these chapters begin to consider the issue of the social forces needed to act as agents for change to achieve a radical transformation of society in Scotland. The contributors are a mix of academics and practitioners, where as often as possible both were partnered together to bring their strengths of rigour and experience to their respective chapters. They are drawn from across the left of the political spectrum, especially on issues of independence, Brexit, and perspectives on social democracy and socialism. Inevitably in such a collection, not all issues could be covered. One obvious example is that Scotland's role on the global stage as an exemplar of 'good' and 'bad' practice is absent.

While all the chapters suggest there is much that can be done within a current and future Scotland to resolve the social problems of society, none believe there are any autarkic answers. So a small country such as Scotland – like New Zealand – can be seen as a social laboratory for certain social classes in other countries seeking to knock back neo-liberalism and ensure the wealth of a nation is equally distributed amongst its populace. Substantial support for independence after its rejection in the referendum in 2014, the pandemic's accentuation of social inequalities and the failure of the Corbyn project reinforce the salience of Scotland in this sense of social experimentation.

PART I

Key Issues

1

The Structural Development of Poverty and Inequality

Carlo Morelli and Gerry Mooney

Introduction

Scotland has higher levels of inequality relative to most other UK regions and nations (see Chapters 8 and 10 especially). Its income inequality is the highest after the South East of England (Morelli and Seaman 2007). Scotland's health inequalities are also widening, with past increases in life expectancy now stalled (Morton 2020). The pandemic has exacerbated these differences, with indicators of poverty, ethnicity and disability all showing that Scotland's population is at greater risk from these than the general population. These inequalities are not the outcome of hidden influences, but the direct result of economic and political decision-making. Inequality is structurally rooted within capitalist economies. In this chapter, we examine the structural nature of inequality, the differences in ideological explanations for its emergence, and the policy focus resulting from these ideological perspectives. Central to the conclusions in this chapter is the recognition that inequality is structurally created, specifically around axes of class, and that remedies for eliminating inequality require actions which undermine these class-based inequalities. We begin by examining the arguments of the proponents of 'trickle-down' economics, and those encapsulated in Keynesian and Marxist approaches. The chapter then places the rise of inequality within these frameworks prior to drawing out the implications this has for devolution and independence.

Trickle-down Economics

The hegemony of neo-classical economics provides the ideological underpinning for contemporary inequality. An evolutionary economic approach sympathetic to capitalist development would suggest that inequality is an inevitable, indeed progressive, outcome of development due to innovation (McCloskey 2017). Rising inequality is a recognition of rapid changes in the rate of economic development. A 'Kuznets curve' exists in which inequality increases due to rapid industrial development. Over time, this inequality reduces via the diffusion of the benefits of economic development spreading throughout the economy (Kuznets 1955). Debates about the extent of inequality and the speed with which it reduces centre upon impediments to market-based economic processes and the efficient allocation of resources. These impediments are then said to prolong and deepen inequality.

Institutionalist economic thinking provides many of the concepts embodied within contemporary neo-liberalism (see, for example, North 1991 and Olson 1971, 1982). North's work identifies the role of defined private property rights and institutional structures maximising the scope for market exchange and market information in economic development. Government, therefore, acts to establish market mechanisms for the efficient allocation of resources, through price mechanisms, and as a result ensures optimal decision-making and outcomes reflecting the marginal value of each individual's contribution to the economy. Olson similarly provides a property rights-based explanation for the failures of economies to continue to grow, and indeed, even decline. Tendencies towards sclerotic decline, brought about by the growth of rent-seeking redistributive coalitions, impede market information, leading to inefficiencies in resource allocation (Olson 1982). These distributional coalitions are then understood as crowding-out opportunities for new innovatory and more efficient investment which then leads to lower growth and economic decline. Schumpeter (1994), within an equally disruptive crisis-focused vein, emphasised the role of 'creative destruction'. Innovation creates new industries while sweeping away older, less efficient forms of production within a revolutionary economic transformation. But these temporary monopoly advantages and inequalities are themselves competed away by new entrants, in line with the predictions of the Kuznets curve. Thus, contemporary advocates of neo-liberalism explain persistence of poverty and inequality as a result of the misallocation of resources. Extending further market-based incentives, whether in the form of privatisation or welfare reform, provides mechanisms not only for economic development, but reducing inequality as a result of individuals actively pursuing their own individual profit-maximising decisions.

It would therefore be mistaken to suggest that neo-classical economics ignores the role of the state. Rather, the state acts as an intermediary body whose role lies in its narrow legal activity of providing a framework for market exchange (North 1991). Private individual market exchange with minimal development of redistributive welfare policies provides the idealised form of economy, thus contemporary neo-liberalism seeks to extend markets into areas where previously non-market decision-making predominated. Hence, 'trickle-down' economics is the means by which equality is argued to emerge over time, and equality of outcome is the means of assessment of the effectiveness of supply-side measures to address inequality.

Keynesian Market Faialure

In contrast, authors who identify market failures as the cause of the rise of inequality, and its social consequences, place greater emphasis upon state intervention within economies to address deleterious impacts of externalities within markets. Private markets can externalise costs in areas where the price mechanism is either absent or too high to allow for the internalisation of economic activities. Thus, pollution, waste and climate change lie outside the cost structure for private markets and highlight the existence of market failures within economic development (Raworth 2017, Meagher 2020). This Keynesian-influenced literature places a focus upon the developmental nature of state intervention, and replacement of market signals by non-market planning and co-ordination for the resolution of market failures. Ranging from economic liberals such as Beveridge (1967) to post-Marxist Keynesians such as Varoufakis (2016), the state is recognised for the redistributive role it plays. Across governments in the developed world, ranging from politically conservative to social democratic, the broad concept of a 'social wage', institutionalising redistributive polices within a system of social security and welfare states, encapsulated these ideas in the post-war settlements (Milward 1992, Alcroft 1993).

This role for the state is itself aimed at further facilitating private markets, generating more rapid growth underpinned by higher levels of government intervention. Importantly, the state then is not simply an institutional body whose role is to deal with market failure, but it is an integral part of the market-based system of production (Krugman 1994: 245–280, Elliott and Atkinson 2016). The state acts to promote innovation, growth and wealth creation. Here, state intervention creates domestic and international frameworks whereby risk can be reduced and managed such that investment, trade and growth can be encouraged. One recent example arises from Mazzucato (2013), who makes the case for an 'entrepreneurial state' in which the state is embedded in the resource allocation decision-making underpinning innovation and development. Whereas under neo-classical thought the state sets the rules of the game, within a Keynesian model it provides a safety net for private risk-taking and innovation.

Institutional barriers to development, structural immobility or lack of access to resources are the means by which inequality is constructed by Keynesian approaches, with its negative impact on human development. Rawls (1985) places an emphasis upon the need for redistributive mechanisms to ensure that fairness and justice can remove structural inequalities in order to facilitate an equality of outcomes. Sen (1995), using a human rights-based philosophy, identifies government action as a mechanism through which structural inequality can again be minimised. Equality of opportunity is primarily the means to address inequalities within these Keynesian frameworks, but using remedial measures to address the inequality of outcomes is a necessity of market failure.

Exploitation and Surplus-value Explanations

Structural inequality deriving from the exploitation of human labour, underpinned by a capitalist mode of production, is the focus of attention for Marxist approaches to inequality. Callinicos (2000) considers the inevitability of inequality within an economic system in which exploitation of labour, through the creation of surplus value, is the primary motivation underpinning the economy under capitalism. Both poverty and inequality are inherent consequences of class-based production systems generally, and within capitalism specifically. This is due to labour income being driven as close as possible to the subsistence level that is required for the reproduction of labour power in the pursuit of maximising absolute levels of surplus value generated in the labour process (Marx 1980: 185–226). Thus, while the owners of capital concentrate surplus value under their control, the producers of this surplus value, the working classes, are kept in a state of insecurity and inequality. Structural poverty and inequalities are inherent within this framework, as sections of the workforce are deemed to be disposable within a 'reserve army of labour' when opportunities for growth emerge. Therefore, while Keynesian and Marxist ideas both focus upon the structural nature of inequality and poverty, the origins of these structural influences differ, with Keynesian approaches identifying market failure and Marxist approaches identifying the form of class-based exploitation.

Marxists' focus of attention in addressing inequality then lies with the agency available to the working-class producers of surplus value, in the form of class conflict. Greater equality arises from the diffusion of working-class self-organisation rather than the diffusion of innovation within the neo-classical Kuznets framework. The decline of labour's agency and power in the form of collective action under globalisation underpins the rise of inequality in the last quarter of the twentieth century in the period of neo-liberalism (Roberts 2016). Competition for accumulation of surplus value therefore creates the necessity for exploitation of the working class, and inevitable class-based conflict emerges in the distribution of surplus value, whether this concerns the wage rate directly or questions of a wider social wage (Shaikh 2016: 638–676).

Why More Equal Societies Almost Always Do Better

Wilkinson and Pickett (2009) provided the most widely known evidence linking income inequality with its wider social implications. They highlighted the consistent social gradient between national levels of income inequality and a diverse range of social and health inequalities. Whether this was levels of addiction, interpersonal violence, imprisonment rates, life expectancy, infant mortality or obesity, they demonstrated a consistent correlation between levels of income inequality and levels of social and health problems. A linkage between economic and social dislocation and income inequality was drawn, with trust, anxiety and socio-evaluative comparison central to an explanation of human wellbeing. Wilkinson and Pickett (2019) then developed this linkage, further highlighting that inequality and social hierarchy increase recognition of inferiority and a social sense of lack of value for individuals, leading to higher levels of stress hormones, evidenced by cortisone levels, in the human body. Higher stress, and thus higher cortisone levels, acts as a means of biological transmission by which social conditions impact upon individual biology, leading to worsening health and social outcomes (Wilkinson and Pickett 2009: 31–45). Importantly, for Wilkinson and Pickett these outcomes varied across economies, based upon their relative levels of collectivism and individualism, and affected those at the top of the hierarchy as well as the bottom. They concluded that the negative impact of inequality could be identified throughout the population relative to more equal societies.

Patrimonial Capitalism and Elephant Curves

Much of the discussion above is encapsulated in contemporary debates over the origins and patterns of income inequality that have occurred from the last quarter of the twentieth century onwards. Income has grown at a very rapid pace for those at the very top of the income distribution. Piketty's (2014) extensive study on the structural concentration of wealth leading to rising inequality is a starting point for this. From the 1980s onwards, the proportion of total income concentrated in the personal ownership of the top income decile returned to pre-First World War levels (Piketty 2014: 1–35). By the twenty-first century, the wealthiest 10% of the population was increasingly a relatively homogenous layer in society. This was constituted by an increasingly elitist layer identifiable as senior managers, business owners and entrepreneurs in the private sector, or doctors, senior government officials or barristers in the public sector, which was able to separate itself from the rest of society through private provision for health, education and housing etc. (Piketty 2014: 279–300). Above these groupings, however, and occupying the richest 1% of the population, lay a still more stable grouping whose position was reliant upon income from inherited wealth and rent rather than labour. The highest income percentile are beneficiaries of the rise of financial capitalism and the rent they derive through the ownership of financial assets, stocks, shares and partnerships (Piketty 2014: 301–303). Piketty thus refers to a concept of 'patrimonial capitalism' to explain this emergence and dominance of these structural inequalities at the top of the income distribution.

Milanovic (2016) identified the emergence of an 'elephant curve' depicting inequality globally spanning an era of two decades from 1988 (see Figure 1.1). For Milanovic, the trunk of an elephant rising exponentially was representative of the rapid increase in income for the wealthiest 5% of the income distribution. This group, and even more so the top 1%, represented a new global elite that gained 40% increases in income in the final two decades of the twentieth century (*Financial Times*, 14 April 2016). Milanovic's explanation identifies deindustrialisation, increasingly flexible labour markets and the weakening impact of unions for redistribution. Stagnating, even falling, real wages in large parts of the developed world led were thus recognised in the emergence of rising inequalities.

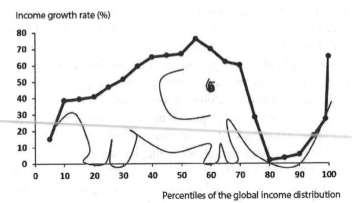

Income growth rate (%)

Percentiles of the global income distribution

Figure 1.1   Income growth by income percentiles, 1988–2008
Source: Freund (2016)

Neo-classical approaches thus suggest that a Kuznets-style 'great moderation' will inevitably see factor mobility ensuring that inequality is reduced over time. Both Piketty and Milanovic's understandings of a broadly Keynesian-based focus for policy interventions are based on identifying proposals for government intervention in the form of regulation and taxation of financial wealth. Roberts (2016: 251–254), from a Marxist perspective, places these changes within a framework of the 'tendency of the rate of profit to fall'. The development of the collective agency of the working class and their organisations, such as formal unions or other collective campaign-based groups, provide the most significant mechanism for increasing equality (Tengely-Evans 2014).

Devolution and Independence

Scottish devolution, and even more so independence, provides one of the governance mechanisms by which policy towards poverty and inequality can be implemented within a 'distinct Scottish model' (Keating 2005). Alternatively, it can be understood within a wider breaking apart of large national state formations in an era when the interconnectedness brought about by globalisation leaves little function for large state structures – as Stiglitz (2002: 21) suggests: 'global governance without global government'. When reduced down to national development utilising models embedded within a framework of comparative advantage, devolution readily spans both neo-classical supply-side economics and Keynesian macro-economic approaches and can be presented as a form of de-politicised technocratic managerialism within a fixed budgetary framework (Stigler 1957, Sloman 1997). However, the understanding of inequality developed above suggests that very different policy approaches are required to address structural inequality. Successive Scottish Governments since devolution have mostly relied upon existing neo-classical models of economic development to trickle down equality and fairness. More Keynesian redistribution policies, with a higher rate of Scottish income tax, have a more limited history since the Scotland Act 2016. However, no policies changing the balance of exploitative relationships within a Marxist framework have yet been attempted. Thus, the existence of anti-union measures weakening working-class agency remains in UK-based legislation. Indeed, even where nationalisation has been introduced, this has remained at the level of legal entities rather than introducing forms of workers' control of production, distribution and exchange.

References

Alcroft, D. (1993) *The European Economy 1914–1990*, third edition, London: Routledge.

Beveridge, W. (1967) *Full Employment in a Free Society: A Report by Lord Beveridge*, London: George Allen & Unwin.

Callinicos, A. (2000) *Equality*, Cambridge, UK: Polity Press.

Elliott, L. and Atkinson, D. (2016) *Europe Isn't Working*, New Haven, CT: Yale University Press.

Freund, C. (2016) 'Deconstructing Branko Milanovic's "Elephant Chart": Does it show what everyone thinks?', 30 November, www.piie.com/blogs/realtime-economic-issues-watch/deconstructing-branko-milanovics-elephant-chart-does-it-show.

Keating, M. (2005) 'Policy convergence and divergence in Scotland under devolution', *Regional Studies*, 39/4:453–463.

Krugman, P. (1994) *Peddling Prosperity: Economic Sense and Nonsense in the Age of Diminished Expectations*, New York: W.W. Norton.

Kuznets, S. (1955) 'Economic growth and income inequality,' *American Economic Review*, 45/1: 1–28.

McCloskey, D. (2017) 'Measured, unmeasured, mismeasured, and unjustified pessimism: A review essay of Thomas Piketty's *Capital in the twenty-first century*', *Erasmus Journal of Philosophy and Economics*, 7/2: 73–115.

Marx, K. (1980) 'Wages, prices and profit', in Marx, K. and Engels, F., *Selected Writings in One Volume*, London: Lawrence and Wishart.

Mazzucato, M. (2013) *The Entrepreneurial State: Debunking Public vs. Private Myths in Risk and Innovation*, London: Anthem Press.

Meagher, M. (2020) *Competition Is Killing Us: How Business Is Harming Our Society and Planet – and What We Do about It*, London: Penguin.

Milanovic, B. (2016) *Global Inequality: A New Approach for the Age of Globalization*, Cambridge, MA: Harvard University Press.

Milward, A. (1992) *The European Rescue of the Nation-state*, London: Routledge.

Morelli, C. and Seaman, P. (2007) 'Devolution and inequality: A failure to create a community of equals?', *Transactions of the Institute of British Geographers*, 32/4: 523–538.

Morton, C. (2020) *Health Inequalities in Scotland: A National Calamity; a Frontline GP View*, www.gla.ac.uk/media/Media_735435_smxx.pdf.

North, D. (1991) 'Institutions', *Journal of Economic Perspectives*, 5/1: 97–112.

Olson, M. (1971) *The Logic of Collective Action: Public Goods and the Theory of Groups*, Cambridge, MA: Harvard University Press.

Olson, M. (1982) *The Rise and Decline of Nations: Economic Growth, Stagflation, and Social Rigidities*, New Haven, CT: Yale University Press.

Piketty, T. (2014) *Capital in the Twenty-first Century*, Cambridge, MA: Harvard University Press.

Rawls, J. (1985) 'Justice as fairness: Political not metaphysical', *Philosophy and Public Affairs*, 14/2: 223–251.

Raworth, K. (2017) *Doughnut Economics: Seven Ways to Think Like a 21st-century Economist*, London: Random House.

Roberts, M. (2016) *The Long Depression: How It Happened, Why It Happened and What Happens Next*, Chicago, IL: Haymarket Books.

Schumpeter, J. (1994) *Capitalism, Socialism and Democracy*, London: Routledge.

Sen, A. (1995) *Inequality Re-examined*, Cambridge, MA: Harvard University Press.

Shaikh, A. (2016) *Capitalism: Competition, Conflict, Crisis*, Oxford, UK: Oxford University Press.

Sloman, J. (1997) *Economics*, Hemel Hampstead, UK: Prentice Hall.

Stigler, G. (1957) 'The tenable range of functions of local government', *Joint Economic Committee, Federal Expenditure Policy for Economic Growth and Stability*, World Bank, Washington, DC.

Stiglitz, J. (2002), *Globalisation and Its Discontents*, London: Penguin.

Tengely-Evans, T. (2014) 'Piketty and Marx', *International Socialism Journal*, 143: 177–186.

Varoufakis, Y. (2016) *And the Weak Suffer What They Must? Europe's Crisis and America's Economic Future*, London: Bodley Head.

Wilkinson, R. and Pickett, K. (2009) *The Spirit Level: Why More Equal Societies Almost Always Do Better*, London: Penguin.

Wilkinson, R. and Pickett, K. (2019) *The Inner Level: How More Equal Societies Reduce Stress, Restore Sanity and Improve Everyone's Wellbeing*, London: Penguin.

2

Towards Climate Justice

Mary Church, Niamh McNulty
and Eurig Scandrett

Introduction

That climate change is the greatest existential threat to society
is now almost universally accepted in all political discourse.
Indeed, with the exception of the ultra-right, all political
parties and policy makers claim to take the climate emergency
seriously. Nonetheless, despite widespread agreement on the
need for action – and the adoption of the Paris Agreement in
2015 – progress towards a climate-safe society is dangerously
slow. The explosion of new climate movements following the
publication of *Global Warming of 1.5°C* (IPCC 2018) has
drawn attention to the discrepancy between popular concern
about the climate crisis and government reluctance to act.
Faced with a scientific consensus that a rise in temperature
of more than 1.5°C above pre-industrial level would be cata-
strophic for life on earth, governments have produced carbon
reduction plans that would see a temperature rise of 3°C or
more. In particular, Global North nations whose power and
wealth are linked to centuries of fossil fuel-driven industrialisation are failing to live up to their responsibilities. Behind the
rhetoric of so-called 'climate leaders' lie targets and plans that
fall far short of climate fair shares (CSO Equity Review 2015)
and are riddled with loopholes that would see a cementing

of neo-colonialism, eking out a few extra decades of decent life for the privileged few before our planet finally becomes a hostile environment for all. This chapter will argue that runaway climate change, global inequalities and social injustices are all rooted in the logic of capitalism, therefore the solution is system change based upon social justice. A broad social justice environmental movement is already active in Scotland and across the world, generating the opportunity for grassroots action and policy innovation to move towards this goal.

Capitalism

At only 1°C warming today, many already live with the devastating consequences of climate impacts, including increased extreme weather events, disruption to weather systems and ability to produce food, bio-diversity loss, ecosystem collapse and extinctions, the loss of livelihoods, cultures and communities, and even whole countries in the case of small island states, mass forced migration of peoples, and the associated social and political instability and violence (IPCC 2018). While the need for a major transformation is clear, it is questionable whether materialistic, individualistic and capitalist societies have the imagination, will and capacity to see this through. That said, many governments' responses to the pandemic have demonstrated that rapid major change is possible.

While some continue to talk about anthropogenic global warming, or humans destroying the planet as if we were all equally responsible, the emergence of a climate justice movement following the failure of COP15 in Copenhagen resulted in a greater focus upon capitalism as the driver of destruction, alongside other structural injustices such as colonialism and patriarchy. This is why we demand 'system change, not climate change'. As the green-left has been saying for decades

– articulated by Fraser (2001: 96): 'Capitalism ... represents the socio-historical driver of climate change, and the core institutionalized dynamic that must be dismantled in order to stop it.' Young people, too, are increasingly expressing their discontent in anti-capitalist terms (Pickard et al. 2020).

The development of fossil-driven industrialisation has accounted for the global temperature increase. Capitalism especially extracts from people and planet, seeing life as a 'resource'. Under this system, we get to the point where multiple environmental limits are breached (Rockström 2010), tipping humanity itself into existential crisis. Whilst individual lives have always been expendable under this and other systems, now all life on earth is at stake. That said, some lives – both at home and overseas – will be and are being impacted first and hardest. Technological and scientific 'progress' since the Industrial Revolution has generated wealth and improved living standards for many. But this has been achieved through the exploitation of labour and the environment worldwide. Alongside this, we have internalised the norms dictated by colonialism, patriarchy and capitalism at personal, organisational and societal levels. Increasingly, we are 'consumers' first, rather than human beings, workers or citizens. Conventional capitalist climate discourses ask us to use its market system to choose different products or pay to offset the carbon from our flights without asking how our choices are limited by a system dependent on ecological destruction. Consumer-lifestyle environmentalism is the only kind tolerated by neo-liberalism.

Justice Lenses

Social justice must be at the heart of a transition away from a climate-destroying economy. Concepts that speak to this, like environmental justice, climate justice and 'just transition', are gaining traction and are increasingly reflected in political rhetoric and policy-making. Environmental justice originated in the movement against environmental racism that grew out of the US civil rights movement, recognising that black communities were, and are, disproportionately impacted by environmental harms. It recognises that the uneven distribution of environmental harms most greatly impacts people at the intersections of race, class, gender and disability, and seeks to challenge their structural causes. Furthermore, it demands that citizens have a voice in decision-making that impacts on the environment as a right and a duty.

Climate justice incorporates issues of equity, historic responsibility and capability to act – principles enshrined in Article 3 of the UN Framework Convention on Climate Change (of 1992). It asserts that countries like Scotland that have grown wealthy through polluting have a historic and differentiated responsibility for addressing the climate crisis. For most of the world to develop its economies sustainably, rich nations must de-carbonise their economies sooner than poor nations and repay their carbon debt by providing support including finance to enable mitigation, adaptation and clean development. 'Climate Fair Shares'[1] analysis, based on these principles, is a useful means of cutting through the rhetoric and assessing nations' relative contributions in responding to the climate emergency. Moreover, climate justice goes further by identifying the need to overcome the common causes of social inequalities and climate damage.

'Just Transition' is rooted in union movements, and refers to the deliberate effort to prepare for a transition away from environmentally damaging industrial practices while promoting decent, socially sustainable jobs for the future. It

---

1   See 'The UK's fair share target', www.christianaid.org.uk/sites/default/files/2020-03/FairShareUK_Infographic.pdf.

puts workers and their communities at the centre of the decision-making process, and should also be internationalist. The union movement's engagement with Just Transition has developed and matured, involving difficult conversations reflecting the contradictory role of unions – representing members in the short term within a long-term socio-economic system rigged against workers.

These concepts have been picked up in other arenas, including at the heart of the Scottish Government. Their meanings have been contested or diluted to range from radical transformation to being vacuously divorced from their roots in justice movements. Environmentally minded leftists must clarify and advocate the links between these ideas: first, to ensure they are not gutted of meaning, and second, to formulate a vision of change built by those who will be engaging in the everyday social practices of a 'green' future. The transition into a climate-safe society will be played out not at climate camps and protests alone, but on the factory floor, in frontline communities and through campaigns focused on people's material needs.

Scotland

Scottish waters hold the majority of UK oil and gas reserves, themselves the second largest reserves in Europe. Scotland also has significant renewable energy resources in onshore and offshore wind, hydro, wave, tidal and solar – with the potential to de-carbonise the economy and become a net exporter of green electricity (FoES et al. 2010, Platform et al. 2019). Despite significant growth in renewable energy generation, associated manufacturing jobs have not materialised. Within the oil and gas sector, a high proportion of workers are worried about job security. According to Platform et al. (2020), many would consider moving into new industries, particularly renewables, but face barriers in 'boom and bust' cycles, agency work, and inaccessible retraining. The opportunity for transition is available. How that transition plays out and whether it addresses a holistic view of economic, social and environmental justice within planetary limits is up for question.

While the mainstream independence movement and the SNP Scottish Government have successfully articulated climate change as a priority, they continue to – increasingly uneasily – combine this with staunch support for domestic oil and gas production. It is important to recognise that transitioning from fossil fuels to renewables is likely to become tightly bound up in nationalist and unionist electoral aspirations. Within this lies the risk of co-option. The coming work of the green-left is to ensure that Scotland, regardless of constitutional outcome, becomes committed to climate and environmental justice through a just transition, and to mobilising against the root causes of climate change.

Currently, however, the Scottish Government's *modus operandi*, along with those of many of the signatories to the Paris Agreement, is that the market will deliver carbon reductions and social justice. This involves nudges and leverage from governments to encourage private capital to be invested in the right direction, and for businesses to acknowledge their social responsibility, all too often contradicted by significant nudges in the opposite direction, not least via vast subsidies to fossil fuel companies (Platform et al. 2019). The few achievements of this approach – the Fair Work agenda, community carbon reduction plans, some voluntary divestments from fossil fuel companies – have largely occurred not because of government leadership or corporate compliance, but because of significant mobilisation from unions, community organisers and environmental campaigners. This limited progress has been undermined by failing to take on Jim Ratcliffe of INEOS at Grangemouth, lost opportunity with BiFab, blind faith in

Carbon Capture and Storage (CCS), the growth of incinerators, and unrealistic plans to meet legally binding carbon emissions reduction targets.

Scotland's Climate Change Plan Update (Scottish Government 2020) relies far too heavily upon unproven negative emissions technologies, with CCS, bio-energy coupled with CCS, and direct air capture and storage together expected to achieve almost a fifth of the 2030 target, increasing to a quarter of emissions reductions by 2032. This is not just about hard-to-treat industrial emissions, but is explicitly envisaged to support de-carbonisation of electricity, heat and transport as well. Furthermore, the prospect of the North Sea as a global dumping ground for carbon is gaining momentum, with an estimated 46 gigaton storage potential in Scottish waters. Scottish Government and sectoral support for this will have an impact well beyond our borders, giving false hope about the delivery of other national and corporate 'net zero' targets.

These targets provide a smokescreen for actual emissions reductions. 'Net zero' leaves the door open to continue emitting greenhouse gases in the short term on the basis that one day they will be sequestered or stored. Furthermore, the targets involve overshooting the global carbon budget for 1.5°C warming (in some cases very significantly) before bringing them back down, by which time the damage of such warming will likely be irreversible (FoEI 2021).

On the Ground

Social justice environmentalism in Scotland ranges from community group initiatives like allotments and bicycle repairs to direct action groups disrupting fossil fuel sites, and campaigns pushing for policy change and making spaces for movement-building in housing and fuel poverty campaigns, unions, health and safety, and anti-toxics activists, and for movements of international solidarity. Green-leftists must work together to keep market-driven, false solutions out and to focus on environmental and climate justice as well as just transitions.

Meeting with likeminded people to envision new futures can be affirming for activists. However, we must recognise how the driving forces of climate change – colonialism, patriarchy and capitalism – show up in our relationships. Our visions of justice must be integrated into our organisational practices in order to retain the energy and voices of those most marginalised and adversely affected by climate change. The criticisms of classism, racism, sexism and ableism in the environmental movement that arose throughout 2019 should be seriously grappled with if we are to hope for a functioning and successful movement.

That said, nearly all environmental progress in Scotland has been pushed from the ground up. A Scotland-wide campaign drove the eight-year fight to ban fracking to victory in the highest-profile environmental win for grassroots activists since devolution. The union movement's demands for a Just Transition found new voice in Scotland with the formation in 2018 of the Just Transition Partnership (led jointly by the Scottish Trades Union Congress and Friends of the Earth Scotland), which in turn led to the Scottish Government's Just Transition Commission (2019–2021, 2021–). Similarly, under immense pressure, Scotland became the first country in the world to announce a climate emergency in 2019, and later that year the Scottish Parliament passed legislation increasing the ambition of domestic climate targets to 75% by 2030 and a net zero target by 2045.[2] The climate justice movement in Scotland is growing and maturing, in part invigorated by the hosting of COP26 in Glasgow. Our strengths lie in our

2 While these targets fall considerably short of Scotland's fair share of climate action, they are an important step in that direction.

diversity of tactics and our ability to demand rapid and radical change while we begin to build new futures, from our community gardens to our energy sector.

Discussion

Whilst it is possible to mitigate climate change without changing capitalist relations of production and consumption, with investors finding new ways to make profit, this will only ever be of temporary and limited effect, and will still reproduce inequalities. The rich can find ways to protect themselves from climate change for a while whilst the poor continue to suffer the consequences. Climate justice cannot be achieved without finding a way for value to be detached from profit. To begin, we must reassess our values and collectively begin practising the future we want. This means looking at the impacts of Scotland's de-carbonisation plans on countries and peoples of the Global South – in terms of pace and ambition, and plans to deliver. It means climate reparations – linked to colonial and slavery reparations – on both international and interpersonal levels. It means not simply substituting fossil fuels with renewables without considering the impact of the continued extraction of resources from the Global South. Corporate profiteering from large-scale renewable operations dependent upon land dispossession, extraction of 'transition minerals' (like cobalt, lithium and nickel) or bio-fuels, and any related job creation, do not constitute a just transition. Further, a Just Transition requires us to expand our concept of what green jobs are into the care, cultural, creative and learning sectors. Britain's furlough scheme showed the possibilities of decoupling work from income, even while governments missed opportunities to use the scheme to operate a just transition away from the climate crisis. We must look towards an economy for social and environmental benefit, for this and future generations. Some of us call this eco-socialism.

There will be no simple manifesto of policies that would implement eco-socialism overnight, but we can build the alliances to undermine capitalism and create the conditions in which a post-capitalist society can emerge. Union collective bargaining can transcend the immediacy of members' interests to imagine a socialised economy, and pre-figurative political action can move beyond utopian experiments to be part of these counter-hegemonic movements. The necessary pressure for this will come from lobbying, demonstrations, direct action, strikes and climate camps, from frontline communities affected by fossil fuel industrial capitalism, the union movement's demands for a just transition, and connections with global movements of Indigenous people, peasants and anti-colonial movements. We can learn lessons – positive and negative – from Scotland's recent history of social movement-building around climate justice, including the achievements of the anti-fracking movement, the failure of corporate takeover of the community waste movement (Mackay 2019), the Just Transition Partnership urging the baby steps of the Commission, the mobilisations around the G8 in 2005 and COP26 in 2020–2021, and the success in forcing Glasgow University to divest from fossil fuels and the Royal Bank of Scotland to stop financing them. By shifting discourse and moving the goalposts towards actual system change, these actions make it increasingly difficult for capital to profit from climate damage and shift costs onto the environment of the poorest.

Whether devolved or independent, what options are there for a way forward for the Scottish Government? The 2021 Scottish Parliament elections showed some steps in the right direction, with the appointment of a Minister for Just Transition, Employment and Fair Work, whilst others, such as the change of title in the climate change portfolio to a Cabinet

Secretary for Net Zero, Energy and Transport, show the emphasis moving in the wrong direction. We urgently need a gear change, with major investment of public resources to transform the economy. At the same time, we must be willing to take democratic control of public goods, many of which are currently in private hands, ensuring the foundations of a sustainable and socially just future. A significant expansion of welfare, health and social care, education, and housing and infrastructure will move the economy away from the corporate domination that is failing to de-carbonise and is incapable of delivering the public goods and wider social benefits required. With social and material needs increasingly met through public provision (via state and other public and community-owned bodies), it will be possible to wean ourselves away from fossil-fuelled consumerism. Combined with a citizens' income of sufficient value, Scotland could actually start moving towards genuine solutions to the crisis of climate injustice.

This is not instant eco-socialism, for we would likely retain a significant private profit-motivated sector, albeit constrained in areas where it is causing the most harm. But it is a realistic direction of travel and provides the opportunity for hope out of crisis. The post-capitalist, ecologically sustainable, democratic and socially just economy is a journey of discovery, not a party manifesto, but for the sake of life on Earth we need to move in that direction, and do so quickly.

References

CSO Equity Review (2015) *Fair Shares: A Civil Society Equity Review of INDCs*, Manila, the Philippines, London, Cape Town, South Africa, Washington, DC etc.: CSO Equity Review Coalition, http://civilsocietyreview.org/report.

FoEI (2021) *Chasing Carbon Unicorns: The Deception of Carbon Markets and 'Net Zero'*, Amsterdam, the Netherlands: Friends of the Earth International.

FoES, RSPB Scotland and WWF Scotland (2010) *Power of Scotland Secured*, Edinburgh, UK: Friends of the Earth Scotland.

Fraser, N. (2021) 'Climates of capital', *New Left Review*, 127: 94–127.

IPCC (2018) *Global Warming of 1.5°C*, IPCC Special Report, New York: Intergovernmental Panel on Climate Change.

Mackay, J. (2019) 'Tackling waste in Scotland: Incineration, business and politics vs community activism', in Harley, A. and Scandrett, E. (eds) *Environmental Justice, Popular Struggle and Community Development*, Bristol, UK: Policy Press, pp. 69–81.

Pickard, S., Bowman, B. and Arya, D. (2020) '"We are radical in our kindness": The political socialisation, motivations, demands and protest actions of young environmental activists in Britain', *Youth and Globalization*, 2/2: 251–280.

Platform, Friends of the Earth Scotland and Greenpeace (2020) *Offshore: Oil and Gas Workers' Views on Industry Conditions and the Energy Transition*, Edinburgh, UK: Friends of the Earth Scotland/Platform/Greenpeace.

Platform, Oil Change International and Friends of the Earth Scotland (2019) *Sea Change: Climate Emergency, Jobs and Managing the Phase Out of UK Oil and Gas Extraction*, Edinburgh, UK: Platform/Oil Change International/Friends of the Earth Scotland.

Rockström, J. (2010) 'Let the environment guide our development', *TEDGlobal*, 10 July, www.ted.com/talks/johan_rockstrom_let_the_environment_guide_our_development?language=en.

Scottish Government (2020) *Securing a Green Recovery on a Path to Net Zero: Climate Change Plan 2018–2032 – Update*, Edinburgh, UK: Scottish Government.

3

Neo-liberalism and Scotland

George Kerevan

Introduction

Neo-liberalism is the dominant political and economic subject framing our era. This chapter examines its impact upon Scotland and its unexpected role in reigniting the popular demand for Scottish self-determination. This might be seen as ironic given that one can argue the neo-liberal capitalist growth model was first pioneered in Scotland. In 1707, Scotland was incorporated against popular will into an economic and political union with an already agrarian, capitalist England. Thereafter, in barely two generations, Scotland was catapulted from feudalism orchestrated by its magnate, landed aristocracy into a modern capitalist entity. This lightning transformation was propelled by access of Scotland's nascent bourgeoisie to England's burgeoning imperial, slave empire. Willing volunteers from backward, feudal Scotland provided the soldiers, slavers, traders and bankers to create the first ever world capitalist empire (see also Chapter 16). Now the twenty-first century finds Scotland a comparative economic backwater amidst a dynamic neo-liberal world order. Scotland adjusted poorly during the post-Second World War industrial boom. Its core shipbuilding, heavy engineering and coal sectors – organised for the most part in middle-sized family firms rather than vertically integrated monopolies – all failed in direct rivalry with re-capitalised European and Japanese competitors. The result was rapid deindustrialisation. Scotland entered the neo-liberal era that opened in the Thatcher-Reagan 1980s having failed to generate the technological and financial gains of the post-war industrial boom.

As a result, the neo-liberal paradigm was imposed in Scotland with an unequalled brutality.[1] The first order of business was to destroy the unions, in a bid to reduce wage costs and create flexibility to introduce new technologies. This class confrontation included the 1984–1985 miners' strike followed by the deliberate wholesale dismantling of industrial sectors where organised labour was also strong (cars, engineering, manufacturing, steel) and the creation of new sectors based on non-unionised labour. This period saw the deliberate closure of vehicle production at Linwood in 1981 and Bathgate in 1986, of the Ravenscraig steel works in 1992 and the complete rundown of underground coal mining in 2002.

The destruction of the old industrial-export nexus in Scotland was followed by a brief flurry of foreign investment in new computer technology, underwritten by state subsidy via the Scottish Development Agency. However, the fantasy of a high-tech 'Silicon Glen' proved short-lived. The bursting of the dot.com bubble at the turn of the new millennium and the rise of post-Mao China as the dominant supplier of cheap labour effectively eliminated Scotland from the new global supply chains that service US high-tech. The neo-liberal trading order reduced Scotland to a niche supplier of raw materials (oil and gas), tourism and agribusiness exports (chiefly farmed salmon and whisky produced by foreign-owned companies).

---

1   Curiously, the predations of neo-liberalism in Scotland were attributed largely to Margaret Thatcher, at least until the crisis of 2008. This political myopia allowed the SNP to facilitate foreign inward investment with religious zeal. Scotland was the UK's top destination outside London for foreign investment for the seven consecutive years to 2020.

One sector where Scotland might have joined the twenty-first-century neo-liberal economy was in banking. Neo-liberal economics is based upon the global free movement of capital, leading to the centralisation of investment decisions. The end of fixed exchange rates in the 1970s, and the wholesale deregulation of banking in the 1980s, opened the global financial markets to heretofore conservative Scottish bank capital. Theoretically, Scotland was in a unique position to access this new order, using the reservoirs of profit accumulated by Scotland's governing elite over two-and-a-half centuries of global plunder.

In reality, Scottish bank capital proceeded to destroy itself. The de-regulated Royal Bank of Scotland (RBS) Group went on an insane international acquisition spree and temporarily became the biggest bank in the world (by assets) in 2008. But the implosion of the global derivatives market following the collapse of the US sub-prime mortgage market led inexorably to the seizure of inter-bank lending on an international scale. RBS suddenly found itself only hours away from insolvency, necessitating nationalisation and a government bailout worth £45.5 billion. Simultaneously, the other major Scottish banking group, Halifax Bank of Scotland, suffered an equally embarrassing implosion and state rescue. Far from being a boon, neo-liberalism opened the door to foreign competition and a hubris that saw an independent Scottish bank capital eliminated as a force (see Fraser 2019).

These economic convulsions had a profound effect on Scottish politics. Deindustrialisation broke up the traditional ruling-class bloc consisting of industrial capital, the conservative Protestant working class, the landed aristocracy and the professional petty bourgeoisie (the latter consisting of the lawyers, bankers and clerics who had retained special privileges under the 1707 Union with England). This led to the eclipse of the ruling Tory Party – which had won a majority of Scots votes in 1955 – followed by the temporary hegemony of reformist Labour from the 1970s onwards.

Labour might have delivered a new devolved model of governance and economic self-reliance for Scotland which could have headed off the rise of nationalism. However, a core section of the Labour Party's Scottish MPs resisted reform and sabotaged the 1979 devolution referendum. Besides, asymmetric devolution for Scotland has never made sense given the continuing domination of London-based economic interests at a UK state level.

As a result, there was almost an inevitability in the rise of the Scottish National Party (SNP) to government after a devolved Holyrood Parliament was eventually created in 1999. Under First Minister Alex Salmond, the SNP narrowly lost an independence referendum in 2014, with major working-class cities such as Glasgow and Dundee voting for secession. In the popular mind, Scottish independence has come to signify both resistance to Conservative austerity policies imposed from London and a naïve hope that a separate Scottish state can manage globalism in Scottish interests.

Reorganisation of Capitalism in Scotland under Neo-liberalism

Some 40 years on, the neo-liberal era in Scotland has had a transformative impact on society. It might be theorised that the lack of a separate Scottish state – one with the financial and political levers to mould domestic change in this turbulence – left Scotland particularly vulnerable.[2] The context of this is that the central dynamic of the economy has switched

---

2   However, we can also follow Tom Nairn in arguing that one of the contradictions of globalism is that it has undermined the legitimacy of the big imperialist states. This has triggered a welter of territories demanding independence (Nairn and Kerevan 2005).

from exporting industrial products to debt-financed consumer demand for imports. This debt is secured by mass home ownership and ever-rising house prices. Using debt-fuelled consumer demand is, of course, a central mechanism in valorising capital investment in the neo-liberal era. It allows the surplus value created by Asian labour to be extracted by finance capital in the West. However, most small European industrial economies retained a significant, high-value, export sector which minimised their dependence upon consumption as the driver of gross domestic product (GDP) growth. Alternatively, Scotland has been displaced from its former role as an advanced manufacturing economy. This is proof, if needed, that neo-liberal competition does not lead automatically to 'modernisation', but can incorporate (or reincorporate) regions in a dependent global role.[3]

Neo-liberalism also brought profound changes at a city level, particularly in the capital, Edinburgh. While domestic Scottish bank capital imploded, Edinburgh began hosting a new wave of inward-investing financial groups and fintech companies, facilitated by the SNP city council's liberal attitude to speculative office development. The city's financial bourgeoisie proved adept at cashing in on the global bull market in equities and bonds triggered by central bank quantitative easing. Its fund managers now have a trillion dollars of foreign assets under local direction thanks to global free movement of capital. Baillie Gifford, a secretive private partnership, is one of the largest global investors in Amazon and Tesla electric cars.

Contemporary Edinburgh has embraced the neo-liberal paradigm in all its glory: the domination of global finance capital, a debt-financed and ultimately unsustainable prop-

---

3   This is a prime example of the process of uneven and combined development which lies at the heart of contemporary globalism. I have examined Scotland in this context (Kerevan 2019).

erty boom that gives the illusion of prosperity, and a local economy based increasingly on entertainment – restaurants, pubs, shops, taxis and hotels. At the same time, Edinburgh is a city of social extremes. It ranks in the top quartile for incomes in Scotland, but is also in the bottom quartile for poverty. The workforce is split between a highly educated professional elite and a precariat whose real income has been static for over a decade. Much of the city's inner core is now given over to Airbnb lets and cheap student property developments, driving ordinary people to live in tract housing developments built on Edinburgh's periphery.

The neo-liberal make-over of Scottish society had its impact on domestic politics. Under First Minister Nicola Sturgeon, the SNP Scottish Government's links with big business grew significantly. In 2016, Sturgeon appointed Andrew Wilson, a corporate lobbyist and former RBS head of group communications, to write the SNP's economic strategy. Wilson (2018) advocated a pro-market vision for an independent Scotland. These developments opened up a split in the ranks of the SNP – especially over the proposal to keep using sterling after independence, effectively binding the Scottish economy to the interests of London finance capital. Many SNP members denounced the report as an ideological justification for pursuing neo-liberal policies. These tensions were one factor in the creation of the Alba political party, led by Alex Salmond, in 2021.

Paradoxically, the SNP leadership's rightward shift towards accommodation with neo-liberalism (or at least with globalist sections of Scottish domestic capital) occurred just as anti-capitalist resistance was growing in England via the Corbyn project within Labour. Corbynism and Momentum had little impact in Scotland because the national question dominated Scottish politics, with Labour pushed into fifth place at the 2019 European Union (EU) election. Defections to the SNP over the years also allowed centrists and avowed Blairites to retain influence within Scottish Labour, even under Richard Leonard's short leadership.

Alternatives to Neo-liberalism

Given the significant intrusion of neo-liberalism into Scottish society, will independence actually change anything? Much depends, of course, on the direction taken by post-independence governments. To date, the SNP seems to have capitulated to the central ideological tenet of neo-liberalism that competition is the only legitimate organising principle for human activity. The party's 2014 independence plan was premised on cutting Scottish corporation tax to 3 pence below the UK, supposedly creating an additional 27,000 jobs. Here, we will consider some potential drivers of resistance to this market-based fixation.

TRADE

The most obvious issue in developing a policy direction for Scotland which is outside the neo-liberal paradigm is how to escape integration into – and domination by – global markets. By this, autarky is not meant. Yet escaping neo-liberalism's reach, even to a degree, means finding some way of securing space for domestic anti-capitalist reforms. These are defined to be related in some measure to non-market distribution of resources and rewards. China manages this by dint of its sheer size. Scotland, with just 5.5 million people, cannot escape a significant degree of integration into global markets and price pressure. But can it pioneer a compromise allowing a non-market, social direction for the economy while retaining limited participation in neo-liberal supply chains and capital flows?

Posing this question raises serious doubts about the SNP's desire to re-join the EU post-independence. Re-joining the Single Market for goods, capital and labour will put the Scottish economy directly under global competitive pressures. One obvious solution for Scotland (as a first step) is to adopt the Norwegian trade model. Norway is not an EU member, but is part of the Single Market. Norwegian goods (except farm produce and fish) are imported tariff-free into the EU. However, Norway is not part of the EU customs union. This means it sets its own tariffs on goods imported from outside the Single Market. Following this route would also allow an independent Scotland to maintain a tariff-free trade zone with England. This arrangement is not without its bureaucratic costs. Nevertheless, the Norwegian model would give an independent Scotland some ability to set tariff walls sufficient to give domestic companies a degree of protection. In Norway, the effect is to protect domestic agriculture. If implemented by Scotland, this would allow a move away from foreign export agri-business towards greater agricultural self-sufficiency, with reduced CO_2 emissions. Developing a managed trade regime would be a major step towards decoupling from neo-liberalism.

INVESTMENT

The essence of the neo-liberal model is free flow of capital on a global scale, uninterrupted by states. This mechanism is not reducible simply to the free movement of foreign direct investment in search of the highest industrial profits, or to capital flows looking for the highest return in global bond markets. The neo-liberal financial system (at least since 2008) is dominated by a centralisation of capital flows under the control, principally, of big US investment banks. For a Scotland seeking to escape the diktats of neo-liberal finance capital

– if only partially – the only recourse is to put domestic capital flows under some form of public direction. In this context, state or community control over domestic savings and investment choices is not to be regarded as a means of dealing with market failure – e.g., supporting access to cheap house mortgage finance for low-income families. Rather, escape from the domination of neo-liberal finance capital means imposing social and political choices decided within Scotland over the hunt by global investment houses, hedge funds, equity investors and property companies for profit and asset value.

Realities of Implementation

The essence of the neo-liberal conundrum can now be posed: how can a small, independent state maintain a balance between popular national control and global market pressures? Recent examples are hardly encouraging – witness the slow-motion collapse of Venezuela. To be specific: can small states successfully control domestic savings and investment flows without provoking international sanctions? If so, how do they maintain productivity growth without succumbing to bureaucratic inertia?

STATE INVESTMENT RULES

The SNP Scottish Government has taken one small step towards putting investment under democratic control through the creation in 2020 of the Scottish National Investment Bank (SNIB). Leaving aside the SNP's appointment of traditional bankers to run it and the bank's limited capitalisation, is it possible for the SNIB to circumvent international state aid rules? The European Single Market (which the SNP seeks to re-enter) forbids the degree of social control over investment flows that would be necessitated by trying to escape the neo-lib-

eral paradigm. For instance, attempts to nationalise the ailing
BiFab offshore energy manufacturing plants were stymied by
EU state aid rules – or at least that was the reason given by the
SNP. The obvious solution first step is to remain outside the
EU proper and so escape direct control by the European Commission. It is also the case that the UK (and *ipso facto* Scotland)
spends a very small proportion of GDP on state industrial
aid – just 0.38% in 2019, so far less than Germany (1.31%)
or Poland (1.59%). An independent Scotland could increase
state-directed investment considerably before encountering
international sanctions. Finally, there are obvious ways of
decentralising investment decision-making to local communities that challenge the legal right of international agencies to
intervene. And public direction of investment flows does not
necessarily imply subsidy (which is subject to legal challenge).
Rather, it involves choosing to invest in sectors or geographical
areas determined by democratic vote, which a profit-maximising system may otherwise ignore. An independent Scotland
could vote on medium-term investment goals and instruct the
SNIB to use them as commercial guidelines. This could form
the basis for democratic planning.

Maintaining Productivity Levels

Marx's 'law of value' describes the way international competition forces global investment towards those sectors generating
the highest average profit rate. This in turn drives capitalist
enterprises to constantly upgrade labour productivity and
cheapen unit costs. The danger arising for an isolated economy
seeking to escape the neo-liberal global market is that it decou-
ples itself from this crude productivity mechanism – witness
Venezuela. Swedish unions produced an elegant solution to this
conundrum in the 1950s in the so-called Meidner Plan. Mandatory sectoral wage bargaining ensures that union strength is

used to accelerate a generalised and regular improvement in real incomes across the economy (a so-called 'solidarity wage policy'). As a by-product, wage costs rise, especially for small and medium-sized enterprises (SMEs). This forces SMEs to invest in new technology, boosting productivity. Active labour market policies are used to push workers into the most productive sectors, and fiscal measures favour long-term investment over profit distribution. Sweden ultimately abandoned its sectoral wage bargaining under internal neo-liberal political pressures. The Swedish model also involved a plan – again aborted under neo-liberal pressure – to sequester excess company profits into union investment funds, socialising the economy over a generation. This idea was revived under Corbyn's Labour leadership for the 2019 UK general election. There remains merit in this model as way of creating a space for meeting progressive domestic objectives while managing (to a degree) globalist pressures. It is a model easily adapted to an independent Scotland.

Coda

Since the 2008 financial meltdown, neo-liberalism has entered a critical new phase. Intensified economic, technological and military competition between the US and China has ruptured the standard model of free trade. With Brexit, Scotland finds itself part of a Tory libertarian plan to turn the UK into a de-regulated offshore island challenging the EU. The SNP under Sturgeon has responded with typical ambivalence, committing itself to re-joining EU after independence while embracing the latest Tory project for low-tax freeports (albeit rebranded as 'Green ports'). The 2021 Scottish Parliament elections gave the SNP one extra seat, but left Sturgeon just shy of an overall majority (which was then resolved via a pact with the Greens). However, she saw off a challenge from the

Alba Party, which failed to make an electoral breakthrough, while Scottish Labour lost another two seats. As a result, Sturgeon and the SNP remain in an unassailable political position within Scotland, at least for the 2021–2025 Parliament. Yet Sturgeon is facing criticism that she is increasingly dependent upon pro-EU, middle-class voters and so is unwilling to pursue anti-globalist, anti-market economic policies, or even do much on independence except passively seek permission to hold a second independence referendum from an unwilling Westminster Government. This suggests there is little appetite in the current Scottish political elite to challenge neo-liberal orthodoxy in any practical way. Yet neo-liberal competition has not served Scotland – or ordinary Scots – well. Independent or not, Scotland and its people will have to escape the siren embrace of neo-liberalism if they are to prosper.

References

Fraser, I. (2019) *Shredded: Inside RBS, the Bank that Broke Britain*, second edition, Edinburgh, UK: Birlinn.

Kerevan, G. (2019) 'Explaining Scotland: The politics of uneven and combined development', *Conter*, 1 (print edition only).

Nairn, T. and Kerevan, G. (2005) 'Scotland in the Global Age', in Hassan, G., Gibb, E. and Howland, L. (eds) *Scotland 2020*, London: Demos, pp. 225–240, www.demos.co.uk/files/Scotland2020.pdf.

Wilson, A. (2018) *Scotland – the New Case for Optimism*, Edinburgh, UK: Sustainable Growth Commission, www.sustainablegrowth commission.scot/report.

4

Economic Democracy and Public Participation

Andrew Cumbers and Robert McMaster

Introduction

With the rise of autocratic regimes and nativist right-wing populisms around the world, the idea that democracy is in crisis has gained a certain traction in mainstream media and commentary. However, typical discussions of what democracy is tend to be fairly narrow or superficial, restricted to realms of electoral politics, voting systems and constitutions. Seldom does debate actually question, in a more fundamental way, the merits of representational liberal democracy – or the subject of how to advance public participation and engagement itself. More fundamental issues of democratic process and the rights of citizens to participate remain largely off the table. If the debate about formal political democracy is somewhat limited, the discussions of economic democracy – that might give citizens some measure of democratic rights, control and decision-making over the key issues that affect their livelihoods – are virtually non-existent. You will struggle to hear or read much on the subject in either UK or Scottish mainstream discourse. It is a largely unremarked, yet quite remarkable, fact that the model of liberal democracy which has dominated the global economy since the 1990s and the collapse of Soviet-style Communism is devoid of any commitment to democracy in the economy. With the exception of the Nordic countries, which are aspirational for many progressive-minded supporters of Scottish independence, and some co-determination structures in western Europe, the workplace is effectively a legitimised and legalised authoritarian regime with considerable power vested in employers. This is especially stark in the growth of casualised employment, such as zero-hours contracts and 'fire and rehire' practices, all of which have been graphically exposed by the pandemic. It is the vulnerable and those on precarious employment contracts who have borne the brunt of the economic fallout of the pandemic and associated policy responses.

Globally, union decline following sustained attacks in the 1980s in Anglophone countries, deindustrialisation and the shift of work to less unionised workforces in the Global South has created serious imbalances in collective bargaining. Alongside the triumph of capital over labour, a neo-liberal policy regime of marketisation and the establishment of the sanctity of private property rights over all else – even human rights and those of the natural environment – have pushed questions of economic democracy firmly into the background of debate.

As part of a lively constitutional debate about Scotland's future, questions of economic democracy should feature more prominently on the radar of politicians and citizens. Many of the grievances against the *status quo* of Scotland's dependent relationship within the United Kingdom have an economic as well as a political character. For instance, continuing structural inequalities between Southeast England and the UK's more geographically peripheral regions and nations, over-centralisation of government revenues and the lack of effective economic decision-making power, despite the establishment of devolved administrations in 1999, all contribute to the profound regional imbalance of the UK's political economy. Indeed, the UK's economic model produces the greatest regional inequalities in Europe. Exiting the European Union in 2020, against the democratic will of the people of Scotland (of those who voted, 62% wished to remain, with majorities in all of the 32 local authority areas), raises other important economic questions regarding trade, market access and a host of other macro-economic questions over which there is little 'local' democratic control. Additionally, as is widely recognised, the 'Singapore' model of free-market Brexiteers of a low-tax, deregulated market environment where workers' rights and protections are greatly reduced is at odds with continued Scottish popular support for a welfare state, progressive tax regime and economic policy that tackle inequalities. This chapter begins by setting out a broad conception of economic democracy, then discusses an economic democracy index (EDI) before investigating the comparative ranking of Organisation of Economic Cooperation and Development (OECD) member states and the relationships between economic democracy and income inequality and poverty. Following this, we discuss the issues with particular reference to Scotland.

A Revitalised Project for Economic Democracy

Re-animating economic democracy for the twenty-first century means coming to terms with a dramatically changing global economic context, characterised by growing inequalities and an increased concentration of wealth. Fundamental changes to the world of work include the emergence of the gig economy, collapse of secure employment, and decline of unions as a powerful countervailing force to capital. Given these unpropitious circumstances, a revitalised project for economic democracy means moving beyond older forms centred upon the workplace and collective bargaining to develop a broader strategy for democratic participation across the economy more generally. Labour rights, unions and collective bargaining will still be important in the struggle for social justice, but a much greater remit is required to democratise the economy.

For us, economic democracy refers to the ability of people to participate in economic decision-making processes. As such, it centres upon individual rights, although it has recognised that all individuals are always embedded in collective social relation networks rather than the atomised individualism of neo-classical economics. The legal framework is central to ensuring that a suitable set of institutional arrangements is in place to enable individuals – citizens, consumers, workers – to meaningfully contribute to economic decision-making. We acknowledge that this presents challenges and there are distinctions between *de jure* (in law) and *de facto* (in reality) rights. Accordingly, the exercise of individual rights usually requires, and indeed should not be seen in opposition to, collective action. Our argument goes beyond consumer choice in a marketplace and workplace-based notions of industrial democracy. Rather, it refers to the transparency of corporate and governmental decision-making processes to ensure accountability and freedom from corruption (such as in procurement practices). Greater economic democracy could include ensuring alternative ownership forms in production, distribution and exchange – whether voluntary or labour co-operatives (see Chapter 6) – can access means to support their endeavours. Urban agriculture and community gardening initiatives are such a case. Ready availability of finance to promote such projects should not require a commercial case. Rather, such support should revolve around community, individual empowerment and improved environmental outcomes. The process of government could include elements of participatory budgeting as well as further devolution of power.

There are such processes, but they tend to be small-scale and rather piecemeal, hence requiring further commitment from government both in terms of securing the financial support to ensure the viability of such initiatives, especially during their establishment, and the requisite legal framework based upon the presumption of individual participation rights.

Rethinking our approach to economic democracy has been at the core of recent research (see Cumbers et al. 2020) and the construction of an EDI.[1] The index is novel in developing a broader definition of economic democracy – beyond the usual focus on union rights or levels of co-operative enterprise – which we term 'associational economic democracy' – to incorporate also individual economic rights, levels of public participation and the nature of economic decision-making. For instance, the index embodies measures of the importance of the corporate financial sector in an economy. As this sector is noted for its concentrated ownership and control, the underlying idea is that such a sizable financial sector as it is presently constituted is not conducive to democratic economic decision-making. Other measures include the extent to which corruption is controlled and the degree to which government structures and decision-making are devolved.[2]

For reasons of data reliability, the index was constructed using 32 OECD members. Figure 4.1 shows their relative EDI ranking using the latest available data (up to 2014 for most countries).[3]

---

1   See A. Cumbers, 'Democratising the economy', https://democratisingtheeconomy.co.uk/2017/12/02/creating-the-democratic-economy/.
2   For further details on the methodology behind the index, see Cumbers et al. (2021).
3   Sources include: European Association of Co-operative Banks data, European Values Survey, Crowe and Meade (2008) Central Bank Transparency Index, ICTWSS database, ILOSTAT, IMF Statistics, OECD Statistics, World Values Survey, World Wealth and Income database and Worldwide Governance Indicators.

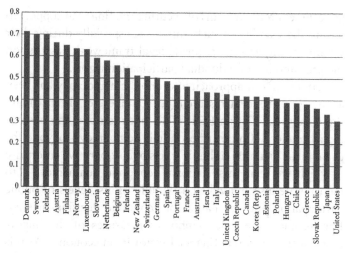

Figure 4.1 Economic Democracy Index: rankings by OECD member state, 2017

The most striking finding is the basic difference between a more 'social' model of northern European capitalism and the more market-driven Anglo-American model. Hence, the Nordic countries score among the best, with their higher levels of social protection, employment rights and democratic participation in economic decision-making. The reverse is true of the more deregulated and less economically democratic economies of the English-speaking world with the US, UK, Australia and New Zealand performing relatively poorly. The best-performing countries – which display high levels of economic democracy – tend to be Nordic or Continental Western European, occupying the top seven places, with Denmark and Sweden clearly ahead of the rest. Notably, the top ten countries all have relatively small population sizes (under 20 million), although our statistical analysis suggests it is not population size as such that is responsible for this. Countries from Eastern Europe are among the worst-performing countries, with Southern European countries, especially Greece, also performing relatively poorly. Estonia is the best-performing post-communist Eastern European country, recording an EDI score comparative to West European standards, and higher than the UK and US.

Our work also reveals that from the year 2000, economic democracy in the OECD as a whole has marginally declined (as measured by the average of our index across member states). We believe this is partly driven by a gradual erosion of workplace (and individual) rights and declining transparency in governance. Within this lies some variability between member states and to some extent for each member state over time. There is an intuitive appeal to this pattern, in that it resonates with unease about the health of democracy in some countries and the growing incidence of less secure employment contracts.

Following the construction of the index, we used statistical analysis to explore the relationship between economic democracy, inequality and poverty. A striking finding is the strong negative and statistically significant correlation between the EDI and poverty and inequality measures. In other words, as EDI rises, poverty rates and inequality fall. Figure 4.2 shows scatter plots of the EDI and poverty as measured by the proportion of households below 50% of median income, and Figure 4.3 shows the EDI and income inequality as measured by the Gini coefficient.[4] We cannot infer causation from these correlations, but we emphasise their statistical significance, which invites further investigation.

Our study questions the celebrated model of liberal democracies with deregulated market economies, trumpeted amidst

---

4   This is a measure of statistical dispersion intended to represent the income inequality or wealth inequality within a nation or any other group of people, developed by the Italian statistician and sociologist Corrado Gini in 1912.

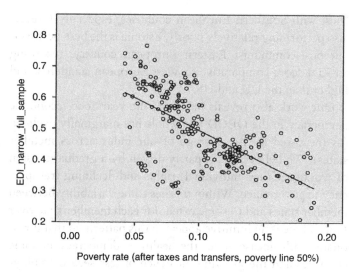

Figure 4.2   The relationship between the EDI and poverty

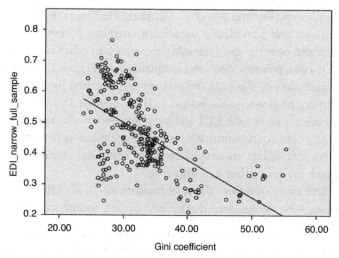

Figure 4.3   The relationship between the EDI and inequality

the capitalist euphoria around globalisation and the collapse of Soviet-style communism (see Fukuyama 1992). In this regard, our findings highlight that those countries with high levels of economic democracy – in our more broadly conceived definition – such as Norway, Denmark and Iceland have much lower levels of inequality and poverty than liberal market economies like Britain and the US. Moreover, they suggest a possible relationship between a combination of individual employment security, decentralised economic decision-making, and greater transparency and democratic engagement in macro-economic decision-making in order to enhance economic democracy, improve equality and lower incidences of poverty. They also highlight the importance of institutional arrangements in the economy – in the form of rights, legal frameworks and devolved governance – in potentially countering inequality and poverty. This challenges much of the conventional policy wisdom of the 1980s onwards regarding the perceived benefits of Anglo-American style flexible labour market policies, deregulated employment and finance, and macro-economic management, suggesting that such approaches may contribute to poverty and inequality.

Academics, think tanks and commentators who advocate economic democracy are well aware, under liberal democratic capitalist regimes, that democracy starts and ends at the ballot box. Not only is political democracy highly restricted – in the UK in particular, which has a limited and somewhat tainted experience of direct democracy – but the contemporary liberal democratic model has a void at its heart when it comes to the economy. This tends to conflate democratic decision-making with purchasing goods or services in market transactions.

Reflecting some of the patterns identified above in the different performance of various models of capitalism in our index, debate on Scotland's constitutional future sometimes pirouettes wistfully to Nordic models. There is recognition of the links between fairer societies and continuing forms of social democracy,[5] proportional voting systems, better collective bargaining, workers and citizens' rights, and modern democratic constitutions. But beyond this, there is a need for a more thoroughgoing approach to the relations between economy, democracy and people. Economic democracy must be considered in its broader and deeper sense of challenging elite domination of wealth, resources and decision-making. For Scotland, that would mean a radical democratic transformation of land and natural resource ownership in particular.

Developing New Practices and Narratives

Just before the 2007–2009 financial crisis, Mair (2013) identified a 'hollowing out' of politics across the Western liberal democracies. While voter alienation from, and disenchantment with, the political establishment was clearly an important problem, Mair also emphasised the perfidious withdrawal of political elites themselves from a meaningful democratic politics. The neo-liberal acceptance of free market discipline to adjust to globalisation in the 1990s went hand in glove with the evacuation of political decision-making from critical spheres of public life – especially in economic but also increasingly in social policy – and their delegation to experts and technocrats. The best example of this post-democratic regime is the tendency for politicians to make central banks 'independent' (Crouch 2004).

The strongest arguments for Scottish independence relate to democratic self-governance; a more comprehensive and deeper sense of 'taking back control' of wealth and resources from corporate, political and technocratic elites. Independ-

---

5 Albeit often eroded by hegemonic values of Anglo-American-inspired neo-liberal governance.

ence would, however, be a somewhat superficial affair without a more radical agenda for economic democracy that challenges the 'top-down' technocratic governance of the hollowed-out neo-liberal state Mair wrote about (see also Chapters 12 and 24). For us, this is about progressive economic policies that challenge elite domination of wealth and economic decision-making. But it is also about new narratives around individual economic rights, public participation and deliberation of the economy itself.

In the first place, alienation from neo-liberal globalisation is fanning the flames of reactionary right-wing economics and xenophobia promoted by Trumpists, and is partly driven by growing individual economic insecurity. This has been produced by disciplinary neo-liberal labour policies around welfare, labour market deregulation and flexibility for employers at the expense of employment security and a growing precarity for workers. Official thinking for almost two decades at the international scale has eulogised flexible labour markets as the solution to the employment problem. Today, the most obvious outcome of this in Britain is the zero-hours economy, with the number of workers employed on these contracts rising from just over 0.1 million to almost 1 million in a decade. This is the 'road to serfdom', to play upon the title of Friedrich von Hayek's 1944 defence of liberalism which criticised the over-weaning state.

Combating these developments in practical terms means rebalancing the labour market from employers to employees, but at a deeper level it requires new thinking and policy about how we generate individual economic freedoms alongside protecting collective bargaining structures – not the freedom to exercise property rights and exploit the labour of others, but freedom to choose how you exercise your own labour. This is an important, but long-neglected, agenda for economic democracy, bringing together the Enlightenment liberalism of

John Stuart Mill with the radical political economy tradition. In this respect, it is worth recalling that it was freedom from economic servitude that most animated Marx.

In an increasingly automated economy, where decent, secure and well-remunerated work becomes ever scarcer, there is a need to rethink how individuals, families and communities secure the income and resources needed to live decent lives (see Chapters 5, 6, 10 and 14). This needs a fresh approach to how work is distributed, new initiatives around working time, and rebalancing of work and leisure around the fundamental individual economic right to a decent sustainable livelihood.

A more genuinely democratic Scotland requires a strong deliberative public sphere where economic ideas and narratives are not the preserve of elites, but are the subject of debate, contestation and even conflict between competing groups (see Chapter 12). The contemporary global economy suffers a knowledge deficit, in the sense that economic discourses – alongside wealth – have become appropriated and concentrated through elite interests and institutions. Economic decision-making should be embedded within the democratic public realm as far as possible, rather than delegated to a remote class of technocratic experts who end up serving dominant vested interests.

The appropriate question then becomes: what kind of economic institutions would be needed to deal with these issues? Ensuring strong collective bargaining rights for workers and unions remains an essential element of a democratic economy, but a citizens' income would also be a good way to promote individual economic rights, set at a level that allows individuals the positive freedom to choose how they sell their labour. And democratic forms of public ownership are one important way to deal with the increasing capture of common wealth on behalf of the elite. The devolution of economic decision-making by the state and the increased use of participatory planning and budgeting forums are also essential ingredients. A functioning democratic economy would require a mix of planning and markets, with the emphasis in the latter on those that deal in use value rather than pure exchange value (e.g., farmers' markets rather than stock markets). But it would require very different forms of social regulation and economic institutions to those currently proposed for the UK's post-Brexit trajectory.

Acknowledgement

This chapter is based upon research conducted under the support of the ESRC Transformative Research Programme (grant ES/N006674/1) and with research assistance from Susana Cabaço, Karen Bilsland and Michael J. White.

References

Crouch, C. (2004) *Post-democracy*, Cambridge, UK: Polity Press.

Cumbers, A., McMaster, R., Cabaço, S. and White, M.J. (2020) 'Reconfiguring economic democracy: Generating new forms of collective agency, individual economic freedom and public participation', *Work, Employment and Society*, 34/4: 678–695.

Cumbers, A. McMaster, R., Cabaço, S. and White, M.J. (2021) 'Income inequality and economic democracy', unpublished paper, University of Glasgow.

Fukuyama, F. (1992) *The End of History and the Last Man*, London: Penguin.

Mair, P. (2013) *Ruling the Void: The Hollowing Out of Western Democracy*, London: Verso.

5

Re-thinking Public Ownership for an Independent Scotland

Alex de Ruyter and Geoff Whittam

Introduction

The debate around the merits of nationalisation and public ownership has waxed and waned over the course of the past hundred years. Pivotal in the drive to state control of key sectors of the economy of course was the experience in capitalist societies of the 1930s Great Depression, the consequent rise of totalitarianism and then the Second World War. The post-war settlement was characterised across the West (albeit to varying degrees) by an expanded state/public sector and Keynesian macro-economic aggregate demand management to maintain 'full employment' (Standing 1997). In Britain, this process saw the nationalisation of key sectors such as coal, railways, telecommunications and aerospace, in addition to the creation of the National Health Service under the Attlee Labour Government.

Disruption during the 1970s, most notably through the oil-price shock of 1973, triggered a period of stagflation and consequent escalation of industrial disputes in Britain, with the 'Three Day Week' in 1974 and 'Winter of Discontent' of 1978–1979 being particularly notable in laying the ground for a resurgence of right-wing ideas seeking to discredit the role of the state and thus ushering in the Thatcherite (neo-liberal) period of 1979 onwards. This was a period typified by privatisation, outsourcing and importation of market mechanisms into remaining public sector bodies (Standing 1997). State ownership was claimed by the advocates of neo-liberalism to have resulted in poorly performing, low-productivity enterprises that required 'market discipline' and 'competition' to revive the economy. To the extent that state-owned firms such as British Leyland after nationalisation in 1975 continued to be plagued by low productivity and poor product innovation, these critics had a point, in that nationalisation in itself was not a panacea for Britain's economic ills – though, as we argue, the market-oriented 'reforms' that followed were even worse.

Hence, in this chapter we argue that the way 'public ownership' is established is pivotal. If one is simply substituting a private monopoly with a public monopoly that continues to be run in a centralised, dirigiste and top-down fashion, then the needs of the wider stakeholder community (such as workers and local communities) will continue to be given insufficient regard. Drawing on Cowling and Sugden's (1999) concept of 'strategic failure', we argue that nationalised enterprises must have corporate governance reforms in the ways decisions are made, enabling such stakeholders to participate in the running of these enterprises. A progressive, independent Scotland offers an opportunity for such ideas to be more widely taken up than the continuing hegemony at Westminster governments would allow for.

So in this chapter we explore opportunities that independence for Scotland could open up in terms of public ownership. We argue that where there is a clear public interest for public ownership (as with natural monopolies or highly oligopolistic industries), this should be taken, but accompanied by a process of economic democracy (see Chapters 4, 6 and 17) to make publicly owned assets accountable to key stakeholders. Prior experiences in the co-operative movement and more recent episodes in Scotland around 'community buy-outs' offer valuable lessons for the implementation of economic democracy and accountability. However, first we will review the theoretical arguments about public ownership, before examining the Scottish experience and finally articulating an agenda going forward.

Economic Rationale for Nationalisation and Public Ownership

From a traditional economic textbook perspective, the ideal of a 'perfect market' with no externalities and other potential market failures results in allocative and productive efficiency. However, when we enter the real world, we are faced with a situation which consists of market failures and income inequalities. Most obviously, this takes the form of monopoly and oligopoly power and the inherent bias towards the supplier of a commodity, due to asymmetric information (which in turn can impose substantial transaction costs upon consumers to overcome a deficiency of knowledge of a particular product). This requires state intervention, which can take a number of forms, from taxation of negative externalities through subsidy of positive externalities to legislation controlling oligopolistic production to outright public ownership.

Policy-makers have also intervened to encourage co-operation between private sector firms and co-operation between different sectors such as the private, the state and university sectors, known as 'the triple helix approach'. These collaborations, which in theory are against the textbook example of promoting the perfect market, typically occur in areas such as research and development, where it is argued that there is underinvestment from the private sector and in certain circumstances it is advantageous to have co-operation rather than competition.

A more widely accepted case for nationalisation is the situation of a natural monopoly and the existence of public goods. A natural monopoly occurs when it is inefficient to have more than one supplier of a good or service. This is the rationale why Network Rail, the public body created to be responsible for rail infrastructure after the private company, Railtrack, collapsed in 2002, has not been re-privatised – and underpins the logic of the proposed creation of a re-nationalised 'Great British Railway' by the Johnson-led Westminster Government.[1]

Public goods are goods which are non-rivalrous and non-excludable in consumption. 'Non-rivalrous' means that consumption by one person does not reduce the amount available for others. 'Non-excludable' means that if something is available to one, it is available to all, so it becomes impossible to levy prices for individual consumption. In practice, the range of goods that qualify as 'pure' public goods is rather limited, being conflated with a wider range of goods known as 'merit goods' that could be (and often are) provided by the private sector (e.g., health, education, public transport), but possess significant positive externalities which the private sector under-provides and, hence, could be better realised under public ownership. Even within the narrow cost-benefit analysis approach of neo-classical micro-economics, it is

---

1   That a *Conservative* Westminster Government should choose to embrace certain policies that some would label as 'populist' but which are antithetical to the ethos of its predecessors over the previous 40 years is interesting and remarkable. As such, it points to the political optics around having to appeal to its new 'Red Wall' base of disaffected former Labour voters in certain areas of the Midlands and North of England. Whilst a discussion of this stance's political dynamics is beyond the scope of this chapter, it does suggest the continued appeal of 'left-wing' ideas and policies in the eyes of a majority of the voting public, as opposed to support for particular left-wing parties claiming to espouse them.

evident 'socially optimal' levels of consumption of such goods are higher than the 'free' market would be willing to provide, as depicted in Figure 5.1.

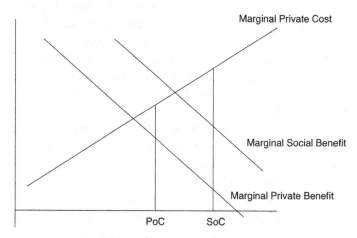

Figure 5.1   Private and social benefits of consumption of merit goods
Note: PoC = private optimal consumption; SoC = socially optimal consumption

Classically, the provision of national defence is cited as a public good. If you provide defence for one civilian, then you provide it for all, and it is difficult to identify how the consumption of one piece of national defence can be measured. The result is that national defence is paid for by all via general taxation, and the consumption is potentially 'enjoyed' by all.

Where we have the existence of large-scale oligopolistic (private sector) companies, wider societal issues come into play. For example, decisions made by a large multinational corporation which provides large-scale employment opportunities within a local community can have a destabilising impact on that community if strategic decisions are made on grounds of profitability alone. Such a company is under no obligation to take into consideration the wider community if it makes a decision to divest from its current location and re-invest elsewhere. The wider stakeholders will be at a disadvantage in comparison to the shareholders of the company, a process which has been referred to by Cowling and Sugden (1999: 363) as 'strategic failure' – that is, 'reasons why the strategic decision-making process in an economy prevents the attainment of a *socially* [our emphasis] desirable outcome'. It would be easier for policy-makers with a state-owned enterprise in a similar location to argue for a policy which incorporated the social cost along with the private cost of ceasing production, and hence potentially reverse the decision to relocate.

There are further examples where competition does not work and there is a case for public ownership – that is, in the case of artificial competition (i.e., that denoted under the rubric of 'contestable markets', which has been used to justify privatisation in areas such as telecommunications and utilities). Such situations are where 'output' would be easier to use with a single provider. A typical example would be deregulated local public transport. The co-ordination necessary for making private provision perform efficiently through, for example, inter-ticketing, cross-subsidisation and sharing of timetables is likely to reduce competition and provide a barrier to entry. Across Britain, the experience of privatisation of local public transport has been a reduction in the number of services and greater difficulty for the passengers who use them. This is particularly the case for remote rural communities, where we have witnessed the establishment of community transport initiatives such as Transport for Tongue (Wyper et al. 2016) in an attempt to overcome the market failure which exists when left to the private sector to provide such services.

Experience of Nationalisation and Public Ownership in Scotland to Date

Prior to devolution, the then Scottish Office had little control over government industrial policy, which presided over the wholesale destruction of manufacturing and extractive industries across Britain. Much of this capacity was under public ownership – for example, coal, steel and, for a time, shipbuilding. Likewise, the accompanying privatisation and consequent job losses affecting sectors such as energy and telecommunications were at the mercy of the Westminster Government. However, since 1997 space has opened up for a different approach to industrial policy and public ownership. This opening up has been accompanied by a gradual realisation across the Western world that market solutions are not always the best solutions, and we have witnessed policy initiatives leading to re-nationalisation and re-mutualisation of many key public services, as with Network Rail.[2]

Since 1999, when the Scottish Parliament gained its devolved powers, there has been less enthusiasm for privatisation in Scotland. For example, whilst water and sewerage services were privatised in England in 1989, this example was not followed in Scotland. Water provision is a classic case of a natural monopoly, hence there is a strong economic argument for maintaining its public ownership. Currently, regardless of measurement, the Consumer Council for Water estimates that 12% of households find their combined water and sewerage bill to be 'unaffordable' (NEA 2021). Hence, there are additional social benefits for public provision of such services. Similarly, privatisation of many services provided under the umbrella of the National Health Service in England has not been followed to the same degree in Scotland. Latterly, the

---

2   See footnote 1.

Scottish Government has intervened to secure the operation of what are deemed essential businesses, such as Prestwick airport, Fergus Marine Shipyard and the BiFab yards. These three examples are not without controversy, but the point is that the Scottish Government stepped in to rescue businesses which were failing under private ownership – which provides a further rationale for public ownership, namely securing sectors and individual businesses which are seen to be of strategic economic importance.

In Scotland, debate on public ownership has been inseparable from the debate on land ownership – and Scotland has one of the highest concentrations of land ownership in the world (see Chapter 17). Even in the twenty-first century, just 85 estates were found to control one-third of the land in the Highlands and Islands (cited in Callaghan et al. 2012: 199). It is significant that when the Scottish Government enacted legislation to reform land ownership, it did not seek to 'nationalise' land, but rather used the means of 'community buy-outs' to democratise land ownership and enable more sustainable development to take place. A similar approach has been undertaken with asset-based community ownership, a means of securing what are deemed as key assets – these could be community centres, a local shop or a local petrol station – within a community setting by key stakeholders within that community. We would propose that a similar approach be adopted for future public ownership of industrial sectors of the economy.

Going forward, there are clear economic cases for public ownership which are deemed to have some elements of natural monopoly attached to them. Here, we can think particularly of the rail sector, which the Scottish Government has already committed to return to public ownership as soon as 2022. We have also identified water and sewerage as a sector with not only aspects of a natural monopoly, but additional social advantages from having a clean water supply and efficient sewerage system. As mentioned earlier, this sector remains in public ownership in Scotland. For other aspects of transport infrastructure, such as buses, we have likewise indicated a rationale for public ownership (see Chapter 18). Indeed, Lothian Buses remains in local authority ownership and appears to be as efficient as the private sector operators whilst offering many more social benefits than its private sector counterparts. We have also highlighted key sectors such as energy and telecommunications as sectors where an economic case can be made for nationalisation, and as the climate emergency unfolds before our very eyes (see Chapter 2), there is an increased rationale for these sectors to be brought into public ownership.

However, we have stressed the importance of democratisation of any move towards public ownership. What we mean by 'democratisation' is local democratic control (see also Chapter 4). Whilst certain activities, because of economies of scale and scope, are better organised at the national level, the principle of subsidiarity should prevail when technically and practically possible. Having said that, it is imperative that this should not be traded off against equity goals, for local autonomy needs to go hand-in-hand with a set of basic economic, social and political rights for citizens irrespective of location (Cumbers 2007). The public ownership of the future needs to have at its core democratic control by key stakeholders like unions and consumer groups, representatives from the local and national administrations, and local communities impacted by the activities of a business organisation within their community.

Prospects for a Democratic Nationalisation in an Independent Scotland

This chapter highlights a key dilemma facing advocacy of public ownership – namely, that simply substituting a private monopoly or oligopoly with a publicly owned one is no guarantee that concerns around economic and industrial democracy and community empowerment will be adequately addressed, let alone improvements achieved. Indeed, there is no *a priori* reason why nationalised ventures would not suffer from the same issues of strategic failure as private sector counterparts if they are dominated by elites whose interests are starkly removed from the local stakeholder communities they are meant to serve. One only has to look back to history – for example, the actions of the National Coal Board in the aftermath of the 1984–1985 miners' strike – to see the effects on local communities of a state-owned monopoly implementing a regressive policy agenda of 'accelerated mine closures without concern for social implications and mining communities' (Turnheim and Geels 2012: 43) and the dangers inherent in simple public ownership.

The possibility of an independent Scotland offers a greater chance to revisit the debate around the merits of public ownership. This has also been forced onto the agenda at the UK level, given the unprecedented state intervention in face of the pandemic. Furthermore, there appears to be some confusion as to the direction of travel for economic policy at the heart of the Westminster Government, with Teesside airport and various rail franchises being taken into public ownership while the Chancellor is seeking to introduce austerity measures to reduce the increased public spending in light of the pandemic. We have argued that increased public ownership in an independent Scotland should not be based upon outmoded 'top-down' notions of nationalisation, but rather upon an inclusive industrial democracy that embraces social justice at its core and thus points to fertile ground in building on what Massey (2008) would refer to as a progressive, rather than a defensive, sense of 'place' that would underpin consequent local community renewal strategies.

So, and in accordance with the 'critical geography' paradigm, scholarly work must continue to contest the spatial socio-political hegemony (Blomley 2006) represented by the current Westminster-centric UK Government regime. However, some have also questioned whether the current SNP Scottish Government is capable of helping to deliver a more radical state of independence (see Chapter 2). As such, the coming years promise to be an interesting time – and opportunity – to work towards this agenda in the knowledge that the nature of any future state of independence – whether neo-liberal, social democratic or socialist – will have a huge bearing upon these issues.

References

Blomley, N. (2006) 'Uncritical critical geography?', *Progress in Human Geography*, 30/1: 87–94.

Callaghan, G., Danson, M. and Whittam, G. (2012) 'Economic and enterprise development in community buy-outs', in Danson, M. and de Souza, P. (eds) *Regional Development in Northern Europe: Peripherality, Marginality and Border Issues*, London: Routledge, pp. 196–212.

Cowling, K. and Sugden, R. (1999) 'The wealth of localities, regions and nations: Developing multinational economies', *New Political Economy*, 4/3: 361–378.

Cumbers, A. (2007) 'Economic democracy and public ownership', in Cumbers, A. and Whittam, G. (eds) *Reclaiming the Economy*, Glasgow, UK: Scottish Left Review Press, pp. 7–22.

Massey, D. (2008) 'A global sense of place', in Oakes, T. and Price, P. (eds) *The Cultural Geography Reader*, London: Routledge, pp. 257–263.

NEA (2021) *NEA's Response to Ofwat's Payment, Help and Debt Guidelines Consultation*, Newcastle upon Tyne, UK: National Energy Action.

Standing, G. (1997) 'Globalization, labour flexibility and insecurity: The era of market regulation', *European Journal of Industrial Relations*, 3/1: 7–37.

Turnheim, B. and Geels, F. (2012) 'Regime destabilisation as the flip-side of energy transitions: Lessons from the history of the British coal industry (1913–1997)', *Energy Policy*, 50/1: 35–49.

Wyper J., De Ruyter, A. and Whittam, G. (2016) 'Are we there yet? Transport for Tongue Limited – a case study of a not-for-profit company in North West Sutherland', *Local Economy*, 31/5: 589–601.

6

Can Democracy Go Hand-in-hand with Efficiency?

David Erdal and John Bratton

Introduction

The global pandemic, with unprecedented job losses and output in Scotland in 2020 falling by nearly 10% year-on-year, has highlighted just how out of kilter our current arrangements are for people making a living. Low-paid and public-facing workers, many classified as 'essential', have experienced economic hardship, ill-health and high mortality rates. Many lower-paid workers, unable to self-isolate without suffering malnourishment, had to carry on working in spite of health risks to themselves and others. Company insolvencies and national lockdowns have disproportionately affected female, young and BAME workers, highlighting long-standing inequalities across society. The dual aim of this chapter is to summarise how the economy is dysfunctional and deleterious to worker and community interests, and to explore a reimagined system aimed at using democratic worker ownership to improve both productivity and equality (see also Chapters 4, 5 and 13). First, we will lay out the dysfunction, before showing what the alternative is. We finish by suggesting how this alternative could be brought about.

Work, Employment and Inequality

In order to make the system work better, we need to start with how it has been working until now. Pre-pandemic, mainstream economic wisdom celebrated economic specialisation and the international division of labour. Neo-liberalism encouraged corporate elites to maximise their self-interest by seeking competitive advantage through minimising their 'core' workforce, outsourcing and contracting the rest, and offshoring factory jobs to low-wage economies. With the use of zero-hours contracts and new technology to create 'gig' work, business risk has been passed onto workers. The consequences of a 'low-road' business model devoid of employment rights and security, exemplified by 'fire and rehire' practices, could hardly be starker. Neo-liberalism also justified deregulating labour and – disastrously – financial markets: leveraged buyouts and leveraging of assets allowed corporate owners to force the disgorging of vast amounts of cash to shareholders, a low point being Philip Green's £1.2 billion dividend, leaving BHS fit only to be sold later for £1, with workers' pensions trashed. Financialisation minimised investment in productive activity in the real economy (Thompson 2013). Ford registered most of its profit from financial activity, leasing rather than manufacturing vehicles. Other financial engineering included buying back and cancelling company shares rather than investing in new technology or training or jobs. This practice increased the share price, justifying obscene CEO salaries and bonuses.

Financialisation impacts firms and workers in important ways. It has fuelled income inequality. In Britain, in 1998–2020, typical FTSE 100 chief executive pay rose from 48 to 120 times a typical full-time worker's pay. Further, financialisation accelerated outsourcing and precarious employment practices. This all reflects and reinforces the shift in power in the institutions of economic life away from working people and towards capital. Inequality rose as union membership fell and the power of the unions declined from the 1970s onwards. Defeating the National Union of Mineworkers opened the way to a series of successful legislative attacks undermining workers' and union bargaining power (Bratton and Gold 2017). This finance-driven system reinforced unfettered powers of corporate elites, intensified by the tendency of web technology to allow huge market dominance to the first successful users of the technology (e.g., Facebook, Amazon, Microsoft and Apple).

Challenging Corporate Elites through Worker Ownership

Each economic institution – each bank, each corporation – is internally structured autocratically, with power flowing from the top down. Subject to few laws, employment contracts give power to the hirer, mostly subject to very few limitations, whether hiring and firing or investing and divesting. Power has long been a preoccupation of rulers and rebels alike. So far, the only established system that when fully implemented prevents the powerful from turning their power into *de facto* dictatorship is public supervision from below, through democracy. But it is, of course, by no means infallible, with some elected leaders becoming elected autocrats.

If democracy has apparently been the only way to keep the powerful in check in the political sphere, it is notable that democracy is almost entirely absent from economic institutions. No corporation allows managers or directors to be, in John Stuart Mill's phrase, 'elected and removable' by the people who do the actual work. Instead, when we go to work, we move from a sphere classed as 'public', where individual autonomy is respected, anyone can seek out information and everyone has a vote, into a sphere classed as 'private', where, by signing an employment contract, one gives up the right to information and influence, and the right to have any share in the wealth our activities create. Those benefits belong to company owners – that is, the people employing us. Increasingly, these owners are the managers of financial institutions: investment and hedge funds and the like, who are often deeply ignorant of the businesses and whose interest is essentially in how much money they can extract by dividends and timing of share sales. Usually, they are entirely without commitment to the business. Yet these financial owners are the ones who have the right to impose the leaders on the people who actually do the work. They can simply ignore the people in it and the community where the firm is located. It is as if the leaders of one country had the right to impose dictators on another country, regardless of what the local inhabitants think.

In 2021, this financial drive was at the heart of the proposed 'European Super League', the breakaway competition designed by a coterie of wealthy owners, deeply ignorant of football, whose aim was enhanced profit extraction. German mega-clubs such as Bayern Munich and Borussia Dortmund were not part of the breakaway group because German clubs are not owned by companies or super-rich elites, but are 'fan-owned' (*Guardian*, 22 April 2021). Club presidents are elected by members. Scottish club Partick Thistle is also wholly fan-owned, a gift from lottery winner Colin Weir. Debate off-field has suggested a similarly democratic model could be implemented in Scotland and England to give power back to supporters.

When a business is owned by those who work in it, the directors are elected by them – that is, by the only productive element in the business: the workers. Director salaries are usually voted on by all workers. Workers have the right to be informed of all factors affecting the business. And the workers vote on what proportion of profit is invested into the business, leaving the rest for distribution among themselves. These types of businesses range from worker co-operatives to employee-owned companies, with the former usually having strong worker-owner rights and small pay differentials. To neo-liberal economists, this system sounds dangerous, for they imagine workers will behave as badly as financial operators, bleeding the company dry rather than investing in developing it for the future, and voting ignorant people onto the board to serve their own short-term interests.

The empirical evidence tells a different story. Numerous peer-reviewed studies since the 1970s have shown that worker-owned businesses invest for the longer term: they are knowledgeable and committed, and really want to make sure their business succeeds. Such businesses create jobs faster than businesses owned by outsiders, they invest at a greater rate, they survive downturns better, and they last longer, sharing the wealth they create among all who work there. Above all, their productivity is higher and grows faster than it does in businesses owned by outsiders, provided the management style is participative (Blasi et al. 2016).

These businesses do have to be managed differently. Since they are not dictatorships, the power of those elected as directors has to be non-dictatorial in the way it is exercised. In other words, leaders have to get used to giving out information, answering questions, listening to – and taking into account – the opinions of those they manage. Since workers are knowledgeable and committed, this generally improves decisions taken, and certainly tends to avoid disasters that occur in new systems designed and imposed by 'experts' on behalf of directors far removed from operations. By democratising a firm's economic activities, workers have the ability to build the business for the long-term, and they do.

This system is distinct from state ownership, which can result in top-down dictatorial bureaucracy. Instead, each enterprise is independent, operating in a market and therefore with the greatest possible incentive to do well for itself and its customers. This is a form of collective ownership that actually works in practice. In an economy crying out for solutions to low productivity, it produces consistently high and fast-growing productivity. In a society crying out for an antidote to ever-accelerating inequality, it spreads wealth widely. Grotesque CEO salaries simply do not get through employee votes, and annual distributions are spread fairly across all the people who work in the company.

Unions' *raison d'être* is to bargain to maximise labour's share of profits and protect members' interests. Wage-bargaining mitigates the worst features of industrial capitalism, but it cannot address the challenges of financial capitalism. Support from union leaders for worker ownership has lagged behind the attitudes of those local union reps who have experienced it in practice. As part of reimagining the role of unions, where they have leverage, unions can help build worker ownership (Martin and Quick 2020). One concern of union leaders is that when workers own businesses, they will not only receive the rewards of ownership, but also be subject to its risks. The illusion of security provided by not taking responsibility for business performance is, however, just that. Senior managers know that in economic downturns their role is shifting the consequences from the owners to the workforce, by redundancies, wage squeezes and so on. Those who really suffer the consequences of poor business performance are workers. As the collapse of the giant construction company Carillion demonstrated, the 'safety net' for the pension funds in bankrupt companies starts by reducing substantially the pensions payable (Wylie 2020). Signing an employment contract does not give any security against even normal business risk. However, while workers bear the risk of the business, they have no say and no part of the wealth they create. Neo-liberals' claim that shareholders need power and vast rewards for bearing risk are nonsense: they diversify their risk of losing some of their money, and when the going gets tough, switch the risk onto workers.

The move to worker ownership, making everyone a partner and giving everyone a share of any wealth created, together with a say over what is done and how, transforms the work situation in a strongly positive way. This is perhaps the main root of the rise in productivity: the way it suits people. Being an informed player with a contribution to make and a share of the rewards, rather than being treated as a mere instrument to be ignored and bossed around, is deeply satisfying. The business is 'ours' rather than 'theirs', so workers have a common interest in making it succeed. This is as good as any safeguard against business failure.

Unions have concerns workers will become capitalists, competing in markets, and that pursuing profit could be damaging. However, a business which does not make enough money to stay in business benefits nobody: it could be sustained only by gift from the state, which in turn gets its funds from profitable businesses. Worker-owned businesses generally do pay their taxes, do not shift the ownership of their assets to tax havens, and by spreading the wealth to those who do the work, they reduce poverty without needing state funding. Competition by democratic businesses results in better goods and services for customers, not in a damaging scramble for growth.

Unions' role changes in worker-owned businesses. Instead of wage-bargaining, workers now have the power to ensure, and also responsibility for ensuring, that the business succeeds: that the right directors are on the board and the right strategy is followed. Union reps therefore face, as do managers, the need for a different culture. They still have a responsibility to represent individuals who are unfairly treated, but everyone is on the same side, seeking to get the constitution properly implemented. There is growing interest in 'social unionism', or in the US, 'bargaining for the common good' (Martin and Quick 2020). In Scotland, it takes the form of a common weal movement striving for common good where what is shared is beneficial for members of a given community, whether defined by geography or online. By making workers owners and active partners, the changed constitution involves all who work in the business in the experience of active democracy. The effects on individual workers are powerful: people are respected; they become informed about the business in which they work; they learn that their knowledge and opinions are valuable; they exercise their votes periodically; and they have an incentive to be creative about how to improve their business. Instead of being subjected to an unelected elite dictatorship, they are encouraged to think and work actively to ensure their enterprise's success for all, including the local community. Instead of being against them, the institution where they work is on their side and under their informed governance. A strand of conventional management thinking aims to get employees to 'think like owners'. In this situation, they really *are* the owners, and most respond to that situation as owners who care.

In 2020, Scotland with 8.2% of the UK population, had some 17% of its employee-owned companies (Robinson and Pendleton 2019). Employee ownership suits the 'Jock Tamson's bairns' strand in Scotland's culture. This preeminence was helped by the funding from 2006 of Co-operative Development Scotland (CDS), an advisory body later merged into Scottish Enterprise, the government business support body, where it remains. CDS found that converting small and medium-sized enterprises into employee ownership was more fertile ground than building new co-operatives. Worker-owned businesses and worker co-operatives are similar in principle and effect.

The rights that need to be transferred to employees for an employee-owned business to function have been analysed by Ellerman (2021). The rights surrendered to the employer/owner by any employee who signs an employment contract are the following: (i) the right to be informed about the business; (ii) the right to appoint or elect the leaders of the business and to supervise their decision-making; and (iii) the right to share in the wealth or loss created by the employees working in the business. These rights are seen as belonging to the owners of the business. However, they are not all, in their nature, ownership rights. In the political world, the right to vote cannot be sold, given away or inherited: it depends on residency in a country. To sell it or hire it out to someone else would be corrupt. Similarly, in a democracy, the right to seek out any information felt to be required is every citizen's right, whether exercised or not. Employee-owned businesses have the same system: workers have the vote because they work in the business; it is not a tradable property right, but a personal right because of their role. Similarly, the right to information is not a piece of property and cannot be sold. What is workers' property is any capital they build through the annual distributions from profit.

The Next Steps

Forty years-plus of neo-liberalism and subsequent financial dominance have left the economy weakened and caused grotesque economic and social inequalities. The pandemic has exposed many weaknesses in globalisation. To address the triple crises facing us – the pandemic, global warming, post-Brexit unemployment – it is increasingly apparent that we need an alternative, more democratic, more environmentally sustainable, economic model. Having saved most of the economy with tax-payer cash, it would be foolish simply to hand it back to the owners of businesses. To challenge economic dictatorship by corporate elites, to move productivity upwards at the same time as distributing wealth rather than concentrating it, governments should support worker ownership. And unions should retrain their organisers to focus on how to make democratic constitutions work in practice in businesses so that they are no longer based upon conflict, but rather partnerships of all who work there, strongly linked into the needs of their local communities and aimed at success over the long term.

Progressive governments should, as soon as they have the powers, introduce democracy into the economic institutions where workers work, as Scottish Labour leader Richard Leonard advocated in 2017. Public policy, as in France and Italy, should give business owners stronger tax incentives than now exist to sell their businesses to their workforces. The workers of any business that is being sold should be given the pre-emptive right to have first refusal to buy it at fair market value. The government, with the help of the professional accounting bodies, should define the system for deciding on fair market value, which will often be less than a predatory acquirer would have paid. Given the benefits, both economic and human, the provision of risk capital to enable such buyouts – such capital is frequently a limiting factor – would fall squarely in the remit of a Scottish national investment bank.

Eventually, as the politicians gain confidence that worker ownership has the desired effects, they should aim for a 'big bang' conversion of all equity into subordinated debt, which will give the owners of those securities no right to interfere in the management of the companies but be just as tradable as shares are currently. *Bona fide* financial institutions such as investment funds and pension funds holding shares to provide income for individuals will still have the same incentives to examine and critique the performance of the companies whose securities they hold – they will have the certainty of knowing in advance what their income will be, and they will gain confidence over time that companies will continue to perform at least as well as they would have done under the conflict-ridden, dictatorial and exploitative system we now have. As well as greater robustness and worker engagement in active democratic systems, the dynamic of the Scottish economy will shift towards more local supply chains, reversing the 40-year trend of offshoring jobs to low-wage economies. Overall, this would create the conditions for high sustainable productivity and wide income distribution as major dynamics built into the economy.

References

Blasi, J., Freeman, R. and Kruse, D. (2016) 'Do broad-based employee ownership, profit sharing and stock options help the best firms do even better?', *British Journal of Industrial Relations*, 54/1: 55–82.

Bratton, J. and Gold, J. (2017) *Human Resource Management: Theory and Practice*, London: Palgrave.

Ellerman, D. (2021) *Neo-abolitionism: Abolishing Human Rentals in Favour of Workplace Democracy*, Ljubljana, Slovenia: Springer.

Martin, A. and Quick, A. (2020) *Unions Renewed*, Cambridge, UK: Polity Press.

Robinson, A. and Pendleton, A. (2019) *Employee Ownership in Britain: Size and Character*, York, UK: White Rose Employee Ownership Centre, https://employeeownership.co.uk/wp-content/uploads/White-Rose-Centre-for-employee-ownership-survey-2019-report.pdf.

Thompson, P. (2013) 'Financialisation and the workplace: Extending and applying the disconnected capitalism thesis', *Work, Employment and Society*, 27/3: 472–488.

Wylie, B. (2020) *Bandit Capitalism*, Edinburgh, UK: Birlinn.

PART II

Policy Areas

7

Towards an Effective Right to Housing in Scotland

Regina Serpa and Emma Saunders

Introduction

More than ten years on from the 2008 global financial crisis, housing remains in crisis in Scotland in terms of supply, quality and affordability. At the same time, barriers to accessing housing continue to contribute to housing inequality in Scotland. In this chapter, we argue that housing inequality is not merely the result of blind, impersonal market forces, but rather and more importantly a consequence of deliberate policies which have protected a market-based approach to housing rather than one driven by regarding housing as a right where homes are to satisfy human need. In other words, under neo-liberalism, the state has been used to structure the processes and outcomes of the market in housing in a certain way and for the benefit of the few and not the many. In some aspects, it has introduced market mechanisms where there were previously none, and in others, relaxed the regulation of capital in the housing market. Such a crisis demands radical reforms to change the system, rather than piecemeal or incremental changes. This chapter outlines the scale of the housing crisis in Scotland, identifies the structural origins of the housing problem, and explains how current constraints can be overcome. We conclude by offering a framework for a progressive housing model. This can result in an achievable right to housing as a cornerstone of a green and socially just society, where energy-efficient housing can be used as a way to tackle climate change and create jobs, provide genuinely affordable and secure housing to alleviate economic stress, and guarantee access to quality homes which protect people's health and wellbeing. Now is the time for the Scottish Government to understand the scale of the housing crisis and seize the opportunity to advance a right to housing in Scotland.

Scale of the Housing Crisis

A comparison between contemporary housing conditions with those in the previous 50 years provides a stark contrast. The landscape for housing in Scotland has significantly shifted: from a policy relying on a largely de-commodified approach, with housing provided primarily through municipal authorities and offering reasonable standards of security and affordability to one where housing is largely valued as a speculative commodity, with public provision relegated to a 'residual' (i.e., housing of last resort) status (Logan and Molotch 2007). Rising prices have followed, whilst progress towards expanding housing rights north of the border has failed to eradicate homelessness.

Just 40 years ago, the majority of Scots were social renters: in 1981, the social housing sector comprised 54% of all housing in Scotland, most of which was provided by local authorities (Robertson and Serpa 2014). By 2016, council and social tenants represented 23% of all tenants. In 1999, the private rented sector (PRS) was home to 5% of tenants, rising to 15% by 2016 (Robertson and Serpa 2014). All the while, homeownership has become the majority tenure (62%), being underlined by large-scale private debt and state subsidy (Scottish Government 2019).

As tenure shifted, the cost of a home skyrocketed: according to the Registers of Scotland, the average price of a residential property in Scotland in 2019–2020 was £182,357. This figure represents an 18% rise when compared with the average price of £154,820 in 2007–2008, and a 400–800% rise from £10,000–20,000 in the early 1970s (Macfarlane 2017). The cost of renting has followed a similar trajectory: average PRS rents in Scotland for a two-bed property have increased by 28% between 2010 and 2020, particularly in the Lothians, Glasgow and the Highlands (Indigo House Group 2020). Similarly, between 2013/2014 and 2019/2020, average rents in the Scottish social housing sector increased by 19.91% (Indigo House Group 2020), closely approximating rent rises in the PRS. Rapidly rising housing costs have had clear consequences for affordability: in the 1960s–1970s, UK renters spent around 10% of their income on housing; by 2016, 36% (Ryan-Collins 2018). Unsurprisingly, the proportion of people in the PRS living in poverty increased by 75% between 2006 and 2016 (Scottish Government 2020a), and in 2020 it was estimated that 40% of social tenants and 33% of private tenants in Scotland were living in poverty (JRF 2020).

Homes in Scotland are expensive relative to their quality: 57% of PRS homes have an energy rating of D or below, and 47% of social homes and over 75% of all dwellings are estimated to be in disrepair, with 57% of homes having disrepair to critical elements. These figures represent an environmental and social cost: in 2019, residential buildings accounted for 16% of total emissions in Scotland and nearly 25% of households, mostly tenants, were estimated to be in fuel poverty, with ongoing exposure to mould and damp having long-term impacts on health (Scottish Government 2020b).

Such shifts have taken place in a context where the building of social housing has decreased by 42% between 1980 and 2010 (Scottish Government 2019). Some 21,292 new-build homes were completed in Scotland over the period 2018–2019, just over a quarter of which comprised social housing (Scottish Government 2019). The number of completed social houses between 2010 and 2020 pales in comparison to figures in the late 1960s and represents a 20% decrease from levels achieved before the 2007–2008 financial crisis. In 2007, the Scottish Government acknowledged that housing supply needed to increase to 35,000 new houses per year to reverse declining levels of affordability (Macfarlane 2017). After 14 years of deepening housing crisis, the achievement of just over half that figure remains inadequate.

Finally, the UK statutory homeless system is unique in that it creates enforceable rights to settled accommodation for homeless households through establishing legal rights to housing (Fitzpatrick et al. 2014). In Scotland, the legal framework for homelessness duties and powers following devolution has sought to expand the rights of homeless households further, instigating a near 'universal' right to settled housing for all homeless people. However, homelessness legislation in Scotland has been criticised for not placing greater prominence on preventative measures, despite being considered to be the closest to a 'right to housing' in Europe (Anderson and Serpa 2013). Nevertheless, rising numbers of households in temporary accommodation and an increasing proportion of social lettings let out to homeless households following the financial crisis have indicated a need to broaden housing rights and entitlements.

Explaining the Crisis

This current housing crisis in Scotland can be explained by the dominance of neo-liberal ideology and associated strategies of commodification, deregulation, financialisation and policy-led gentrification. Housing has become a key commodity in an inflated and financialised global market. The commodification of housing as an asset can be traced back to fiscal calamity and restructuring following the International Monetary Fund crisis of the mid- to late 1970s. The deregulation of building societies and the liberalisation of mortgage credit promoted by Conservative governments, alongside the Conservatives' ideological drive for homeownership through 'Right-to-Buy', ongoing policies aimed at undermining public housing, and post-2008, ongoing attempts to 'kickstart' the economy through an array of incentives for first-time house buyers, have all given rise to homeownership as the dominant tenure in Scotland (Robertson and Serpa 2014). As housing has been increasingly privatised, a 'rentier' economy has emerged, whereby it is ownership of assets (rather than work) which determines one's wealth (Christophers 2020).

Processes of deregulation have led to growing costs and insecurity, which more recent legislative attempts have failed to redress. Tenants' protests throughout the twentieth century ensured that some measure of rent controls remained in place until the Housing Act 1988 deregulated rents on new private lets and introduced Assured Shorthold Tenancies in Scotland (Wilson 2017). The rapid subsequent increase in the PRS as a proportion of total housing stock and equally rapid rises in PRS rent levels are strongly related to the repeal of rent controls, alongside the restricted availability of social housing. Following sustained campaigning, in 2016 the Scottish Government introduced reforms, such as the Private Residential Tenancies (PRTs) and the possibility for local authorities to implement rent caps in areas called 'Rent Pressure Zones' where rent increases were deemed to be 'excessive' (Indigo House Group 2020). Despite these reforms, PRS tenants still lack a right to decent, affordable housing in Scotland.

Financial markets play a growing role in housing provision. Houses are increasingly seen as investments offering financial security, in the face of stagnating wages and decreasing pensions. Subsequently, access to mortgage finance has lubricated rising demand for homes. Increasingly, the boards of housing associations tend to be dominated by those with expertise in finance, accountancy and law, as decreasing government funding requires a search for new forms of credit. Banks and traditional lenders make up the majority of the shortfall, but 20% of lending now comes from pension funds, bond and capital markets (Scottish Housing Regulator 2020). The current financialised social housing model therefore involves minimal government funding, strong reliance on investment markets, high interest levels on loans and pressure on housing associations to seek funding through cross-subsidies and rent increases.

Lastly, neo-liberal ideology has redefined the definition of affordable housing and promoted 'mixed-tenure' neighbourhoods as a means to gentrify formerly working-class communities. In 2012, the Westminster Government established a new category of 'affordable rent' whereby social housing rents could reach up to 80% of market rents, measuring rents in relation to market values rather than income, thus making 'affordable housing' largely inaccessible to low-income households. In Scotland, there is no clear definition of 'affordable housing', and while there is evidence that affordable rent rarely rises to the maximum 80% of market levels, the deliberately confusing use of the term makes assessment of genuinely 'affordable' housing output (based on residual household income) almost impossible to determine and has fostered the commodification of social housing. For instance, new forms of tenure now portrayed as 'affordable' include: mid-market rent, shared ownership and new supply shared equity, introducing mortgaged property and even 'Build-to-Rent' into the social housing domain. At the same time, social housing has been 'residualised' as a tenure of last resort, and formerly working-class areas of social housing stigmatised as 'areas of concentrated poverty' to justify further transformation into 'mixed communities'. In practice, this has often meant destroying former social housing in favour of building more expensive housing targeted at a wealthier population, yet an inverse process of 'mixing' is rarely promoted in more affluent areas.

Securing Housing Rights

Persistent problems of housing supply, quality and affordability offer considerable challenges for housing policy some 20 years following devolution in Scotland. Despite the expansion of rights for the homeless, private tenancy reform and improvements to housing condition standards, we believe the Scottish Government needs to be bolder in its ambition on housing. Crucially, we propose a new social agenda, one which guarantees universal access to high-quality, genuinely affordable housing through both expanding the supply and standards of new homes and regulating the existing public, social and private stock. This would also see housing becoming a cornerstone of achieving a better society and meeting Scotland's climate targets. A right to housing has the potential to positively impact multiple domains of social life (for example, economic security, mental and physical health and safety, employment opportunities, community feeling, civic participation and other aspects of citizenship), given that ensuring adequate housing offers the potential to realise a range of related benefits. An effective right to decent housing as set out above is therefore part of a series of economic and social rights. Taken together, these rights can challenge significant disparities in material wellbeing and strengthen the foundations of a just and democratic society. Importantly, achieving such a right requires radical political, material and ideological changes, away from a market ideology that sees housing as an asset, and towards ambitious policies that cement redistribution and equality.

The human right to housing is not merely a right to shelter, but should be interpreted more broadly as the right to live in security, peace and dignity. For housing to be considered adequate and to realise the right to housing, we believe there are seven key conditions which must be met. These include: security of tenure; availability of services, materials, facilities and infrastructure; affordability; habitability; accessibility; location; and cultural adequacy (SHRC 2020). Locating a right to housing within a human rights framework moves the debate beyond means-testing and distinctions between deserving and undeserving groups (on which many welfare systems are premised), and instead focuses on a universal entitlement to an acceptable standard of living. Upholding that universality is an ideological shift: everyone should have access to a home to live in, rather than the current situation where *some* should be supported to profit from owning houses, whilst others should provide a stream of income.

Realising radical change means articulating a popular challenge to the interests of the property and financial elites and their lobbyists, and implementing a strategy to de-commodify housing. Promoting a right to housing requires reversing the stigmatisation of social housing as an 'ambulance service', and returning to 'general needs' housing. To this end, the Scottish Government must invest in building genuinely affordable Passivhaus standard public and social homes, daring to achieve numbers of new-builds replicating the 1960s–1970s (i.e., 30,000–40,000 p.a.), alongside a programme to buy back housing lost through 'Right-to-Buy'. Councils should also immediately stop the short-sighted selling-off of their remaining land to private developers, and instead use available land to build the housing needed. The Scottish Government should increase funds to allow community buy-outs of private land, where a variety of mutual financing models can provide genuinely affordable housing alongside that of the state.

We want to imagine housing as an essential means for Scotland to achieve its climate targets: sequestering carbon through house building and addressing the carbon footprint of existing and new houses. The Scottish Government should introduce net zero carbon building standards for all new builds and launch a co-ordinated programme of retro-fitting social and private homes, relying on incentives, including: subsidies for registered social landlords; interest-free loans for homeowners; national co-ordination of refurbishment (including mapping of best practice, training workers and procurement streamlining); and enforceable energy efficiency requirements. The Scottish Government should work with the Westminster Government to harmonise VAT so that refurbishment (20% VAT) is on a level playing field with demolition and new-build (0% VAT), and to introduce green bonds to fund such ambitious plans.

Housing provision should be accompanied by enhanced regulation, to address issues of affordability and security. Refurbishment work should not be paid for by the tenants, and no tenant should face 'renoviction' – eviction following rising rents after a renovation. This is why the Scottish Government should introduce a practically enforceable system of rent controls which is based on quality, location, size and other relevant factors with clear appeal mechanisms, limiting exponential increases in rents and associated growing poverty in the PRS. In the social sector, a similar system of rent controls should be instituted alongside the expansion of tenant participation initiatives, thereby reforming social landlords' rent consultation processes.

The Scottish Government should enhance the regulatory protections of tenants, specifically private tenants, by re-categorising existing grounds for evictions as discretionary alongside the appropriate pre-action requirements, and by updating the Private Residential Tenancy to address the needs of joint tenants and closing regulatory loopholes around short-term lets and student housing, to return houses to their primary use – as homes, not income streams. All these measures should be accompanied by greater powers of enforcement locally and nationally to ensure that landlords fulfil their obligations. Such reforms would open up the possibility of changing the very relationship between people and housing: enabling the democratisation of access to land, continuing to support community land ownership and community buy-out (see Chapter 16), revisiting the vision of co-operative housing or locally managed housing associations and for tenants building their power through tenants' unions, to empower the fight for a genuine 'right to housing', now and in the future.

As a final point, the emergence of the COVID-19 pandemic has reinforced deep, structural inequalities within society – not only with respect to health, but in all aspects of social life, including housing. At a time when many are required to socially isolate, we have been reminded of the crucial importance of safe and quality housing and its connection with other rights, including rights to health, work and education. Prior to the public health emergency, concern was raised over both homelessness and the inadequate provision of housing in the UK by a variety of United Nations Treaty Body Committees and by the UN Special Rapporteur on Extreme Poverty and Human Rights. The predicted dramatic economic consequences of the pandemic mean that many more people will require housing support. Emergency funding and measures have been designated to respond to the crisis, but these have been patches to structural issues rather than systemic reforms. The next five years provide an opportunity for the Scottish Government to offer a bold vision, based on ensuring that people have access to decent, secure and genuinely affordable homes, and in so doing addressing the scale of the economic and environmental crisis that threatens our society. We hope that the Scottish Government rises to this challenge, because Scotland's residents can no longer afford to wait.

References

Anderson, I. and Serpa, R. (2013) 'The right to settled accommodation for homeless people in Scotland: A triumph of rational policy making?', *European Journal of Homelessness*, 7/1: 13–39.

Christophers, B. (2020) *Rentier Capitalism: Who Owns the Economy, and Who Pays for It?* London: Verso.

Fitzpatrick, S., Bengtsson, B. and Watts, B. (2014) 'Rights to housing: Reviewing the terrain and exploring a way forward', *Housing, Theory and Society*, 31/4: 447–463.

Indigo House Group (2020) *Rent Better: Wave 1 Baseline Report*, London: Nationwide.

JRF (2020) *Poverty in Scotland 2020*, York, UK: Joseph Rowntree Foundation.

Logan, J. and Molotch, H. (2007) *Urban Fortunes: The Political Economy of Place*, Berkeley, CA: University of California Press.

Macfarlane, L. (2017) *The Housing Land Market in Scotland: A Discussion Paper*, Inverness, UK: Scottish Land Commission.

Robertson, D. and Serpa, R. (2014) 'Social housing in Scotland', in Scanlon, K., Whitehead, C. and Arrigoitia, M. (eds) *Social Housing in Europe*, Oxford, UK: Wiley Blackwell, pp. 43–58.

Ryan-Collins, J. (2018) *Why Can't You Afford a Home?* London: Polity Press.

Scottish Government (2019) *Housing Statistics 2019: Key Trends and Summary*, Edinburgh, UK: Scottish Government.

Scottish Government (2020a) *Poverty and Income Inequality in Scotland 2016–2019*, Edinburgh, UK: Scottish Government.

Scottish Government (2020b) *Scottish House Condition Survey 2019: Key Findings*, Edinburgh, UK: Scottish Government.

Scottish Housing Regulator (2020) *Summary of the Annual Loan Portfolio Returns at 31 March 2020*, Edinburgh, UK: Scottish Housing Regulator.

SHRC (2020) *Housing Rights in Practice*, Edinburgh, UK: Scottish Human Rights Commission.

Wilson, W. (2017) *A Short History of Rent Control*, Briefing Paper 6747, 30 March, London: House of Commons Library.

8

Creating a Healthier Scotland

Iain Ferguson and Gerry McCartney

Introduction

Scotland's health has dramatically improved over the last 150 years. It is now rare for mothers to die in childbirth or babies to die in infancy, and most live into pensionable age and do so in relatively good health. However, relative to other European countries, and to the rest of Britain, improvements in these headline health indicators lag behind others, leaving life expectancy lower than in comparable populations. The causes of the lagging overall trends, widening health inequalities and excess mortality – even after accounting for the higher poverty and deprivation in Scotland compared to the rest of the UK (the 'Scottish/Glasgow Effect') – are now well understood. Historical urban and public policy decisions generating higher numbers of poor-quality, peripheral housing estates, accelerated deindustrialisation, and creation of new towns and associated selective migration all left Scotland more vulnerable to the introduction of neo-liberal policies from the 1980s onwards compared to other areas (Walsh et al. 2016). The rise in income, wealth and power inequalities associated with the mass privatisations and disinvestment of the subsequent decades caused a rapid increase in health inequalities and rises in alcohol-, drug- and violence-related mortality (Scott-Samuel et al. 2014).

Over the last decade, the health challenges facing Scotland have intensified. Improving life expectancy rates have now effectively stalled for both sexes since 2012. Average trends hide worsening premature mortality rates for people living in the most deprived 40% of areas. The most likely causes of this are austerity policies introduced since 2010, including declining real-terms value of benefits (and increased conditionality), increased precarious work and squeezed funding for public services (particularly local government) (ScotPHO 2021). The trends are particularly bad for working-age adults living in the most deprived areas of Scottish cities, where mortality rates are rapidly increasing, not least because of an exponential rise in drug-related deaths (Walsh et al. 2020). Mortality statistics are only part of the experience of health, and are not a good measure of other aspects of health, specifically mental health. It remains one of greatest limits to people living in good health. Over the last decade, it has worsened for those impacted by changes to social security (Wickham et al. 2020, Taulbut et al. 2018) and prescribing for mental ill-health has increased in the population overall (ScotPHO 2016).

The pandemic has exacerbated many existing trends. Both the direct impacts of mortality and morbidity from the virus, and the indirect impacts on incomes, employment, education and social isolation, have impacted disproportionately on the people living in the most deprived areas, those in working-class jobs, and on ethnic minorities. Although the direct impacts have impacted most on men and the elderly, the indirect impacts have disproportionately affected women and the young (Douglas et al. 2020). The role of government in exacerbating the impact has been widely aired, and the strategic approach to managing the pandemic has not always been clear or coherent. The extent to which the Scottish Government has been tied into a broader UK-wide strategy can be debated, but the lack of independent financial powers to fund policies such as furlough has meant that the Scottish approach has tracked the UK approach to a substantial degree (Horton 2020, Ferguson and Gall 2021, Calvert and Arbuthnott 2021).

This chapter explores the ways in which health and social care services in Scotland have changed in recent decades, and the wider economic and political forces shaping these changes. The social determinants of health referred to above – poverty, inequality, poor housing and so on – are by far the main factors affecting the health and life chances of people in Scotland (as elsewhere). Access to publicly provided health and (to a lesser degree) social care services which the post-war welfare state provided marked a huge step forward for working-class people, so it is important to assess and critique the ways in which access has been expanded or constrained in recent years by the policies of both Westminster and Holyrood Governments.

Causes

The primary causes of Scotland's health problems do not arise because of a failure of health or social care services. Even less are they the product of 'poor choices' or individual behaviours. Rather, their roots lie in an economic system which promotes inequality and insecurity (see Chapters 1 and 10), in a decade of austerity during which the poorest and most vulnerable have been made to pay for the banking bail-out in 2008, in failure by both national and local governments to challenge austerity policies, and in the historical legacy of policy and institutions that Scotland has been exposed to. So the causes are rooted in social determinants of health. It is therefore unfair to expect health and social care services to be held responsible for these trends. That said, health and social care services have been subjected to change, so it is relevant to understand that they have been able to respond to increasing needs. Most hospital services in Scotland are provided through the territorial health board structures which provide a network of District General Hospitals and tertiary specialist hospitals. Primary care services are delivered through a mix of direct provision (whereby the NHS runs some GP surgeries and dental clinics) and a large series of contracts with other providers (including GP partnerships, dentists and pharmacies). There have been some increases in direct provision of GP services over the last decade, with more '17C' practices (which are run by health boards, with GPs directly employed rather than being independent contractors). However, there has also been a trend towards some entrepreneurial GPs employing nurses and doctors in 'mega-practices'.

During the 'new' Labour years, funding for the NHS increased markedly, leading to a renewal of much of the physical infrastructure in both primary and secondary care in Scotland. However, many of the new hospitals and surgeries were built under the Private Finance Initiative (PFI) or Public–Private Partnerships (PPPs), leaving health boards with large recurrent revenue costs for modest capital investments. There has been less movement towards direct provision of healthcare services by the private sector in Scotland compared to elsewhere, not least because of changes to legislation introduced in 2007. However, there remain risks of creeping privatisation, as represented by the more entrepreneurial end of the independent contractor model for primary care and the Strathcathro treatment centre in Tayside (Kirkwood and Pollock 2017).

If the NHS in Scotland has not experienced the degree of privatisation that it has south of the border, the same can hardly be said of social care. Since the welfare state's creation in 1948, there has been a glaring disparity between a national health service free at the point of need and funded out of general taxation and a fragmented social care system which rations services on the basis of charges and ever-tighter eligibility criteria. Despite these limitations, until the early 1990s social care remained overwhelmingly a local authority-provided service, albeit one which was often paternalist and 'top-down' in dealing with service users and which relied heavily on women's unpaid labour within families. The NHS and Community Care Act introduced by the Conservatives in 1990 changed this. It created a market in social care, based upon a 'purchaser/provider' split. The role of local authorities was transformed from being direct care providers to purchasers and commissioners of services which were increasingly provided by private or 'third sector' providers, based on competition for contracts. The end result was 'the biggest privatisation in history' (Gosling 2008/2011). The stated aim was to improve quality, choice and control for service users. But the opposite has been the case (Blakely and Quilter-Pinney 2019). Private providers have less training for staff, higher turnover and lower pay – and the private care market has proven volatile, with large operators using highly leveraged business models, leading to their collapse, as in the case of Southern Cross. Moreover, small nursing and residential homes have provided better care. Despite this, the economies of scale these large providers offer can prove difficult for cash-strapped councils to resist. Given the impact of these market failures, it is deeply concerning that the Scottish Government-commissioned Feeley Review (Scottish Government 2021) ruled out recommending nationalisation of social care. While it made some progressive recommendations, its central recommendations – establishing a National Care Service and replacing 'markets with partnerships' – are likely to be no more than good intentions while social care continues to be dominated by firms such as HC One which shape the market for other providers and whose primary concern is their profits.

Nor is health and social care integration, the dominant policy for more than a decade, the panacea it is often claimed to be. Kempe (2021) argued that it has so far met with little obvious success:

> The chasm between primary and secondary care on the NHS remains and, with Health and Social Care Partnerships (HCSPs) close to financial collapse, the evidence suggests that neither the NHS nor councils have the resources to make them work.

From a different direction, the policy of integration has been met with suspicion and sometimes outright opposition from many disabled activists. Daniels and Williams-Finlay (2021), two leading members of the disability movement, argued:

> Many decent people remain confused as to why the agenda for the integration of Health and Social Care structures is so dangerous and oppressive. For decades, disabled people and their organisations have fought against the medicalisation of their lifestyles. They view the integration of services, culture, and planning based on such medicalisation as turning the clock back.

It is that same opposition to the dominance of the bio-medical model of health, professional and ideological, that has also led some social workers to question about the alleged benefits of integration. Thus, Turbett (2021) argued:

> The health service in its many forms is a giant compared to social work and social care and this partial merging of functions has not served social work well. It has only led to further marginalisation of its role and functions, additional to the processes already taking place since the 1990s. Health

and social work have different underlying philosophies and, rather than complimentary and mutually beneficial practices developing, the former has become dominant.

In fact, professional social work has suffered enormously from a managerialist agenda. Returning to a community social work model, managed by qualified social workers and with closer links both to community groups and to other local authority departments such as education and housing, is increasingly seen by many in the profession as the best way forward, rather than its continued subordination to health managers whose primary concern is often with relieving the problem of 'bed-blocking'.

There have been many opportunities within health and social care to take a different path. Much of the additional resource provided between 1997 and 2008 was diverted into private contracts. Wage differentials across the NHS remain stark even with some progress in increasing the wages of the lowest-paid social care workers, most of whom are women, as a result of union-led legal action rather than pre-emptive policy change. Finally, experimentation with directly elected health boards, in recognition of disconnected governance of the NHS from either local or national democratic processes, has not engendered substantial engagement from the public, and the governance structures remain unreformed.

Achieving Step-change

To achieve improved health and wellbeing and narrow health inequalities, we require all policies to support health. This means that economic and industrial policy has to serve the population's needs by providing adequate and decent jobs, incomes, goods and services so that inequalities in income, wealth and power reproducing health inequalities are driven down. Housing and public transport need to be high-quality, affordable, accessible and equitable. Our physical and social environments must provide a context in which we can flourish. And our health and social care services also need to play a role here.

Thus, the first and most important step in improving Scotland's population health record is to ensure the impact of health is seen in all policies, and that any policy that negatively impacts on health or inequality is avoided. Then, healthcare services should be provided directly by the NHS (including GP services, dentistry, pharmacy and physiotherapy). The continued provision of some healthcare by the private sector, or independent contractors (such as GPs and dentists), represents unfinished business from when the NHS was created, with the independent contractor model being established as a compromise with the medical profession. Direct NHS provision is more effective in meeting needs equitably, thereby effectively tackling the 'inverse care law' in which it is seen that there is greater unmet need where there is greater market involvement (Tudor-Hart 1971).

The NHS is also the biggest single employer and procurer in Scotland. Through the NHS, substantial inroads into wage inequalities could be made by converging the pay of higher and lower grades and between professional groups. A substantial proportion of NHS spend is on pharmaceuticals, which have often been created and produced with the benefit of publicly funded scientific research. It is difficult to redress this within Scotland, but an international collaboration in which the NHS contributes scientific knowledge and receives in turn its share of the 'intellectual property' would help to stop financial 'leakage' into 'big pharma'. Taking back ownership of the privately owned buildings (PFI/PPP contracts) is another way by which unnecessary financial 'leakage' occurs. This would augment resources for healthcare.

There is often debate about the best method of democratic accountability for large publicly owned services such as the NHS. As often demonstrated by local hospital campaigns, NHS managements seem unaccountable to the public. The current governance arrangements comprise a board of executive (senior health board employees) and non-executive directors (usually comprising a mix of experts and local councillors), with the board chair being directly accountable to the Cabinet Secretary, and a union-nominated Employee Director. This arrangement does not appear to have created the power-sharing arrangement between the Scottish Government, local government, workers and the public that is needed. However, it is not yet clear how best to improve on this, not least because of the need to avoid substantial local variation in a national service.

Conclusion

Between the 1920s and late 1970s, life expectancy improved, health inequalities narrowed, and available measures of well-being were at a historical high. In addition to creating the NHS, achieving this required the welfare state's creation, highly progressive taxes, increased power for organised labour, state pensions, reduced income and wealth inequalities, and the building of hundreds of thousands of council homes. In the subsequent decades, all of these institutions and policies have been undermined or underfunded, driving the decline of many health trends. To achieve substantial reductions in health inequalities and to raise life expectancy improvements again, a further change in economic direction is required such that economic policy supports the funding of public services and social security, thereby ending austerity so that income, wealth and power inequalities start to narrow, and eliminating precarious work and poverty. Even in the shorter term, moving away from austerity and increases in poverty levels would make a big difference given the particular impact they have had over the last decade. However, simply re-inventing the institutions and structures of the post-Second World War settlement would represent a misstep. As there is a more productive economy now, it is no longer necessary (if it ever was) for people to work long hours and to forgo leisure time. We cannot afford to have the fossil fuel consumption of the twentieth century if we are to avoid climate chaos. We also need to learn from democratic experiments, not least the recent citizens' assemblies.

Health and social care services should be free at the point of use, publicly owned and accountable, and provided according to need. The agenda for a future government should therefore be to put in place policies across government that actively improve health and reduce health and social inequalities. Within health and social care services, the opportunities to use the spending on staff and goods should be much more actively used to reduce wage inequalities and to create publicly owned supply chains that retain value for workers and the public rather than concentrate it with the already wealthy. There is also an opportunity to put in place new democratic structures to give the public and workers a much more manifest role in the governance of services to ensure genuine ownership and accountability. Given the reluctance of Holyrood Governments since 1999 to challenge either the austerity policies emanating from Westminster or the powerful industrial, financial and landowning interests which continue to rule Scotland, these much-needed reforms are unlikely to be realised unless we are able to create a powerful grassroots movement which insists that our health and social wellbeing should take precedence over the interests and priorities of neo-liberal capitalism (Ferguson and Mooney 2021).

References

Blakely, G. and Quilter-Pinney, H. (2019) *Who Cares? The Financialisation of Adult Social Care*, London: Institute for Public Policy Research.

Calvert, J. and Arbuthnott, G. (2021) *Failures of State: The Inside Story of Britain's Battle with Coronavirus*, London: Mudlark.

Daniels, S. and Williams-Finlay, B. (2021) 'Is Health and social care integration the panacea?', in Ferguson, I. and Gall, G. (eds) *People before Profit: The Future of Social Care in Scotland*, Glasgow, UK: Social Work Action Network/Jimmy Reid Foundation.

Douglas, M., Katikireddi, S., Taulbut, M., McKee, M. and McCartney G. (2020) 'Mitigating the wider health effects of covid-19 pandemic response', *British Medical Journal*, 369: m1,557.

Ferguson, I. and Gall, G. (eds) *People before Profit: The Future of Social Care in Scotland*, Glasgow, UK: Social Work Action Network/ Jimmy Reid Foundation.

Ferguson, I. and Mooney, G. (2021) 'Neoliberalism with a heart? The reality of life under the SNP', in Fotheringham, B., Sherry, D. and Bryce, C. (eds) *Breaking Up the British State: Scotland, Independence and Socialism*, London: Bookmarks, pp. 338–372.

Gosling, P. (2008, updated 2011) *The Rise of the 'Public Services Industry'*, London: UNISON, www.cheshireeastunison.org.uk/files/resources/19.pdf.

Horton, R. (2020) *The Covid-19 Catastrophe: What's Gone Wrong and How to Stop It Happening Again*, Cambridge, UK: Polity Press.

Kempe, N. (2021) 'Towards a set of principles for a national care service', *Scottish Left Review*, 121: 6–7.

Kirkwood G. and Pollock, A. (2017) 'Patient choice and private provision decreased public provision and increased inequalities in Scotland: A case study of elective hip arthroplasty', *Journal of Public Health*, 39/3: 593–600.

ScotPHO (2016) *Scottish Burden of Disease Study*, Edinburgh, UK: Scottish Public Health Observatory, www.scotpho.org.uk/comparative-health/burden-of-disease/overview.

ScotPHO (2021) *Recent Mortality Trends*, Edinburgh, UK: Scottish Public Health Observatory, www.scotpho.org.uk/population-dynamics/recent-mortality-trends/.

Scottish Government (2021) *Independent Review of Adult Care in Scotland* (chaired by Derek Feeley), Edinburgh, UK: Scottish Government.

Scott-Samuel, A., Bambra, C., Collins C., Hunter D., McCartney G. and Smith K. (2014) 'The impact of Thatcherism on health and well-being in Britain', *International Journal of Health Services*, 44/1: 53–71.

Taulbut, M., Agbato, D. and McCartney, G. (2018) *Working and Hurting? Monitoring the Health and Health Inequalities Impacts of the Economic Downturn and Changes to the Social Security System*, Edinburgh, UK: Public Health Scotland, www.healthscotland.scot/publications/working-and-hurting.

Tudor-Hart J. (1971) 'The Inverse Care Law', *The Lancet*, 297: 405–412.

Turbett, C. (2021) *Struggling to Care: Why Scotland Needs to Reform the Role of Social Workers*, Glasgow, UK: Common Weal, https://commonweal.scot/policy-library/struggling-care.

Walsh, D., McCartney G., Collins, C., Taulbut, M. and Batty, G. (2016) *History, Politics and Vulnerability: Explaining Excess Mortality*, Glasgow, UK: Glasgow Centre for Population Health, www.gcph.co.uk/publications/635_history_politics_and_vulnerability_explaining_excess_mortality.

Walsh, D., McCartney, G., Minton, J., Parkinson, J., Shipton, D. and Whyte, B. (2020) 'Changing mortality trends in countries and cities of the United Kingdom: A population-based trend analysis', *BMJ Open*, 10/e038135: 1–9.

Wickham, S., Bentley, L., Rose, T., Whitehead, M., Taylor-Robinson, D. and Barr, B. (2020) 'Effects on mental health of a UK welfare reform, Universal Credit: A longitudinal controlled study', *Lancet Public Health*, 5/3: e157–164.

9

Improving Learning: Education after the Pandemic

Brian Boyd, Larry Flanagan, Henry Maitles and Mary Senior

Introduction

Scottish education continues to be held in high regard, despite a persistent political undertone which echoes the ill-founded mantra: 'Scottish education used to be the best in the world and now it is only mediocre.' Pre-pandemic, most parents expressed confidence in the education and learning provided to their offspring, and the experience of the pandemic and home schooling has only served to confirm the importance of schools to children's wellbeing and resilience. More broadly, there is general support for no tuition fees in higher education, and a well-founded belief that our colleges and universities have manifest strengths. Notwithstanding such positive framing, much remains which can be improved. Thatcherism witnessed introducing market forces into all sectors of education across Britain – marketisation, testing, league tables, privatisation, managerialism, commercialisation and various metrics. Scottish education, particularly schools, fought hard to resist, but was not immune. Nonetheless, the return of the Scottish Parliament in 1999, with education being a wholly devolved area, created opportunities for a different approach in Scotland.

Consequently, the Curriculum for Excellence (CfE) framework for education for ages 3–18, allowed the early years sector (ages 3–8) to embrace the type of play learning associated with effective educational systems like Finland. However, the Scottish Government also imposed Primary 1 Standardised Assessment in spite of contrary research evidence. Moreover, the secondary school senior phase has found it difficult to create space for deeper learning, maintaining breadth of study, interdisciplinary learning and parity of esteem between 'vocational' and 'academic' subjects because of high-stakes exam pressures. It is eminently possible here to create new approaches as part of an educational recovery. For two years, exams were replaced by teachers' professional judgement, witnessing confidence and trust of students and their families, compared to wholesale rejection of the Scottish Qualifications Authority's algorithm-driven system and its in-built bias against schools serving the poorest communities.

That challenge – of addressing the impact of poverty on educational attainment at all levels – remains the single biggest issue to be tackled as we look to build an educational recovery. This was highlighted *vis-à-vis* schools by the Auditor General's 2021 Report (*Herald*, 23 March 2021). In Scotland, as elsewhere, the gap between rich and poor and the consequent educational inequality are major issues. Its impact upon education is far-reaching. It is far harder for young people to move out of poverty and areas of deprivation than had been previously assumed. Schools can – and do – make a difference, but the challenge facing the Scottish Government is to use macro-planning to tackle poverty at source, and not tinker around the edges.

The pandemic highlighted inequalities and failings, and underlined the critical role of education. But it has also afforded a new moment of political opportunity to start building an education system that works for pupils, students, staff, communities, and the broader society and economy. Following this introduction, we suggest some areas in which early years and primary schooling could be enhanced. We then examine the specific areas in secondary education relating to high-stakes exams and their impact upon areas such as creativity and citizenship. Further education and higher education are examined in terms of the negative impacts of marketisation and casualisation. Finally, we make some recommendations.

Foundations of Comprehensive Education

In primary schools especially, there has been strong support for the CfE and the interdisciplinary learning and active learning inherent in it. It fits with the teachers' understanding and perspective. For example, in Holocaust Education, primary teachers regularly bring history, geography, modern studies, science, music, art and literature to bear. However, there is growing concern that children start formal learning too early (years 4–5), partly ignoring play-based learning's importance. Some of the most successful school systems, notably in Scandinavia, do not begin formal schooling until around the age of 6 in order to allow pupils to learn through play, to focus upon creativity and to facilitate outdoor learning. Children there are not prevented from learning how to read and write. Rather, these skills develop through the medium of play. Sahlberg's (2014) three-point plan for healthier kids – 'play, play, play' – sums up the philosophy. Many schools in Scotland are taking on these ideas and embedding them into primary education, complementing the experience of early learning. To build this further, consideration should be given to making such early years provision statutory, universal, free to access and paid for out of general taxation. The CfE paved the way for *Realising the Ambition* (Scottish Education 2020). It suggested that building better health through being outdoors would require parent and teacher support to ensure proper clothing and smaller class sizes to make this manageable. Initial teacher education programmes in universities should make it central to teacher education.

Secondary Schools: Beleaguered by Exams

Secondary schools face numerous challenges. First, transitioning pupils from primary to secondary is not universally coherent or progressive, and pupils are sometimes let down by lack of continuity and responsibilities. Second, while abolition of selection of pupils for different schools was fundamental to the comprehensive ideal of 1965, it has been replaced too often by selection *within* schools. The practice of 'setting' or 'streaming' by ability means that 'bottom sets' are likely to be disproportionally populated by boys from deprived areas. Examinations are often used as the reason for this. However, abundant research evidence suggests otherwise. Third, in secondary schools there are unacceptable hierarchies of subjects between 'academic' and 'practical', the former being the preserve of pupils destined for university, and the latter being for those destined for lower-paid jobs or for further education colleges. More recently, STEM (science, technology, engineering and mathematics) subjects have been seen as more important than the social sciences and arts (history, modern studies, music, art, drama and dance). Parity of esteem is lacking, and there is no reasonable argument for one group being more important than others. Fourth, concentration upon exam targets can impact on attempts to develop better-rounded students (Gillborn and Youdell 2000, Maitles 2005). Creativity and citizenship are often only valued if they improve exam results. The examination system has for decades been inherently biased in favour of more advantaged schools and pupils. The pandemic highlighted this, and made the case for re-evaluating upper-school assessments and associated algorithms. Indeed, the Organisation for Economic Co-operation and Development has highlighted this (OECD 2021), and the Scottish Government has announced that the Scottish Qualifications Authority is to be replaced and has pledged to re-evaluate senior-phase qualifications. The pandemic has also shown up inequalities in home learning in terms of equipment and environment.

Teacher Empowerment and Collaborative Approaches

The CfE argued that educational policy-making should be constructed upon the foundation of trust in teachers. There is also growing demand amongst teachers for greater professional autonomy and a more collaborative approach in schools. The Scottish Government, local authorities and teacher unions should work together with salient stakeholders to improve the system. The Educational Institute of Scotland (EIS) union has set out some key areas which would benefit from teacher empowerment, including devolving more funding to schools, ring-fencing education spending, providing more support for Teacher Learning Communities, and greater consultation and collegiality on curricular matters. Importantly, pupils' voices should also be heard and parental involvement should constitute more than attending parents' evenings.

Further and Higher Education

Further and higher education have the potential to do much better. Colleges often continue to cater for their local areas, and staff have a commitment to an ideal of college provision for the less able and high-quality vocational learning alongside feeder courses into local universities. Universities remain free for Scottish-domiciled students, although most do not receive grants. Scottish universities combine strong research areas with positive teaching, and most students most of the time are content with the quality. Nonetheless, marketisation has been ubiquitous across both sectors. Colleges have found their public service role being questioned, experiencing pressure to respond to 'customers' needs' – these being not students, but employers – and facing competition with other colleges to do so outside the traditional communities they have served. This shift has led to a demarcation between teaching staff in colleges and management teams. Marketing functions have been developed, structures and processes stripped of public accountability, and income sought from private sources. This has led to conflict with lecturers, who see their role as defending pedagogic cultures against attacks of 'management by spreadsheet'. The drive for efficiency and quantification of all activities has led to an unsettled sector. A code of governance (Scottish Government 2017) laid out procedures, and following a major dispute, incorporation ended, national bargaining and conditions returned and colleges were reframed as public sector providers. Yet the sector has seen repeated turmoil as EIS members have had to strike against poor governance and disrespecting of staff. So colleges still need to re-establish their links with local communities and become part of the process of closing the learning gap.

Universities in Scotland are locked into a philosophy and practice of external and internal markets (Valentine 2019). Performativity, casualisation, competition and league tables are now widespread manifestations, channelling learning and academic research into crude algorithms. Competition is embedded into every senior leadership team's way of thinking (Maisuria and Cole 2017). Harvey (2007) argued that marketisation had been so deep, intensive and all-encompassing as to become almost 'natural', in that the neo-liberal agenda has normalised the narrative that defines universities. Most universities have now developed a strongly corporate management team with strong potential for patronage and a divorce between senior management and staff, reflected in large increases in salary for senior managers. Following significant union pressure, change to governance has been introduced with the Higher Education Governance (Scotland) Act 2016. Now unions have nominees on governing bodies, there are elections amongst staff and students for the university senior governor (chair of the governing body), and there is renewed scrutiny of how things are run. How these new requirements may make a meaningful difference to how universities operate is only just beginning to be seen, especially with remuneration committee proceedings. Nevertheless, there is still a long way to go to temper principals' runaway salaries. The demand for implementation of an outstanding recommendation from the 2012 von Prondzynski review of higher education governance (Scottish Government 2012) is still relevant – principals and senior staff should be included in national pay negotiations and framework agreements so they are placed on pay scales in relation to other university employees.

Although some 50% of Scotland's school leavers are in higher education, there are still glaring inequalities. Universities in Scotland are populated by the children of the better-off. Despite the spotlight shone on this by the Commission on Widening Access (CoWA), and the subsequent appointment of the Fair Access Commissioner, the inequality gap persists, so there is still more to do. In Scotland, the measure used is the percentage coming from Scottish Index of Multiple Deprivation20 (SIMD20), the lowest 20%. Currently, it stands at some 15.9% (Scottish Government 2020). It should be acknowledged that this meets the initial CoWA target and was, after years of stagnation, a significant step in the right direction. It is also the case that retention rates in 2018–2019 for SIMD20 fell by 3% to 86.8%. Further, these students are overwhelmingly in the newer universities. Higher Education Statistics Agency (HESA) figures for 2020–2021 (*Herald*, 12 February 2021) show that, if anything, the figures across Britain expose even greater inequalities, with 40% of the 'top' universities seeing a fall in numbers of entrants from state schools. And it can be argued that when 'top' universities do take working-class students, they are continuing to cream off the most able of the pupils from deprived areas, rather than making a genuine attempt to reduce inequalities.

Setting of targets for fair access needs to continue and increase in order to address the additional challenges which have arisen due to the pandemic. This means continuing to increase numbers of funded places to avoid any 'crowding out', provision of additional outreach activities, reviewing minimum course entry requirements in light of the moves to school teacher assessment and interrupted education, and addressing digital poverty. It is also vital to address ratios between students and staff so that academics and professional support staff have the capacity and resources to provide vital one-to-one input for students that is the difference for some between graduation or dropping out.

Whilst the pandemic has been disruptive to learning and social interaction with implications for mental health issues, Scottish education has always had a breadth and depth. The value of the four-year undergraduate degree is a case in point. The fact that the first year enables students to study a wide range of subjects before specialising is a strength. It is one we cherish and should nurture at this point.

Although there are no undergraduate tuition fees for Scottish-domiciled students in Scotland, it would be incorrect to suggest that Scottish universities are impervious to market influences. First, there are some voices arguing that Scottish universities cannot compete, as in England the £9,250 p.a. student fee exceeds the £6,500 p.a. Scottish Government income per student. Indeed, there is a gap in teaching funding, with institutions not receiving the full cost of teaching from the Scottish Funding Council grant. Second, the fee model has been rigorously applied to the rest of UK students and international students (which from 2021 includes EU students) such that universities claimed that as the pandemic developed in 2020, without this income some universities would fail and most others would need to retrench, making cuts. Further, the post-Brexit decision to withdraw from the Erasmus provision has already had a deleterious impact upon European students wishing to come to our universities (and vice versa) and to academic exchanges and research potential. The Turing scheme as a replacement has been criticised for being grossly underfunded by comparison, only lasts one year and lacks the reciprocity of Erasmus, which enabled staff and students to benefit from learning in a different country. The University and College Union is pushing for Scotland to attempt to remain in some way involved in the Erasmus scheme.

Marketisation has altered aspects of the university relationship, principally the shift from an academic–student one to a teacher–consumer/customer one, and created unhealthy expectations as regards degree classification. Indeed, 75% of students/consumers achieved a 1st or a 2-1 across Britain in 2016–2017, up from just under 50% in 1996–1997 (*Times Higher Education*, 28 June 2018), and it is not uncommon for programme leaders in Scotland to be questioned if they fall below this 'target' as it makes the programme/university look less efficient than others, both within and outside the university. It reduces the relationship to one of individual material gain rather than a collective pursuit of knowledge.

One key issue has been casualisation of the workforce, with the use of casual contracts proliferating particularly in the past decade. For 2019–2020, HESA (2021) indicated that 33% of academic staff were employed on fixed-term contracts (25%

full-time academic staff and 49% part-time academic staff). Casualisation undervalues staff, limits professional development and is generally damaging for staff who lack security. This all undermines students' experiences. Addressing casualisation and pay inequalities have been key aspects of the annual claim campus unions have sought for many years. The pandemic has starkly exposed this neo-liberal model in universities – from students unnecessarily being on campus and in halls of residence (to justify fees and rents) to university managements restructuring with consequent redundancies – and led to the university unions (both staff and student) waging an ongoing campaign against its effects.

Suggestions for an Alternative Approach

Boyd et al. (2021) discussed many of the aforementioned issues at greater length and made a large number of detailed recommendations and proposals. Here, we have selected just a few of the major ones:

- Play is a crucial aspect of learning. It should be a part of learning in early years and beyond. There should be a stronger emphasis on play and outdoor learning, based upon the Scandinavian model.
- Early years education is capable of enabling all children to fulfil their potential, and as such, should be part of statutory state provision.
- More professional autonomy should be given to teachers in order to discuss aspects of the curriculum with students.
- The role of testing and exams needs urgent reform – in particular the National Qualifications at levels 5–7 – and consideration given to an exit qualifications approach to enable deeper learning and greater breadth in study.

- The curriculum in secondary schools should be further based on active and interdisciplinary learning to enable it to tackle the global issues of our time.
- The rights of students should be recognised, with additional support needs as a requirement across colleges, and not based upon postcode lotteries.
- The neo-liberal model of education provision should be effectively eliminated. From early years to universities, education should be paid for out of taxation and seen as a public good. Co-operation between universities should be encouraged, and league tables and destructive competition should be discouraged.
- The curriculum needs a thorough review for decolonisation and for strengthening of human rights/citizenship underpinnings.

Two other issues require immediate attention. The first issue is concerns raised through the Black Lives Matter movement, and in education, the linked area of decolonising curricula. The Welsh Government announced in March 2021 that the Welsh curriculum will include mandatory teaching of BAME histories. This could help prioritise the practice across all the nations of Britain and all education sectors. The Scottish Government should enable this. The second is misogyny, sexual violence and inappropriate behaviour. Recent evidence from the *Everyone's Invited* website suggested there was a rape and misogynist culture in schools and in at least 80 British universities (*Herald*, 15 April 2021). The sectors and the government must ensure this is stamped out.

The challenges for the Scottish education system are clear. Inequalities in education, especially those linked to external factors like income inequality in society, need a concerted approach from all sectors and from all government branches for them to be rooted out. Our greatest asset is our workforce, professional and highly skilled. When they can be empowered to further develop student-centred learning, Scottish education can flourish.

References

Boyd, B., Kelly, J. and Maitles, H. (2021) 'Liberal education in a neo-liberal world: Re-culturing and recalibrating', Glasgow, UK: Jimmy Reid Foundation.

Gillborn, D. and Youdell, D. (2000) *Rationing Education*, London: Open University Press.

Harvey, D. (2007) *A Brief History of Neoliberalism*, Oxford, UK: Oxford University Press.

HESA (2021) *Higher Education Staff Statistics: UK, 2019/20*, 19 January, Cheltenham, UK: Higher Educational Statistics Agency.

Maisuria, A. and Cole, M. (2017) 'The neo-liberalisation of higher education in England: An alternative is possible', *Policy Futures in Education*, 15/5: 602–619.

Maitles, H. (2005) *Values in Education: We're Citizens Now*, Edinburgh, UK: Dunedin Press.

OECD (2021) *Improving Schools in Scotland: An OECD Perspective*, Paris, France: Organisation for Economic Co-operation and Development, www.oecd.org/education/school/improving-schools-in-scotland.htm.

Sahlberg, P. (2014) *Finnish Lessons: What Can the World Learn from Educational Change in Finland?* New York: Teachers College Press.

Scottish Education (2020) *Realising the Ambition: Being Me – National Practice Guidance for Early Years in Scotland*, Livingston, UK: Scottish Education.

Scottish Government (2012) *Report of the Review of Higher Education Governance in Scotland* (chaired by Professor Ferdinand von Prondzynski), Edinburgh, UK: Scottish Government.

Scottish Government (2017) *The Code of Good Governance for Scotland's Colleges*, Edinburgh, UK: Scottish Government.

Scottish Government (2020) *Fair Access to Higher Education: Progress and Challenges*, Edinburgh, UK: Scottish Government.

Valentine, J. (2019) *Neo-liberalism and the New Institutional Politics of Universities*, Glasgow, UK: Jimmy Reid Foundation.

10

Income, Wealth and Inequality in Scotland

Mike Danson and Francis Stuart

Introduction

Income inequality increased hugely across Scotland and the UK in the 1980s, and has remained at historically high levels since. In Scotland in 2017–2020, the top 10% had 43% more income than the bottom 40% combined after housing costs were accounted for (Scottish Government 2021). Whilst overall measures of income inequality, such as the Gini coefficient and the Palma ratio, have not shown a further clear increase since the early 1990s, extreme inequality appears to be rising, with the net incomes of the top 1% growing more quickly than those in other sections of the income distribution (Eiser et al. 2017). In addition, earnings inequality before tax and benefits are accounted for has been on an upward trend, pointing to structural issues within the labour market (Eiser et al. 2017). Wealth in Scotland is distributed even more unevenly than income. In 2016–2018, a typical household in the top 10% of the wealth distribution held £1.6 million in financial, physical, property and pension wealth, whereas a typical household in the bottom 10% held only £7,500. Wealth inequality increased between 2014–2016 and 2016–2018, although there was not a clear trend in the years preceding this. Using *Sunday Times* 'Rich List' data for 2021, the combined wealth of Scotland's top ten 'Rich Listers' increased by 12% from £19.8 billion to £22.4 billion. Scotland's two richest families now have as much wealth as the poorest 20% of the population, whilst Scotland's 14 richest families are wealthier than the bottom 30% of the population combined (*Sunday Times*, 23 May 2021; Scottish Government 2020). Figure 10.1 shows the distribution of household wealth and income across Scotland during 2016–2018.

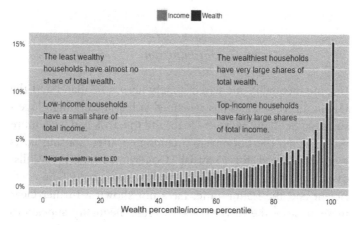

Figure 10.1   Share of total wealth in each 2% wealth band, and share of total household income in each 2% income band, Scotland, 2016–2018

Source: Scottish Government (2020)

As in any society, ownership and control over the means of production, distribution and exchange (PDE) – productive capacity and other resources in an economy – primarily determine most of the inequalities in income and wealth in Scotland. Private ownership has become the norm, including over the commanding heights of the economy and infrastructure – especially utilities, energy, transport and finance. Many of the owners in these sectors are arms of foreign states, earning profits from Scottish households, businesses and the public sector. Their private interests are driven by profit-generation. Whilst these contribute to Gross Domestic Product (GDP), this merely highlights how inappropriate GDP is as a measure of the nation's economy and the wellbeing of those within it. Neo-liberal Britain works for big capitalists, operating through monopoly powers and inefficient markets, with undue influence over governments and regulators producing unfair outcomes for families, workers and smaller businesses. An economy based on significant amounts of precarious work, flexible labour markets and workfare (rather than social security), financialisation and an overly important arms/defence sector generates distortions in markets and lives, unaddressed negative externalities and unavoidable costs forced upon the poor, workers and the environment.

Having laid out these dimensions of inequality in income and wealth, this chapter will examine their three primary roots before turning to creating alternative policy solutions to these social and economic problems and how these might be realised.

Roots of Inequality

UNION MEMBERSHIP, COLLECTIVE BARGAINING AND STRIKES

In Britain in the late 1970s, around 58% of workers were union members and 82% of workers' wages were set by collective bargaining. According to the Department for Business, Energy & Industrial Strategy (2021), by 2020 these figures had fallen to 24% and 26% respectively, whilst in Scotland, 29% were members, and collective bargaining covered 36% in Strathclyde and 33% in the rest of Scotland. This decline in membership and bargaining coverage has coincided with a fall in the share of income going to wages. Figure 10.2 shows the labour share of national income in the UK since the late 1950s. Whilst Scottish-specific labour share data are not readily available, the situation in Scotland is anticipated to be broadly in line with UK trends.

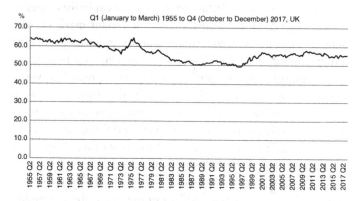

Figure 10.2 The labour share, unadjusted for mixed income

Source: Office for National Statistics (2018)

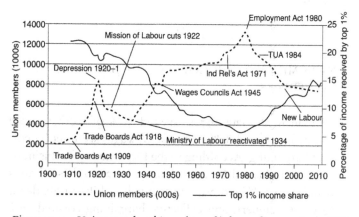

Figure 10.3 Union membership and top 1% share of income in the UK

Source: McGaughey (2015: 21)

The fall in membership and bargaining has also coincided with large increases in income inequality. Figure 10.3 shows membership alongside the top 1% income share in the UK over the last century, and demonstrates the clear negative relationship.

As membership declined, so did strike action, and this is also associated with rising inequality because it indicates that workers generally – and union members specifically – have less leverage to gain their bargaining demands such as higher wages (see Figure 10.4).

These figures confirm what organisations like the International Monetary Fund and the Organisation for Economic Co-operation and Development argued recently, namely: inequality is a function of institutional changes, particularly in

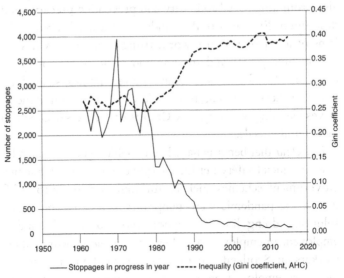

Figure 10.4 Number of industrial stoppages (UK) and income inequality (GB)

Source: Authors' analysis based on Office for National Statistics and Institute for Fiscal Studies data

labour market institutions (Denk 2015, Jaumotte and Buitron 2015).

Social Security as a Solution to Inequality?

Scotland faces huge challenges of poverty and inequality, with families struggling to feed and clothe themselves, pay bills, heat their homes, service debts and participate fully in society. Social security payments continue to be the lifeline for those unable to work or struggling on low incomes from underemployment or low wages. Social security is a crucial component in helping ensure everyone has access to an adequate standard of living and to pursuing a more equal society affording dignity to all. It is not just about providing income security, but also promoting social solidarity and preventing precarity and destitution. Even before the pandemic, Scotland faced problems of low pay, insecure work, rising child poverty despite low unemployment, and growing household debt. Subsequent pandemic lockdowns saw many more families struggling. Many workers, including those in key industries, found themselves claiming Working Tax Credits or Universal Credit to meet family needs.

It is clear that benefits have been unable to provide an adequate financial safety net for everyone during the pandemic. Government schemes such as furlough and the £20 uplift during the pandemic were temporary and, for some, scant solutions, doing little to support those previously underemployed, unemployed or otherwise unable to work. Many workers in Scotland are in insecure employment, including those employed on zero-hour contracts, agency, casual or seasonal workers, and the low-paid self-employed. Using sanctions to suspend social security payments has also become a growing issue with an increase in conditionality.

The current social security provision not only has problems of inadequacy of income, but also issues of dependability of income. Claimants find the process of assessment stressful and difficult, and design features such as the delay to start of payments further reduce the reliability of income. Moreover, enhanced conditionality, benefit caps and sanctions all serve to increase stress and insecurity of income for individuals and families.

Economic Structures, Ownership and Control

Before 1914, the economy in Scotland was dominated by indigenous companies dependent upon British imperial markets. Today's economy is overwhelmingly externally owned and controlled, with many higher functions located outside Scotland (Danson 1991, Scottish Trades Union Congress [STUC] 2020a). Outwith the public sector, the Scottish economy mirrors the sectoral breakdown of most other regions and nations. Nevertheless, its manufacturing sector has declined further and faster than most other European countries, with this workforce declining over 25 years from 346,000 to 179,000. In many cases, these well-paid unionised manufacturing jobs have been replaced by low-paid, precarious service jobs and out-of-town retail outlets (Danson and Trebeck 2011). Compared with other small open economies, especially Nordic ones, Scotland has much higher degrees of external ownership and control, and this heavy reliance upon branch plants in manufacturing and services means truncated career and occupational ladders within Scotland. As a result, and in the context of procurement and other regulations being set at the UK level under reserved powers, supply chains – and therefore jobs and incomes – are similarly often located outwith Scotland. Complementing these neo-liberal projects have been strong UK drivers to increase numbers of low-income self-employed entrepreneurs and a precariat of poorly organised and insecure workers. These long-term structural transformations have collectively led to the under-development of the Scottish economy, precipitating lower shares of GDP for workers and entrepreneurs than in comparative economies (Danson 1991). Collectively, Scotland has been put into a cycle of low productivity/low incomes/low investment/low profitability/low productivity. To break this cycle, manifestly radical change is needed.

Alternative Policy Solutions

Historically in Britain, the development of council housing, the NHS, and nationalised industries and services was the primary method through which inequality was addressed by the state. And in Scotland in the last 20 years, the main reason for slightly lower levels of inequality compared to the rest of Britain is because its housing stock has not been financial-ised to the same extent (Joseph Rowntree Foundation 2019). Despite more than a decade of austerity, public services are more valuable than cash benefits to all decile groups in the UK, including those at the bottom of the income distribution. They are also more likely to maintain public support (Curtice et al. 2020). Similarly, although the Nordic welfare states have generous social security systems, their primary means of redis-tribution is through public services. Whilst tackling poverty and inequality will require investment in social security as dis-cussed below, as a collective endeavour, public services can be an extremely efficient way of providing resources to enable people to participate in society. So they should be viewed as a crucial weapon in the fight against poverty and inequality.

Restructuring the Scottish economy through a 'just tran-sition' is necessary for a better, greener and fairer Scotland. A radical restructuring of ownership and use of the country's resources and outputs must be the basis for moving Scotland towards a new path which seeks to deliver improved well-being rather than growth, leaves no one behind and raises living standards for all. The (re)construction of local economies, building community wealth, and prioritising abolition of poverty and a green recovery should be at the heart of economic development. As with the Nordic countries, with their strong economies built on cohesion, smart specialisation and inclusion, Scotland should pursue a progressive tax regime, with a better balance between taxes on corporations and workers, and closing loopholes over evasion and avoidance. An economy based on a more equal distribution of incomes, utilising the skills and experience of the workforce, will generate higher wages and other benefits. A revitalisation of Scotland's skills development and enterprise agencies, promoting and facilitating local and national companies and workforces within reinvigorated and new supply chains to meet both community and national demands and exporting where appropriate, offers a future more closely matching the successes of Nordic countries than the continuing stagnation under the neo-liberal UK model.

Citizens' Basic Income (CBI) is defined as a 'periodic cash payment unconditionally delivered to all on an individual basis, without means-test or work requirement' (Basic Income Earth Network 2020). The general concept, which can be dated as far back as ancient Greece, is based on offering every individual, regardless of existing welfare benefits or earned income, an unconditional, regular payment. Rising inequality, economic insecurity, precarious work and the potential for labour to be displaced by technological change have led to a resurgence of interest in CBI in recent years. It is seen as a way of promoting social justice and equality, reducing poverty and income inequality, removing work disincentives, addressing job insecurity and increasing freedom to make choices. However, its appeal suffers due to high costs and, thus, possible repercussions for tax increases, and perceptions of its potential to encourage labour market withdrawal and promote state dependency. There are also concerns a CBI might divert funds from those most in need, risking the removal of other social programmes. Available evidence suggests a CBI could impact upon a wide range of employment, social and health outcomes, but there is a need for piloting to assess the effects on long-term service use, poverty and wider economic impacts (Gibson et al. 2020). The Citizens' Basic Income Feasibility Study Steering Group identified substantive and complex legislative, technical and delivery challenges associated with institutional arrangements for a pilot in Scotland (CBIS 2020).

Achieving and Implementing Solutions

Besides the high point of union membership in the late 1970s, it is worth considering what we can learn from history about the forms of working-class and community organisation that have successfully challenged inequalities of income, wealth and power. Arguably the high-point of housing struggle in the UK was during 'Red Clydeside' in the 1910s. Led by working-class women, the rent arrears revolt led to the UK government passing rents restriction Acts – the main basis of tenant protection and rent controls for the following 75 years. Living Rent, Scotland's tenants' union, is now leading a welcome resurgence in locally led housing campaigns. The unemployed workers' movement of the 1930s had some success in fighting benefit cuts and increasing economic support to areas most impacted by the Depression. Subsequent attempts to organise in a similar fashion have been less successful – arguably because the unemployment benefits system became increasingly centralised. However, both examples illustrate the potential of grassroots organisation, unions and political parties to combine to bring about manifest change at a local level. With the Corbyn project's demise at the UK level, there may well be a 'local turn' from those on the left towards policy and institutional change at community and council level. The community wealth-building work being pioneered by North Ayrshire Council (Cullinane 2020) and others is of particular interest here (see Manley and Whyman 2021).

Across most political parties and organisations representing workers, businesses and consumers, there is a consensus on the need for an effective national industrial strategy that offers Scotland a fairer and greener future based on promoting wellbeing and sustainable development (Danson 2021). That new economic strategy needs to be consistent with the aspiration for contributing to meeting the UN's Sustainable Development Goals with performance indicators and targets set in a refreshed National Performance Framework (NPF). The terms and path for a 'people's green recovery' have been established by the STUC (2020b), the Just Transition Commission (JTC 2021) and others such as Common Weal (2020). As Danson (2021) found, there is a remarkable degree of consensus across the proposed strategies from these bodies about what needs to be done and how it can be done. Recapturing more value added by Scottish workers means growing public, co-operative and private enterprises under local and national ownership so that surpluses stay in Scotland and are recirculated around the economy. A more holistic approach to public investment should ensure that public procurement supports and privileges supply chains which encourage entrepreneurs and suppliers in Scotland, rather than importing products and services which do not meet criteria of fair work, addressing negative externalities and tax avoidance. Creating and nurturing local and Scottish businesses and supply chains consistent with the Sustainable Development Goals and an NPF offer a more economically and environmentally sustainable future than one based upon importing and assembling from elsewhere. Re-establishing ownership and use of the means of PDE in these ways would allow society in Scotland to move towards a more equal and efficient economic system with greater equity and rights embedded in the pre-distribution of incomes, opportunities and skills.

However, consensus and good ideas do not necessarily lead to change. With BiFab's renewable yards, it was only through the GMB and UNITE unions undertaking a workplace occupation in 2017, along with local community, wider union movement and environmental organisations' support, that those yards still exist to build an industrial base in offshore wind. The barriers identified to piloting CBI alongside the current social security system mean that neither the Scottish Government nor local authorities alone could implement a CBI. Within the current constitutional arrangements, considerable commitment from the UK Government would be required to make the necessary legislative, technical and procedural changes for a pilot of CBI. This exploration of CBI in Scotland was picked up by the Social Renewal Advisory Board and translated into a call for action for a commitment to a Minimum Income Guarantee, based on a Minimum Income Standard, as a long-term aim (Social Renewal Advisory Board 2021). It is likely, given current devolution arrangements, that this will be pursued through a series of uplifts to current social security provision, perhaps with a focus upon child payment and disabled people, and possibly other uplifts aimed at reducing poverty. Moreover, this does not address issues relating to conditionality and associated stigma and stress, nor the problems of sanctions and those with no recourse to public funds. Whilst this is a move in the right direction, it is likely that much more radical social security reform will be required to address the income inequalities experienced in Scotland.

The inequalities and inequities in income and wealth inherent to the neo-liberal economic system of Scotland and the UK have been revealed in fine detail since the pandemic. A comprehensive and integrated approach is needed to address the failings and to deliver outcomes which promote wellbeing for all rather than for the few, including empowered union and community organisations (see Chapter 23). To realise these benefits for the whole of society requires a simultaneous institutional capacity to manage the terms and conditions facing workers, entrepreneurs and enterprises so that changes in procurement laws and practices, in fair work and fair trade, in access to supply chains and investment opportunities can be actioned. As well as changes in attitudes and behaviours by local and national government and other players within Scotland to support Scottish workers and suppliers, this also means that controls over employment law, public sector and pension fund investments, procurement and many Treasury rules need to be repatriated to the Scottish Parliament, otherwise UK neo-liberal interests will continue to undermine hopes and efforts for a better Scotland.

The changes required to decarbonise the economy whilst also tackling inequality require massive investment that far exceeds what the Scottish Government alone can access under the current financial settlement. That poses a constitutional challenge: for those who support the union, how do you raise billions of pounds to decarbonise and create green jobs under a Tory Government? For those who support independence, how do you raise the required finance under the SNP's Growth Commission proposals? The need for an alternative strategy is paramount.

References

Basic Income Earth Network (2020) 'About basic income', https:// basicincome.org/about-basic-income/.

Department for Business, Energy & Industrial Strategy (2021) *Trade Union Statistics 2020*, London: House of Commons Library.

CBIS (2020) *Assessing the Feasibility of Citizens' Basic Income Pilots in Scotland: Final Report*, Edinburgh, UK: Citizens' Basic Income Feasibility Study Steering Group, www.basicincome.scot/__data/assets/pdf_file/0024/175371/Draft-Final-CBI-Feasibility_Main-Report-June-2020.pdf.

Common Weal (2020) *Resilient Scotland: Rebuilding a Better Nation Post-virus*, Glasgow, UK: Common Weal.

Cullinane, J. (2020) 'Community wealth building – the beginning of a new economic order', *Scottish Left Review*, 120: 6.

Curtice, J., Davies, C., Grollman, C., Hudson, N., Kolbas, V., Montagu, I., Taylor, I., Wishart, R. and Yarde, J. (2020) *British Social Attitudes Survey 37*, London: NatCen, https://natcen.ac.uk/our-research/research/british-social-attitudes/.

Danson, M. (1991) 'The Scottish economy: The development of under-development?', *Planning Outlook*, 34/2, 89–95.

Danson, M. (2021) 'Progressive consensus versus neo-liberal stagnation', *Scottish Left Review*, 121: 11–12.

Danson, M. and Trebeck, K. (2011) 'Whose Economy? An introduction', *Whose Economy* seminar paper, London: Oxfam.

Denk, O. (2015), 'Who are the top 1% earners in Europe?', OECD Economics Department Working Paper 1274, Paris, France: Organisation for Economic Co-operation and Development.

Department for Business, Energy & Industrial Strategy (2021) *Trade Union Statistics 2020*, London: House of Commons Library.

Eiser, D., McQuigg, R. and Stuart, F. (2017) *Building a More Equal Scotland: Designing Scotland's Poverty and Inequality Commission*, London: Oxfam.

Gibson, M., Hearty W. and Craig P. (2020) 'The Public health effects of interventions similar to basic income: A scoping review', *The Lancet Public Health*, 5: E165–E176.

Jaumotte, F. and Buitron, O. (2015) *Inequality and Labor Market Institutions*, New York: International Monetary Fund.

Joseph Rowntree Foundation (2019) *Poverty in Scotland*, York: Joseph Rowntree Foundation.

JTC (2021) *Just Transition Commission: A National Mission for a Fairer, Greener Scotland*, Edinburgh, UK: Scottish Government.

Manley, J. and Whyman, P. (2021) (eds) *The Preston Model and Community Wealth Building: Creating a Socio-Economic Democracy for the Future*, Basingstoke, UK: Routledge.

Office for National Statistics (2018) *Estimating the Impact of the Self-employed in the Labour Share*, London: Office for National Statistics.

Scottish Government (2020) *Wealth in Scotland 2006–2018*, Edinburgh, UK: Scottish Government.

Scottish Government (2021) *Poverty and Income Inequality in Scotland, 2017–20*, Edinburgh, UK: Scottish Government.

Social Renewal Advisory Board (2021) *'If Not Now, When?' – Social Renewal Advisory Board Report: January 2021*, Edinburgh, UK: Scottish Government.

STUC (2020a) *Scotland's Renewable Jobs Crisis and Covid-19*, Glasgow, UK: STUC.

STUC (2020b) *The People's Recovery: A Different Track for Scotland's Economy*, Glasgow, UK: STUC.

11

Fiscal Policy in Scotland: Under Devolution and Under Independence

Jim Cuthbert

Introduction

This chapter is about fiscal policy in Scotland, under the contrasting scenarios of devolution and independence. It argues that fiscal policy-makers in today's devolved Scotland are in an impossible position. They are being forced to operate a fiscal settlement which is subject to rigid constraints on what can be done with the levers of tax, and there are inherent design flaws which mean the system will operate inefficiently. But even worse: implicit in the design of the system is a particular set of neo-liberal beliefs which is inconsistent with those held by a majority of those living in Scotland. In contrast, the challenges under independence, whilst huge, are do-able. The main problem as regards fiscal policy would be to set about the fundamental redesigning of the tax system which would be inherited from the UK: a tax system which has been designed primarily to benefit a rentier class, and which, in effect, presently treats Scotland as a colony. This chapter begins by setting the context for this discussion. It then looks at the devolution settlement. Following this, the scenario of independence is laid out.

Context

The commonly quoted headline measure, the net fiscal balance, measures the difference between public sector expenditure and public sector revenues. According to the Government Expenditure and Revenue in Scotland (GERS) report (Scottish Government 2020), since 2010 Scotland's net fiscal balance, including its geographic share of North Sea oil revenues, has been in large deficit – typically at 8% or more of Gross Domestic Product (GDP). Partly, this reflects the decline in oil revenues. Over this period, Scotland's net balance has worsened considerably relative to that of the UK as a whole: since 2015/2016, Scotland's net fiscal deficit has commonly been about 6% larger relative to GDP than the deficit for the whole of the UK. Over the medium-term past, Scotland's net balance, including oil revenues, has tended to move in parallel with that of the UK as a whole, but has commonly been about 2% worse as a share of GDP. Further back still, in the 1980s, Scotland's balance was large and positive, when North Sea revenues were high. It is worth making three points about these figures.

First, in the past, when Scotland's funding was largely determined by the Barnett formula, the level of public spending in Scotland did not depend directly upon the amount of tax revenue raised in Scotland. This position has now changed, and is likely to change further in the future, because of the implications of the post-independence referendum fiscal settlement introduced in 2016. Second, Scotland's present net fiscal balance tells us about how the present constitutional settlement is operating: it does not say what Scotland's fiscal position would be under independence. Nevertheless, the current level of deficit represents a starting constraint which a newly independent Scotland would have to reckon with. Third, the presentation in GERS arguably distorts because it focuses attention upon Scotland in isolation relative to the UK as a whole. The Office for National Statistics (2019) now produces GERS-type analyses for all of the countries and regions of the UK. These figures for 2018/19 show that only three of the 12 countries/regions of the UK had a positive net fiscal balance for that year. What dominates the figures is the large positive fiscal balance in London and the South East. In fact, five areas (North East, North West, West Midlands, Wales and Northern Ireland) had larger net fiscal deficits per head than Scotland. What the figures demonstrate is the extent of regional imbalance in the UK, and the extent to which the UK economy is unhealthily dominated by the heavily financialised economy of the South East of England.

Fiscal Policy under the Post-referendum Fiscal Settlement

The Scottish Government raises just over 30% of its revenues through devolved taxes, principal among which, since 2016, is tax on non-savings, non-dividend income. Apart from very limited borrowing powers, the remainder of the Scottish Government's budget is funded via a block grant from Westminster, delivered by the well-established Barnett formula. Under the old Barnett formula, changes to the block grant received by Scotland were equal to the per capita change in expenditure on the aggregate of comparable services in England. One of the key points of the 'vow' made to Scotland before the 2014 referendum was that the Barnett formula would be maintained. Under the post-referendum fiscal settlement, therefore, each year there would be a deduction, or 'abatement', from the block grant as calculated by Barnett, to allow for revenues which the Scottish Government would be raising by its own taxes. The tricky question was: how should this abatement be increased each year? The solution finally agreed to was that the abatement for income tax, the dominant element, should be indexed by the percentage growth in corresponding income tax receipts in England, adjusted for the relative growth rates of population in Scotland and England.

This means that if Scotland grows its per capita income tax receipts at the same rate as England, then Scotland will receive the same funding as it would have done under the old Barnett formula. Scotland will do better if it achieves a higher growth rate. But if the rate of growth of per capita tax receipts lags behind England, Scotland will be penalised. Effectively, the fiscal settlement thrusts Scotland into a fiscal race with England, where, if it wants to do as well as it would have done under Barnett, it has to grow its per capita tax receipts as fast as England. As will now be argued, this is a retrograde deal for Scotland, and puts fiscal policy-makers in Scotland in a very difficult position.

First of all, the range of powers available in Scotland is actually very limited. For one thing, the only really major tax which is largely under Scottish control is that on non-savings, non-dividend income. But it is also true that the non-tax levers available to Scottish policy-makers are also very limited: in particular, the areas of employment, and trade and industry, crucial to growing the economy, are largely reserved. Second, if Scotland lags in the growth of devolved tax receipts, it will be progressively penalised under the abatement mechanism. Moreover, Scotland is likely to be intrinsically weak in this income tax race. For example, even before devolution of income tax to Scotland in 2016/17, per capita receipts in Scotland of that element of income tax which was going to be devolved were just over 80% of the level of corresponding receipts per head in the rest of the UK (Scottish Government 2020: T4.4). Third, fiscal policy-makers in Scotland have to operate within a system which is basically unstable. As noted by Bell et al. (2016), the system is unusual in international terms in lacking stabilisers, since it provides 'virtually no insurance for future economic shocks or trends that affect Scotland's devolved revenues and welfare more than they do equivalent spending in the UK' (Bell et al. 2016: 57).

Finally, there are detailed design flaws and weaknesses in the current system. Here are two examples. One is that Westminster is still responsible for setting the lower threshold at which earners enter the tax system. Because of differences in income distribution between Scotland and England, a decision by Westminster to raise the lower-rate threshold is likely to have a disproportionately adverse effect on the Scottish Government's revenues. Another is that the income tax system, largely devolved to Scotland, cannot articulate properly with the system for national insurance, which is reserved to Westminster. As a result, in 2021/22, the marginal rate of income tax plus national insurance in Scotland for employees earning between £43,662 and £50,270 was 53%. This is more than 20% higher than the marginal rate for employees with similar earnings elsewhere in the UK.

All this is bad enough. But in addition, it is a clearly stated belief of the Scottish Government that somewhat higher taxes than in the rest of the UK, over most of the range of taxable income, is a price worth paying in order to undertake socially beneficial expenditure. By contrast, when I put it to a very senior Treasury official, just before the fiscal settlement was finalised, that the Scottish Government would not have sufficient powers to make the new system work, he disagreed. He said the Scottish Government would need to reduce taxes on income and out-compete the rest of the UK as an attractive destination, particularly for high earners: that was the way for Scotland to win the fiscal race with the rest of the UK. In other words, the Scottish Government finds itself trying to make a system work where that system was specifically designed to operate under a set of hard-line, neo-liberal, low-tax beliefs which are the direct opposite of the Scottish Government's own belief set. This fatal inconsistency, together with the limited powers the Scottish Government has, along with the poor design of the system itself, mean it will be well-nigh impossible for a Scottish government to develop a successful fiscal policy under devolution.

Fiscal Policy under Independence

Before considering more broadly the opportunities and challenges of fiscal policy under independence, it is worth stepping back and looking at the wider characteristics of those aspects of the tax system in Scotland which are not devolved to Scotland, but which an independent Scotland would, in the first instance, inherit.

TAX ON LAND

The UK tax system on land is notable for having no way of taxing the unearned increment in land value as it accrues. The situation is worsened by the existence of several loopholes which mean large estates are not effectively taxed on the death of owners. All this has had a particularly bad effect in Scotland, and has led to Scotland having one of the most unequal distributions of land ownership among advanced economies – and, arguably, one of the least efficiently used stocks of land (see Chapter 17).

TAX ON NATURAL RESOURCES

As regards hydrocarbon reserves, the UK system of taxation is one of the most generous in the world. According to Boué (2020), the loss to the UK Exchequer due to the UK's oil taxation regime over the period 2002–2015 was about £250 billion compared to what might have been collected if it had similar taxation regimes to Norway, Denmark, Holland or Germany. As regards the development of renewable sources like onshore wind, this interacts with the system of land taxation in a way which has meant a huge, and unearned transfer of wealth to certain landowners.

CORPORATE TAXATION

The UK has been particularly lax in seeking to apply corporation tax effectively to the operation of large corporations. This is true as regards achieving an equitable tax take from large multinationals which exploit the UK market, but then, by means of transfer pricing, pay little tax. For example, Google paid UK corporate tax of only £65 million in 2018, despite its total UK revenues for that year being estimated at £9.4 billion (Christophers 2020: 223). And it is also true in the converse direction, of industries where production is based here, but earn substantial profit by selling their product abroad and still manage to pay relatively little UK tax. The classic example is Scotch whisky, which generates global sales worth an estimated £30 billion from production in Scotland. However, Professor John Kay estimates that only about 2% of this total actually comes back to the Scottish economy, after allowing for tax by foreign governments and profits of the producers of whisky, who are predominantly non-Scottish-owned (quoted in Bruce-Gardyne 2018).

CONCEALED LEVIES

The concealed levy on utility customers implicit in utility pricing models is akin to a tax, other than that it goes straight into the pockets of privatised utility owners. This is a very strange, peculiarly British, pathology. The pricing models operated by the utility regulators to compensate the owners for the capital cost of utility networks have long been flawed, and have resulted in grotesque overcharging (Cuthbert 2012). If the utilities had been owned, as they used to be, by the state, this would have been a straightforward, if concealed, tax: and at least the public sector would have benefited. But the British state, in its wisdom, sees fit to operate this system for the benefit, not of the state, but of the private owners.

There is, in fact, a common theme which runs through these instances. In each case, decisions on tax can be regarded as specific actions which have been taken in the interests of a rentier class – namely, the owners of land and other assets, particularly financial assets. There is a term for this: rentier capitalism (Christophers 2020). Christophers is in many ways a direct intellectual descendant of Lenin (1965), for Lenin saw that finance capitalism as a key driving force behind the expansion of colonialism, particularly in the latter part of the nineteenth century, and that Britain was playing a leading role in this, turning itself in the process into what he called a 'rentier state'. The following quotation from Lenin refers to Britain, and Britain's rentier income from abroad: 'The income of the rentiers is five times greater than the income obtained from the foreign trade of the biggest "trading" country in the world' (Lenin 1965: 121, emphasis in original).

In many ways, the UK rentier state as it is now and as analysed by Christophers (2020) can be regarded as the inevitable outgrowth of the process described by Lenin. The engine of finance capital demands fuel, in the shape of new classes of asset to justify the never-ending expansion of credit. One choice of the British ruling class, faced with the end of Empire, was to turn this process inwards, like an ingrowing toenail, and start assetising and exploiting the resources and people of their own state. Hence the features of the UK state we have already observed.

If one regards the Conservatives as the political wing of the rentier class, rather than the wider capitalist class (including most obviously industrial capitalists), then this makes sense. This is not a new insight. Marx (1852) noted:

> Up to 1846 the Tories passed as the guardians of the traditions of Old England .... The fatal year, 1846, with its repeal of the Corn Laws ... proved that they were enthusiasts for nothing but the rent of land.

What Marx did not foresee was the way the Tories would survive and dominate by broadening their position on rent from land to all types of assets, particularly financial, and how they would become, in effect, the political arm of the rentier class as a whole. Given that, the current UK system of taxation makes perfect sense as the manifestation of the ideology of Britain's main party of government when confronted with the realities of coping with the end of traditional colonialism.

But this analysis indicates some of the key steps an independent Scotland would have to take in redesigning the tax system. Policy would have to be reformed so that an equitable share of the current rewards to rentiers sticks with people and public finances stay in Scotland. This is not just a question of tax, for changes to industrial policy would have to be undertaken in lockstep, particularly as regards the creative use of licensing. But here is a suggested 'shopping list':

- Introduce a land value tax to give an incentive to bring land into productive use. This could be tailored to size of holding to encourage the break-up of vast estates. And to avoid problems with trusts, and multiple holdings, taxation of land could be on penal terms for other than land owned by local residents.

- On hydrocarbon reserves, create a tax system more in line with international norms, conjoined with an approach to licensing that makes it a condition that ancillary work should be sourced in Scotland.

- Implement a realistic approach to harvesting a share of windfall profits stemming from renewables, together with similar licensing conditions as for hydrocarbons to ensure that ancillary work is sourced in Scotland.

- On corporation tax, for industries like whisky, where production necessarily takes place in Scotland but the product is sold internationally, there should be a licensing scheme, where licences would only be issued if a fair share of profits were taxed in Scotland. For companies like Google, which are international but sell into Scotland, another form of licence would give the right to participate in the Scottish market on condition that a fair share of the resulting turnover results in profits which are taxed here.

- There is a strong case for widespread re-nationalisation of utilities. But in any event, a new regulatory regime would be required for all areas other than water (which is the only utility not currently regulated at a UK level). Regulators should be given a much tougher remit to avoid regulatory capture. And the nonsenses which were perpetrated around previous pricing models for capital investment should be swept away.

The task for an independent Scotland in implementing these or other similar taxation system reforms would not be easy. In each area, it would involve upsetting powerful vested interests. It is, however, worth recording two points. First, it would be essential for an independent Scotland to undertake these tasks. It is not just the importance for a new state of securing tax revenues, for there is also the question of market confidence. An independent Scotland, like other states, will have to borrow in the international capital markets. The ultimate security for such borrowing is a country's revenue base. Unless a country can show that it is willing to secure and maintain that tax base, the borrowing terms will be penal. Second, the chances of meaningful fiscal reform are greater under independence than under any feasible continuation of the union. As long as Scotland continues in the union, then reform will be dependent upon consent by the popular political will in England, which appears increasingly aligned to the powerful vested interests opposing reform. Even federalism, which might appear to offer a way out, is ruled out by the lack of appetite in England for such an approach and by the fact that, because of numerical superiority, England would dominate at the federal government level. The conclusion is stark: independence is a prerequisite for any chance of meaningful reform.

References

Bell, D., Eiser, D. and Phillips, D. (2016) *Scotland's Fiscal Framework: Assessing the Agreement*, Working Paper W16/05, London: Institute for Fiscal Studies.

Boué, J. (2020) *The UK North Sea as a Global Experiment in Neo-liberal Resource Extraction*, London: Public and Commercial Services Union.

Bruce-Gardyne, T. (2018) 'Is Scotch whisky Scottish enough?', *Scotch Whisky*, February, https://scotchwhisky.com/magazine/opinion-debate/the-debate/17782/is-scotch-whisky-scottish-enough/.

Christophers, B. (2020) *Rentier Capitalism: Who Owns the Economy, and Who Pays for It*, London: Verso.

Cuthbert, J. (2012) *Excessive Profits and Overcharging: Multiple Errors in the UK's Model for Setting Utility Prices*, Glasgow, UK: Jimmy Reid Foundation.

Lenin, V. (1965) *Imperialism: The Highest Stage of Capitalism*, Beijing, China: Foreign Languages Press.

Marx, K. (1852) 'The elections in England: Tories and Whigs', *New York Daily Tribune*, 21 August.

Office for National Statistics (2019) *Country and Regional Public Sector Finances: Financial Year Ending 2019*, London: Office for National Statistics.

Scottish Government (2020) *Government Expenditure and Revenue in Scotland 2019–20*, Edinburgh, UK: Scottish Government.

12

Governing Scotland

*Robin McAlpine, James Henderson
and Claire Bynner*

Introduction

Governance is seldom a subject of much interest in the public debate on democracy. Indeed, it is often not even an element of that debate. We tend to see it only when particularly significant failures of governance take place – like banking regulation and the financial crisis. Even then, it is often seen as failures of individuals doing the governance rather than systemic failures of governance. This is a grave error, because it is governance which often actively defines and shapes governments' ability to achieve any form of economic or social change. By governance, we mean the governing and decision-making processes across the whole of society – for instance, those relating to the state and public realm, as well as those relating to economic institutions and enterprises, and communities, associations and networks. Few of these processes can currently be considered fully democratic – as in governed by or as delegated by 'the people'. And the degrees and types of democracy and aspirations for becoming more democratic vary dramatically within Scotland and further afield. In this chapter, we cannot cover each of these three broad areas of state, economy and civil society in depth, so we focus upon democratising the state. For economy and society, see Chapters 4, 5, 22 and 23. Here, we concentrate upon the central and local states (and associated community governance) which are respectively critical to power and resources distribution and crucial to deepening democratic participation in Scotland.

Issues of governance are often seen as secondary to issues of policy and ideas. They are important, but in practice, the ways policies are shaped, developed and executed are often more important in terms of their successes or failures. If social and economic reform advocates are unable to see the inextricable link between failures of policy and failures of governance, they will continue to feel frustration when their 'big idea' gets on the agenda and does not seem to make much difference in practice. We are not, however, offering a negative perspective or a call for a greater realism about what is possible (which is, ironically, a fundamental feature of current governance culture). Rather, we offer a positive perspective, looking at the opportunities to change the machinery which mangles the product.

Local Governance

Taking local government, we can explore the failures of democratic governance. Scotland has one of the democratic world's most centralised forms of government and one of the least 'local' local democracies (Bort et al. 2012). By almost every measure, Scotland stands out markedly from European norms. This leads to the following consequences: (i) governance is centralised and remote, covering comparatively enormous constituencies both in terms of geography and population where power is significantly more distant from communities than in comparable countries; (ii) there are low levels of participation in local democracy both in terms of people standing for election and people voting in elections; (iii) the conjunction of this remoteness and the decline of local journalism leaves local government little scrutinised; (iv) the legitimacy and authority of councillors is greatly weakened by their representation of only a small part of these very large administrative units; and (v) governance is largely conducted and dominated by a professional-managerial class (PMC) (Winant 2019, Lui 2021; see also Chapter 21 in this volume) which administers both elected councils and local public services and enterprises.

Unsurprisingly, evidence shows that trust in local councils to make fair decisions has declined to 28% in 2019, with only 8% believing local councils should have the most influence over how Scotland is run (Reid et al. 2020: 22, 30). Local government is a weakened and neglected democratic institution, which is reflected in the attitudes towards it and the influence it has or should have. This might be explained by the lack of meaningful opportunities to participate, physical remoteness of institutions and/or the difficulty in gaining a clear picture of what is being done on citizens' behalf. This disconnection is concurrent with rising cynicism and distrust in political institutions and elected representatives (Dalton 2005). It is compounded by the global nature of economic decision-making, roles of corporations and investment bodies, and use of technology (Steiner 2016).

Societal Trends

This democratic alienation and frustration increasingly permeate local, regional and national governance across the globe. At the heart of this democratic hollowing out has been the rise of the neo-liberal state (Cochrane 2007, Baston and Ritchie 2021) and the rolling out of its political, economic and social agenda:

- The post-war social democratic welfare state and the expectation of the shared roles of state, business and unions in economic development declined from the 1970s, and were dismantled aggressively in the US and UK in the 1980s and 1990s.

- This was replaced with largely economic, partly cultural, neo-liberal ideologies, including extreme individualism, removing the post-war belief in the transformative power of political institutions, and replacing it with 'market fundamentalism' and emphasis upon global financial liberalisation.
- Along with the economic determinism of neo-liberalism came 'New Public Management' (NPM); in the supposed absence of a political ideology, government would be driven by 'technocratic administration', bringing market-style thinking into public service provision and moving parts out to the free market via privatisation.
- In the 1990s and 2000s, there was also a conscious move to transform the civic sector along these lines: US 'New' Democrats and UK 'New' Labour defined large NGOs as 'delivery partners', outsourcing aspects of core government policy delivery to them.
- With the move from the politics of ideology to that of technocratic managerialism came an inevitable institutional capture by the PMC which populates the machinery both of government and the economy.

This PMC works with economic elites to make and sustain key policy decisions that shape our economy, services and society. It is pivotal not just in the public and private sectors, but also NGOs, the creative industries, media and universities. The technocratic NPM ethos of the PMC has limited interest in political and democratic engagement as its concern is inevitably cost-efficient and profit-extending running of the neo-liberal state. It is therefore a barrier to developing genuinely democratic governance and more equitable social and political economic change.

The long-term consequences of neo-liberal dominance and paternalistic NPM 'insiderism' of our public governance and decision-making has been predictable: (i) inequality: economic, social and health inequalities and related poverty are the primary social outcomes of the neo-liberal era; (ii) externalities – the decline of industrial towns, drug deaths, the climate emergency and so on – have become coincidental or 'external' to the process of government, and there has been little serious attempt to resolve social-ecological crises over the last 40 years; and (iii) in terms of exclusion, the 'participation gap' has increased as the neo-liberal system has become more closed and accessible only to those who understand its 'language' through working in and around the PMC.

Rising Alternatives

So does the rise of neo-liberalism with its NPM and PMC mean we should resign ourselves to a deepening democratic deficit with increasingly unequal and ecological unsustainable outcomes? Of course not – because it is possible to build new democratic alternatives. There is a growing, international evidence base (Escobar and Elstub 2019, Escobar 2020, Fung 2015, Fung and Wright 2003) demonstrating the potential of processes of: (i) participatory democracy, seeking to involve diverse stakeholders meaningfully in governance; (ii) deliberative democracy, where citizens have opportunities to participate in making considered judgements on key policy decisions; and (iii) direct democracy, empowering citizens to engage directly in and with state decision-making processes.

These practices can be adjusted to fit particular contexts – whether local, centralised or transnational – although these aspects will be crucial: (i) recognising diversity – approaching issues from a wide range of experiential backgrounds and perspectives creates more rounded understandings of the potential impacts of decisions; (ii) building deliberation – supporting participants to deepen their discussions and adapt their judgements and views through their interactions so that thinking processes becomes less entrenched in opposing and unresolvable positions; and (iii) creating legitimacy – improving confidence in democratic decision-making by ensuring that citizens see that 'people like me', other citizens, and not just the PMC, have been involved.

We now have a 'toolkit' of widely applicable democratic approaches and innovations. Among them are sortition (the random selection of participants to reflect wider society) and 'mini-publics', multi-stakeholder approaches (where all groups with an interest have a right to equal representation), and deliberative approaches which require people to engage directly in considering alternatives and making recommendations (e.g., citizen juries and assemblies). But careful process design and execution of these democratic innovations are crucial to prevent capture and manipulation by the PMC.

Applying these democratic practices can generate a significant improvement in governance in Scotland. If increasing managerialism has shut many people out, these alternatives can help do the opposite. Failed approaches are more likely to be challenged, whilst ideas and concepts previously absent from public policy debate are more likely to find traction. The implications are potentially significant: the current vast inequalities of power can begin to be reversed as democratic empowerment spreads more evenly.

Envisioning the Future

So what could this look like in Scotland? Here we propose four initiatives which would go a long way to kick-starting vast governance improvements before concluding by thinking further about what else is needed to make progress.

NEW TIER OF LOCAL GOVERNMENT DEMOCRACY

For people to participate in public governance, the starting point has to be local democracy. Closeness to communities generally facilitates greater physical – and social – accessibility, with greater visibility of consequent actions. But one of the most important roles of local democracy is to act as a stepping-stone; in most countries people, particularly women, who go on to become involved in regional and national politics start out at local levels (Maguire 2018). The lack of this stepping-stone is one of the reasons national politics in Scotland is so heavily populated with (often male) political and PMC insiders. Scotland is so far outside the norm of European democracies in lacking strong local tiers of government that it now needs an extra, properly local tier of democracy at town, rural community/district and urban community/district levels. Many organisations have proposed elements of how we can achieve this – for example, McAlpine et al. (2018) developed detailed proposals for 'Development Councils'.

LOCAL PROGRESSIVE MUTUALISM

There is a growing body of community organisations, enterprises and networks across Scotland (like community-controlled housing associations, development trusts, community enterprises, community-led health organisations, credit unions and community finance, community media and arts, community groups and networks, tenant organisations and unions, and local equalities and anti-poverty groups). These create a system of local mutualism which can be supported and further developed in terms of their capacity and democratic governance in a range of ways through skills and knowledge development, building local digital resources, support for community-led plans and deliberation, and funding for initiatives which counter centralised and market power, such as citizen journalism and advocacy groups. They can be supported through a national policy programme which prioritises working-class communities and working people more generally, and enables community ownership of assets like land and energy generation, facilitates initiatives to support people's ability to participate such as minimum income guarantees or a basic income, citizen allowances, and universal public services, and supports related economic reform to promote community wealth-building (Bynner 2016, Henderson et al. 2020).

GOVERNANCE ACADEMY

An education and training institution – a Governance Academy – could help to drive these democratic aspirations. Its roles would be to improve skills and knowledge of modern participatory governance practice, and to embed the use of participatory and deliberative processes. Lack of 'governance literacy' among those who are outside the formal governance system and lack of awareness of new governance practices among those who are inside the system are major barriers. Adequately resourced, a Governance Academy would tackle these issues by working with community bodies to enable people to better understand good governance, how to get involved in it, and how to use it to achieve change. This would be a key element of investing in those on low and precarious incomes and other marginalised groups. Its second role would be to develop a participatory democracy programme which would require institutions to start to use these approaches throughout their core work, such as requiring stakeholder elections for their boards, using mini-publics for policy-shaping and using deliberative inquiry at the very early stages of policy development. Its role would be to identify anywhere the PMC is effectively governing and to open that up. This would mean identifying methods of decision-making which are closed and inaccessible and making them participatory. Consideration would need to be given to how the Academy could ensure this happens and that it does not simply lead to a series of negotiations where the other partner has the dominant hand.

CITIZENS' CHAMBER FOR HOLYROOD

A key characteristic of a governing class is its ability to manage its accountability to others by influencing the judgement of its work, especially via controlling the political discourse. A second Citizens' Chamber of the Scottish Parliament could therefore have a powerful reforming impact upon democracy. It could be selected through sortition and weighted for key demographic features to fully resemble Scotland's social make-up. Members could serve one term, full-time and fully paid, returning to their lives thereafter, closing off the risk of creating another self-perpetuating insider class. Direct lobbying could be prohibited, so the distorting impact of money in politics would be curtailed. The Chamber could be given a formal role in contributing to the development of legislation in the Parliament, have the power to hold inquiries into any aspect of the work of government in Scotland it chose, and have the ability to consider and propose any policy ideas it wished. It could not pass legislation, but could have a very powerful impact upon national debate and greatly strengthen citizens' scrutiny. It could also contain a representative panel which would represent social interests not present in the Chamber – such as children/young people, future generations, those who live beyond Scotland (e.g., the Global South) and ecological systems (e.g., wildlife, nature). This panel would have the role of advocating through dialogue with the Citizens' Chamber and MSPs to support serious consideration of 'all our futures'.

These are four examples that could have a radical transformative effect – or they could pay lip service to democracy, providing cover for 'business as usual'. The climate crisis is placing pressure on elites to change, but it is the PMC which will shape this change, with the likelihood that existing power structures will simply replicate themselves. Leadership is required to make this happen – but it is the current form of leadership which has created the problem. One key step, therefore, will be taking very practical steps to share power by tackling the participation gap. Currently, this is large, and for many it is insurmountable for the following reasons: (i) material – e.g., financial stresses (poverty), employment patterns and/or caring roles; (ii) knowledge/skills – lacking the expected skills to participate effectively; and (iii) culture – lacking the confidence that they have crucial knowledge to offer.

There is no shortcut to overcoming these barriers. To fully open up and localise governance, we need to take economic inequality and poverty seriously and challenge exclusion and prejudice. We must invest in working-class communities and the wider body of working people who face these barriers – including women with caring responsibilities, ethnic minorities and faith/belief groups, disabled people and people with mental health problems, and both younger and older people. This will require a multi-faceted strategy that includes providing childcare, grants and rights to enable people to take time off work, physical infrastructure where effective participation can take place, and supportive services to help people take the first step to participation and more. This is not a 'possible addition' to reforming the processes of governance in Scotland, but is rather an essential pre-condition if a new, diverse countervailing and democratic leadership of people, organisations, institutions and sectors is to emerge that challenges the PMCs and their maintenance of the *status quo*.

Finally, there is also a need to explore what role constitutional change for Scotland could play in catalysing the reforms advocated above. All of the proposals could be achieved under the current devolution settlement, and none would require additional powers. Indeed, the pattern of increased centralisation in Scotland over recent years does nothing to suggest that Scotland is in any way immune from the centralisation of power and dominance of the PMC across the governance structures of the UK. However, pursuit of a second Scottish independence referendum, in the context of wider constitutional crisis in the UK and Europe, offers opportunities to develop alternative, countervailing leadership, expand participatory and deliberative democratic processes, and bring the global social-ecological crisis centre-stage.

References

Baston, L. and Ritchie, K. (2021) *Turning Out or Turning Off? An Analysis of Political Disengagement and What Can Be Done about It*, London: Electoral Reform Society.

Bort, E., McAlpine, R. and Morgan, G. (2012) *The Silent Crisis: Failure and Revival in Local Democracy in Scotland*, Glasgow, UK: Jimmy Reid Foundation.

Bynner, C. (2016) *Rationales for Place-based Approaches in Scotland*, Glasgow, UK: What Works Scotland.

Cochrane, A. (2007) *Understanding Urban Policy: A Critical Approach*, Oxford, UK: Blackwell.

Dalton, R. (2005) 'The social transformation of trust in government', *International Review of Sociology*, 15/1: 133–154.

Escobar, O. (2020) 'Futures in common: Democratic life beyond the crisis', in Hassan, G. (ed.) *Scotland after the Virus*, Edinburgh, UK: Luath, pp. 119–126.

Escobar, O. and Elstub, S. (2019) 'Introduction to the Handbook of Democratic Innovation and Governance: The field of democratic innovation', in Elstub, S. and Escobar, O. (eds) *Handbook of Democratic Innovation and Governance*, Cheltenham, UK: Edward Elgar, pp. 1–10.

Fung, A. (2015) 'Putting the public back into governance: The challenges of citizen participation and its future', *Public Administration Review*, 75/4: 513–522.

Fung, A., and Wright, E. (2003) (eds) *Deepening Democracy: Institutional Innovations in Empowered Participatory Governance*, London: Verso.

Henderson, J., Revell, P. and Escobar, O. (2020) *Building the Community Economy in Scotland*, Glasgow, UK: What Works Scotland and Policy Scotland.

Liu, C. (2021) *Virtue Hoarders: The Case against the Professional Managerial Class*, Minneapolis, MN: University of Minnesota Press.

Maguire, S. (2018) *Barriers to Women Entering Parliament and Local Government*, Bath, UK: Institute for Policy Research, University of Bath.

McAlpine, R., Pearson, L. and Dalzell, C. (2018) *Development Councils: A Proposal for a New System of Local Democracy in Scotland*, Glasgow, UK: Common Weal.

Reid, S., Montagu, I. and Scholes, A. (2020) *Social Attitudes 2019: Attitudes to Government and Political Engagement*, Edinburgh, UK: ScotCen.

Steiner, N. (2016) 'Economic globalisation, the perceived room to manoeuvre of national governments, and electoral participation: Evidence from the 2001 British general election', *Electoral Studies*, 41/1: 118–128.

Winant, G. (2019) 'Professional-managerial chasm: A sociological designation turned into an epithet and hurled like a missile', *N+1 Magazine*, 10 October, www.nplusonemag.com/online-only/online-only/professional-managerial-chasm/.

13

Decent Work in Scotland – a Charter for Change

Jane Carolan, Ruth Dukes and Eleanor Kirk

Introduction

The pandemic laid bare the reality of working life in Scotland. The extent of 'in work' poverty for 700,000 Scots facing low pay and precarious conditions was revealed through unprecedented food bank use (Trussell Trust 2020), followed by waves of evictions (Shelter Scotland 2020). The work of largely female 'key' social care workers was exposed as low-paid, undervalued and insecure. The limited reach and worth of our employment laws became clear when many workers found they had no right to personal protective equipment or to sick pay (Ewing and Hendy 2020). If they tested positive for COVID or came into close contact with someone who had the virus, they faced a choice of going into work anyway or staying home and isolating without wages. As statutory sick pay amounts to only £95.85 per week, even those who were owed it could not always afford to stay home. And since the COVID crisis began, Scotland has suffered a higher percentage of job losses regionally than anywhere else in Britain, and the second highest degree of 'job disruption', including furlough, job losses and lost hours or pay (McCurdy 2020: 2). This is particularly worrying given the pre-existing prevalence of 'bad jobs' in the country, such as those where workers are involuntarily part-time, in non-permanent work, or on a zero-hours contracts (ZHCs), with no guaranteed shifts (Fair Work Convention [FWC] 2020: 45).

The world of work in Scotland is also riven with inequalities. Young workers and those from minority ethnic groups are disproportionately likely to find themselves on low pay or ZHCs (FWC 2020: 44, 46). In 2019, nearly 12% of workers aged 16–24 were on ZHCs (FWC 2020: 44), comparing unfavourably with the UK figure of 9.9% for the same age group (Office for National Statistics 2020). Scottish women are still paid much less than men, with a current gender pay gap across the country of 13%. As the Glasgow City Council equal pay dispute demonstrates, local authorities are themselves guilty of paying women workers significantly less than their male counterparts for work of equal value. Meanwhile, the disability pay gap in Scotland is as high as 16.2% (FWC 2020: 43).

Conditions such as these do not arise through accident or fate. Employment practices develop in a social, cultural and ideological context that is expressed in the system of employment law. Such practices are shaped in part by the paucity of strong and effective legal rights for workers and their ability to enforce those rights easily and affordably. And they are shaped by the presence or absence of unions in workplaces, giving voice to workers' interests. To secure decent jobs for people in Scotland – women and men, BAME and white, young and old, disabled and able-bodied – urgent action is needed. If the Conservatives in Westminster will not act, there are important steps the Scottish Government can take, as we explain below.

We begin this chapter by describing in more detail the shortcomings of our employment laws. We then discuss the Scottish Government's efforts to improve wages and working conditions in Scotland under the banner of 'Fair Work'. Finding weaknesses with this, we draw upon the work of the Institute of Employment Rights (IER) to propose a Charter of

Workers' Rights for Scotland and a more robust approach to ensuring that those rights are respected by employers.

Multiple Failures of Employment Law

Worker and union rights are fundamental human rights, enshrined in several charters and treaties and in international law. Since the 1980s, Britain has failed to abide by these provisions. Beginning with Thatcherite neo-liberalism, and continuing today, a series of deliberate legislative changes diminished and sidelined unions' roles in defending workers' interests. Union rights to access workplaces, to organise workers and to take industrial action were significantly curbed, effectively curtailing union activities and influence. Without the protection membership of strong unions affords, increasing numbers of workers found themselves vulnerable to ill treatment and low pay. Between 1997 and 2010, the Labour Government under Blair and Brown took only very limited steps to reverse these changes. It introduced a national minimum wage and a new statutory recognition procedure for unions, but left the highly restrictive rules around strikes and picketing largely untouched. Indeed, Blair (1998) boasted that Britain had 'the most lightly regulated labour market of any leading economy in the world'.

Unions exist to defend their members' interests. Membership is voluntary, and union decision-making is democratic. Workers as individuals have almost no power relative to their employers; unions can seek to rebalance this equation by requiring employers to negotiate with the workforce rather than with workers on an individual basis. Collective agreements between unions and employers can set pay and other terms and conditions, tailoring these to the needs of a particular workplace and workforce. Sectoral collective bargaining sets pay and other standards for whole industries or sectors.

Sectoral collective bargaining was important in Britain for much of the twentieth century, and remains common in many European countries.

In 1980, 70% of British workers benefited from collective agreements (Waddington 2019). By 2020, this had dropped to 25.6%, though coverage in Scotland was somewhat higher, at 35.7% in Strathclyde and 32.8% in the rest of Scotland (Department for Business, Energy & Industrial Strategy 2021). Without collective bargaining, a 'take it or leave it' (Hayes 2017) system has developed, in which workers have little choice but to accept whatever terms an employer offers. Employers can compete with each other to drive down labour costs and wages in search of competitive advantage. As a result, the UK Parliament has had to intervene to use legislation to create minimum standards. These minimum standards are insufficient, however, to ensure that people can live healthy and secure lives. For example, the national minimum wage as of April 2021 was set at only £4.62 per hour for the under-18s, rising to £8.91 per hour for the over-22s – still less than the living wage calculated according to the cost of living of £9.50 per hour. In other words, even if you are employed full-time in a minimum-wage job, you may not earn enough to support yourself and your family.

Minimum standards can be difficult and costly to enforce, requiring workers to bring a legal claim before an Employment Tribunal. In the current 'take it or leave it' system, some employers have taken to drawing up contracts which falsely state that the worker in question is self-employed. They do this in order to escape legal obligations to pay national insurance, pension contributions and the minimum wage, and to provide breaks and paid holidays. The 2021 Supreme Court decision concerning Yaseen Aslam and other Uber drivers showed it is possible for workers to prove their written contracts are false: that they are workers with employment rights

(Dukes and Streeck 2021). But, again, this is difficult, costly and potentially very time-consuming. In low-pay sectors, including hospitality and catering, social care and retail, employment laws are routinely breached by employers, with the result many workers earn less than the minimum wage. Across the board in Scotland, 36% of workers are in 'bad jobs' which do not provide them with security or a decent standard of living (FWC 2020: 40).

Fair Work in Scotland

Even in the midst of the pandemic, and in light of all that it has uncovered about the extent of bad jobs and inequalities in this country, the Tory Westminster Government has no plans to strengthen worker and union rights. In June 2021, it delayed the plans it had to introduce minimal reforms. Because some of our employment laws have their origins in European Union law, there is even a concern that Brexit will be used by the government as an opportunity to weaken workers' rights yet further.

In Holyrood, there has been recognition of the need for government action to improve the lot of working people. Since 2016, an independent body called the Fair Work Convention has provided advice and recommendations to the Scottish Government aimed at making Scotland a 'fair work' nation by 2025. The FWC's 'Fair Work Framework' has five dimensions aimed at facilitating work that provides workers with an effective voice, opportunity, security, respect and fulfilment. These dimensions cover various aspects of pay, conditions, equal treatment and collective bargaining, amongst other things.

The Fair Work Framework comprises admirable goals which go well beyond the position of the Westminster Government on workers' rights. What is missing, however, is a sense of urgency about the implementation of these goals. Proposals set out in a 2019 Action Plan were primarily promotional and aspirational, constrained by a desire to please everyone, most notable in the wish to develop a 'business case' for workers' rights. When it comes to ensuring that employers treat workers fairly, the Action Plan and associated campaigns fall short (Gall 2021), placing the emphasis on businesses pledging voluntarily to pay the living wage and to avoid making 'inappropriate use' of zero-hours contracts – raising the question of whether zero-hours contracts can ever be appropriate.

Scottish unions have been publicly supportive of Fair Work, but have continually demanded that more be done. The proposals contained in the recent (Feeley) Independent Review on Adult Social Care (Scottish Government 2021) and the Inquiry into Fair Work in Construction are again very welcome, but manifest action is by now long overdue. The FWC's (2020) report goes some way to recognising this is the case. Most recently, disappointment has been expressed by the STUC at the years-long delay to plans to devolve authority over employment and other tribunals to Scotland (*Scottish Legal News*, 8 June 2021).

A Charter of Workers' Rights

The case for workers' rights does not depend upon the wishes of employers. 'Bad' employers will never be persuaded that it is 'good' for businesses to pay workers a decent wage, provide regular hours or recognise a union. It is true that the possibility of employment law reform in Scotland is currently limited by the devolution settlement and the designation of employment law as a so-called 'reserved matter'. While the Scottish Government is therefore unable under current constitutional arrangements to legislate to improve workers' rights, it is far from powerless in this respect.

In 2019, the Institute of Employment Rights published a draft Scottish Charter of Workers' Rights for consultation with the STUC and Scottish unions (Carolan et al. 2019). Work on the final version of the Charter is ongoing, but has been delayed as a result of the pandemic. The IER is a think tank for the union movement. The aim of its Charter is twofold. It proposes a set of rights for workers and unions in Scotland, and it identifies steps that could be taken now, in Holyrood and by local authorities, to promote and implement those rights.

In respect of workers' union rights, the Charter aims to replace the current 'take it or leave it' system with something much better. It proposes a new system, in which workers are both protected from ill and unfair treatment by employers *and* empowered to participate in setting their own wages and terms and conditions. Specifically, the Charter proposes rights for workers' to be paid at least a living wage, to have transparent and predictable working hours and to be paid an increased overtime rate when working on after a shift has ended. It proposes that workers have rights to be treated equally whatever their gender, race, ethnicity, age or disability. And, it proposes that workers should be protected from unfair dismissal from their first day on a job.

The Charter recognises that differences in pay between women and men are caused by multi-dimensional factors, societal and organisational, thus requiring a range of legal and policy responses. While current devolution arrangements mean the Scottish Parliament is unable to legislate to improve equal pay laws, it could engage in awareness-raising among workers and employers, highlighting that it remains unlawful to pay a woman less than a man for doing the same or similar work, regardless of the narrowing of an employer's gender pay gap. It could increase the provision of state-funded childcare to 50 hours per week, allowing parents to combine work and childcare commitments. And it could supplement the legal duty to report on the gender pay gap with a duty to produce a mandatory action plan for addressing that gap.

The Charter also recognises the importance of collective rights and collective bargaining. It is now no longer in doubt that an efficient and productive economy is critically associated with strong workers' rights and high levels of collective bargaining coverage (International Labour Organisation [ILO] 2013; see also Chapter 10 in this volume). Over and above the contribution it can make to economic goals, collective organisation is a necessary condition both of workers' freedom and of a free society more generally. Strong unions and collective bargaining improve democracy, help achieve social justice, and help ensure respect for the rule of law and the international standards that Britain is bound by. It is not enough for the government to guarantee workers' rights to form and join unions and to call members out on strike. The government must also take positive steps to promote union recognition and collective bargaining within workplaces and employing organisations and at sectoral level so that these rights have effects.

Implementing Employment Rights in a Devolved Scotland

When it comes to implementation of these rights, the IER Charter emphasises that the Scottish Government and all local authorities are themselves employers and should lead by example, treating their own employees fairly and equally and recognising unions for the purposes of collective bargaining. In addition, the government in Holyrood could create structures to promote workers' interests, including importantly a dedicated department within the Scottish Government, with its own Cabinet-level minister responsible for workers' rights.

While lacking legislative authority in respect of workers' rights, the Scottish Government has wide-ranging administrative powers it could use to encourage compliance with workers' rights. Apart from making clear public policy expectations, there are coercive powers available to the devolved parliaments in the form of contracts and licences. The government in Holyrood and local authorities alike could make it a condition of contracts and licences that the company in question treat its workers well, as is intended with the Welsh Government's Draft Social Partnership and Public Procurement (Wales) Bill (see Ewing et al. 2021).

Furthermore, it is not enough to merely encourage employers to comply with various standards: it is essential that they be required to comply. In contrast to Fair Work's reliance upon promotion, encouragement and benchmarking (Gall 2021), the IER Charter makes two sets of concrete proposals. It proposes first that a new Scottish Cabinet Secretary for Labour should collaborate with union and employer representatives to establish a register of employers which commit to the Charter, and create a robust machinery for reporting and monitoring compliance by these employers. The model for this purpose would be the ILO monitoring machinery which requires states to submit regular reports about their compliance with the treaties by which they are bound, with unions (and employers) having the right to comment upon these reports. Further, the new Cabinet Secretary should act to ensure that registration and compliance with those provisions of the Charter which can be made mandatory without legislation are a relevant consideration in public procurement and licensing decisions.

Secondly, the Charter proposes that the government oversee a programme of rolling out sectoral collective bargaining, beginning where necessary with sectors where there is the greatest need and the greatest opportunity. There is already a form of sectoral collective bargaining in Scottish agriculture (which survived the abolition of its counterpart in England and Wales). A modern equivalent should be introduced for social care (both residential and peripatetic), hospitality, construction, and early learning and childcare as a matter of some urgency. As in agriculture, collective agreements in these sectors would set out minimum pay and standards to apply to all workers regardless of union membership.

Conclusion

It is difficult to exaggerate either the scale of the need for a programme to strengthen employment laws and to revitalise collective bargaining, or the importance of the Scottish Government's role in making this happen. International evidence clearly demonstrates that sectoral bargaining can raise wages and enhance worker protections. It is also associated with other benefits, such as (i) closing the gender pay gap, (ii) enhancing workers' voices and job security, (iii) eliminating private competition for public services on low wages alone, and (iv) preventing the exploitation of agency workers. As debates on constitutional matters continue, both the Fair Work Convention and the IER have begun the important work of demonstrating that where there is political will, there is certainly a way.

References

Blair, T. (1998) 'Foreword', in *Fairness at Work White Paper*, London: The Stationery Office.

Carolan, J., Dukes, R., Ewing, K., Kirk, E. and McCorkindale, C. (2019) *Draft for Consultation: Charter of Workers' Rights*, Liverpool, UK: Institute of Employment Rights.

Department for Business, Energy & Industrial Strategy (2021) *Trade Union Statistics 2020*, London: House of Commons Library.

Dukes, R. and Streeck, W. (2021) 'Putting the brakes on the spread of indecent work', *Social Europe*, 10 March, https://socialeurope.eu/putting-the-brakes-on-the-spread-of-indecent-work.

Ewing, K. and Hendy, J. (2020) 'Covid-19 and the failure of labour law: Part 1', *Industrial Law Journal*, 49/4: 497–538.

Ewing, K., Hendy, J., Jones, C. and Shears, G. (2021) *Draft Social Partnership and Public Procurement (Wales) Bill: A Consultation Response from the Institute of Employment Rights*, Liverpool, UK: Institute of Employment Rights.

Fair Work Convention (2020) *Fair Work in Scotland*, Glasgow, UK: Fair Work Convention.

Gall, G. (2021) *Critique of Scottish Government's 'Fair Work' Policy*, Glasgow, UK: Jimmy Reid Foundation.

Hayes, L. (2017) *8 Good Reasons Why Adult Social Care Needs Sectoral Collective Bargaining*, Liverpool, UK: Institute of Employment Rights.

ILO (2013) *Collective Bargaining Essential to Overcome Global Income Inequalities*, 17 December, Geneva, Switzerland: International Labour Organisation,

Office for National Statistics (2020) *People Employed in Zero Hours Contracts*, London: Office for National Statistics.

McCurdy, C. (2020) *Local Differences: Responding to the Local Economic Impact of Coronavirus*, London: Resolution Foundation.

Scottish Government (2021) *Independent Review of Adult Care in Scotland* (chaired by Derek Feeley), Edinburgh, UK: Scottish Government.

Shelter Scotland (2020) *Briefing Paper for the Local Government and Communities Committee*, Edinburgh, UK: Shelter Scotland.

Trussell Trust (2020) *End of Year Stats for 2019–2020*, Salisbury, UK: Trussell Trust.

Waddington, J. (2019) 'United Kingdom: A long-term assault on collective bargaining', in Waddington, J., Muller, T. and Vandaele, K. (eds) *Collective Bargaining in Europe: Towards an Endgame, Volume 3*, Brussels, Belgium: European Trade Union Institute.

14

Alienation and Exclusion to Empowerment and Inclusion? Human Rights in Scotland

Carole Ewart, Janis McDonald and Sean Whittaker

Introduction

Ensuring people have their dignity respected and their rights as humans fulfilled remains an enduring political challenge. Although the Scottish Parliament has had the power to use human rights to make Scotland fairer, a divide quickly emerged between theory, rhetoric and practice. Now there is evidence of the divide being bridged, resulting in collaboration as well as collision. Despite Brexit, the UK's eco-legal system remains centred on the Human Rights Act 1998, which gives domestic effect to the European Convention on Human Rights (ECHR). Change beckons as the Westminster Secretary of State for Justice has announced a major overhaul of the Act before the next general election.

The constitutional settlement in the Scotland Act 1998 also places a duty upon Scottish Ministers to comply with the ECHR, and with 'international obligations' in how they deliver devolved functions. This legal power was confirmed by the UK Supreme Court in October 2021 when it did not challenge the right of the Scottish Parliament to incorporate a UN treaty into domestic law, but did rule that specific articles in the UN Convention on the Rights of the Child (Incorpora-tion) (Scotland) Bill had wandered into reserved matters and needed to be amended by MSPs before Royal Assent could be granted.

Constructing a human rights architecture must address concerns about defining the respective roles of the individ-ual, state and private enterprise, facilitating commitment to equality between human beings and agreeing rights in law. Practitioners focusing upon delivering positive outcomes need to collaborate with those for whom rights and duties are con-tested and enforcement mechanisms challenged. Writing on 'natural morality', Biggar (2020: 325) addresses the problem of defining rights by arguing that 'rights fundamentalism' con-flates morality with legality, reducing the former to the latter. 'Rights fundamentalism' proceeds to take rights as given, and by asserting at the beginning what is properly a conclusion, pre-empts and shuts down ethical deliberation. That is why 'rights-talk' has a tendency to push all other moral considera-tions off the table.

Biggar (2020) also addresses the role of the courts and judges. In many cases, the arguments centre on interpreting legislation agreed by the sovereign parliament, and the breach of human rights arises from the interpretation or the abuse of state power and its failure to protect the human being. Citing a case in Canada where a right was not established in law by parliament, Biggar (2020: 2) poses the problematic question concerning 'how it was that an oligarchy of judges presumed to take to themselves the responsibility for making such a politically controversial decision'. Whitty et al. (2001: 55) offer a solution: 'if civil liberties law is to negotiate, explain and critique this new era, it must discard its history of legalism and atheoreticism, and embrace literature which is still most often outside the mainstream legal curriculum'. That literature, examining non-judicial remedies as well as the work of practitioners, informs this chapter.

Whilst the expectations of many in the Global North on the interpretation of rights may be different to many in the Global South, we argue we must share minimum standards such as the right to food and a shared community benefit from a healthy, accessible environment. The belief that 'the state will provide' rings hollow for many due to abundant evidence of failure, including levels of child poverty, homelessness and health inequality. We highlight communities of interest around human rights, such as the links between those with hearing loss and those who face systemic exclusion from everyday opportunities.

In this chapter, we cast a critical eye over the Scottish Parliament's efforts since 1999 to define human rights, promote a culture of rights delivering a fairer society, collectively and individually, and establish an infrastructure with accessible enforcement. Politicians voted unanimously to pass the aforementioned UN Convention on the Rights of the Child (UNCRC) Incorporation Bill, and so far have not shown the regressive revisionism on human rights articulated by Westminster. Political unity may fracture when incorporating economic and social rights, and the identity of rights holders becomes an issue, along with financial concerns. We focus on three areas: deafness, environmental justice and law-making.

Deaf to Rights

Over a million people in Scotland are directly affected by deafness, about 20% of the population. We all know someone impacted, but we will also know many more who are unaware of their hearing loss. It can take 4–15 years for a person to realise they have a problem. Repeated miscommunication between friends and family as well as colleagues is understandable, but the growing isolation caused along the way has proven to be a cause of poor mental health and early-onset dementia. A quick fix is to widen the practice of inclusive communication so that it becomes standard across services. Moving away from marginalising the issue to mainstreaming the solution is a political matter. It requires a focus on culture, funding, practice and strategic change. Politicians from all parties and key decision-makers are slow to take targeted action.

Deafness has been normalised and consistently ignored for decades, resulting in multiple abuses of human rights. Even writing this is controversial, as people get defensive and tend to blame the 'victim' for not trying harder to understand what is being said or criticising them for not being assertive enough. Many wrongly judge that the 'deaf community' has failed to campaign effectively and convey succinctly the extent of exclusion, discrimination, isolation and misery. But to suggest that the over 1 million people affected are all the same is another mistake. In Scotland, there are Deaf/British Sign Language (BSL) users, there are Deafened people, Deafblind people and Hard of Hearing people (McMenemy et al. 2021). Each key pillar of deafness indicates different barriers and solutions. Any strategy cannot be based on a 'one size fits all' approach.

These figures can be further broken down to help design action. For example, 40% of those aged over 40, 60% of over-60s, 70% of over-70s, and 90% of those aged over 75 have hearing loss. That loss defines their lives and opportunities. Language can also be problematic, because it reflects misunderstanding: a 'BSL user' is not a Deaf person or hearing loss person, but is a person using a defined and recognised language under human rights law. Not all people affected by deafness use BSL or other sign language, so that needs to be factored into decisions too.

Gradually, doors are being opened because of the breadth of evidence concerning the impact and experience of excluded voices, poorly designed services and unequal outcomes. The pandemic has exacerbated problems across health and social care, welfare and employment. The adoption of a digital-first approach means telephone helplines are inaccessible and online services depend on skills and software that people cannot use or that are routinely unavailable. Many must pay more for accessible technology. Face coverings are a noticeable barrier, and physical distancing has exacerbated personal isolation too. Hearing aids usually only work up to a metre's distance.

Human rights are easy to identify as a framework for solutions. The state and its agencies are required to deliver rights with equal outcomes across economic, social, cultural, civil, political and environmental matters. It is not a process of seeking equality with a poorly paid worker, it is about realising the equal 'right to enjoy just and favourable conditions of work which ensure fair wages' (Article 7, *International Covenant on Economic, Social and Cultural Rights*).

Understanding rights is a matter for rights holders as well as duty bearers. For example, a survey created by Totaljobs (2016) in partnership with five deaf charities revealed that 56% of deaf employees have experienced discrimination during their career which led to 25% of them leaving a job, 25% of workers stated there was no provision for deaf employees at their workplace, and 19% had not told their employer they were deaf or had experienced hearing loss.

Adopting a human rights-based approach offers opportunities to identify the problems as well as focus upon designing and delivering solutions. The PANEL principles (Scottish Human Rights Commission n.d.) frame delivery in terms of (i) *participation*, which depends on inclusive communication so that all voices are at the table to inform decisions; (ii) *accountability*, where the conversation is flipped so that key decision-makers have to justify why they are excluding those affected by deafness; (iii) *non-discrimination*, with a plethora of evidence demonstrating unequal outcomes so it can be used to drive forward the pace and detail of change; (iv) *empowerment*, acknowledging that a person owns rights and the state cannot take them away, so the terrain moves to asserting entitlement; and (v) *legal*, where the requirement to work differently is embedded in Scots law.

Currently, inclusive communication is included as a process in specific laws such as on social security or to promote a specific language, such as the British Sign Language (Scotland) Act 2015.[1] The Scottish Parliament has voted to deliver global standards on human rights, and mainstreaming inclusive communication needs to be core to every aspect of that agenda.

Cost of Environmental Justice

Scottish court procedures that guarantee access to environmental justice are undergoing a period of scrutiny and reform. The pace and detail of the reform are a matter of concern, but they nonetheless provide an opportunity for useful learning about the barriers to improving access to justice generally, and on Scotland's implementation of the Aarhus Convention in particular. Through the United Kingdom's ratification of the 1998 United Nations Economic Commission for Europe's Convention on Access to Information, Public Participation in Decision-making and Access to Justice in Environmental Matters (commonly known as the Aarhus Convention), Scotland is obliged to ensure that individuals and non-govern-

---

1 See S6 and S9 of Coronavirus (Scotland) Acts, S6(7)(b) of Consumer (Scotland) Act 2020, S4(2) of Social Security (Scotland) Act 2018, British Sign Language (Scotland) Act 2015 and Gaelic Language (Scotland) Act 2005.

mental organisations (NGOs) have access to 'fair, equitable, timely and not prohibitively expensive' review procedures to challenge environmental decisions of public bodies (Article 9(4)). Individuals and NGOs primarily challenge environmental decisions via judicial review, and these obligations are critical in ensuring that the judicial review procedure, and thus access to environmental justice, is accessible to all.

Despite these obligations, in 2014 the Aarhus Convention Compliance Committee (ACCC) found that among other breaches, the costs of initiating a judicial review in Scotland were too onerous and unduly restricted the right to access environmental justice. This led to various reforms to the Court of Session's rules on judicial reviews in 2018, specifically in relation to costs and protective expenses orders.[2]

A key feature of these new rules governing protective expenses orders is that as a default position, the liability of applicants seeking judicial review in environmental matters is limited to £5,000 or lower if 'justified on cause shown' (Chapter 58A.7(1)(a)). This liability cap is intended to ensure that the cost of seeking judicial review is kept as low as possible, thereby ensuring that individuals and NGOs are not inhibited from accessing environmental justice due to cost barriers. Additional revisions to the Court of Session's rules, including a limit to the cost for unsuccessful protective expenses order applications to £500, further seeks to reduce the impact of financial barriers on how individuals and NGOs challenge the environmental decisions of public authorities. However, these reforms do not wholly eliminate the financial barriers to environmental justice in Scotland. Under these new rules the default liability cap can be raised as well as lowered if 'justified on cause shown'. Additionally, if a decision made by the Outer

---

2   Chapter 58A – Protective Expenses Orders in Environmental Appeals and Judicial Reviews, Court of Session Rules.

House of the Court of Session is appealed, applicants must re-apply for a protective expenses order. These issues increase the financial risk applicants are exposed to, potentially deterring them from initiating judicial review proceedings (ACCC 2020, Christman 2019). It has also been suggested that the £500 cost for an unsuccessful protective expenses order application may deter applicants (Pedersen 2011).

These issues are symptomatic of a broader recurring problem in Scotland. Despite continued efforts by the Scottish Government, the ACCC continues to find Scotland in breach of its obligations. The current approach of relying on judicial reviews to provide access to environmental justice is unfeasible (Pederson 2011), and the Scottish Government may be better creating an environmental-specific forum for hearing cases rather than tinkering with pre-existing procedures. The Scottish Government is obliged, under S41 of the Withdrawal from the European Union (Continuity) (Scotland) Act 2021, to launch a consultation on the effectiveness and sufficiency of the laws guaranteeing access to environmental justice in Scotland. The findings of this consultation might be what triggers the Scottish Government to consider creating an explicitly environment-centric review body and (potentially) resolving the pernicious problem of guaranteeing access to environmental justice in Scotland.

Ditching Theory to Practise Rights

In February 2006, the Scottish Parliament's Justice 1 Committee asked:

> In a country where actual breaches of human rights are extremely rare and in a country with open, independent and robust legislative and judicial systems, the question is

whether we need to create a public body charged with promoting best practice in human rights?[3]

The Committee agreed it was 'not in a position to recommend to the Parliament whether the general principles of the [Scottish Commissioner for Human Rights] Bill should be agreed to or not'.[4] Compromise led to a law establishing a Commission, not a Commissioner, to comply with the coalition agreement between Labour and the Liberal Democrats. MSPs opted to specifically prohibit the funding or pursuance of individual cases. The very reason why people from all political parties can support human rights seemed to be one of the greatest threats: human rights are owned by individuals and communities, and they place specific obligations on States to deliver them with equal outcomes.

The Committee's conclusions demonstrated that the new parliament trusted public institutions to comply with human rights law, a view not shared by the civil society submissions on the bill. Although the Scottish Commission for Human Rights was eventually set up in 2008, its annual budget of £1 million was immediately cut, and its funding is still below that in 2021.

MSPs have used their powers to approve specific human rights delivery measures outwith the courts, such as the Freedom of Information (Scotland) Act 2002 with simple, free enforcement through the Scottish Information Commissioner. MSPs also passed the Commissioner for Children and Young People (Scotland) Act 2003, including functions relating to the UNCRC. The Commissioner's functions have since been expanded to include casework.

---

3   *Stage 1 Report on the Scottish Commission for Human Rights Bill*, para. 188, http://archive.scottish.parliament.uk/business/committees/justice1/reports-06/j1r06-01-vol01-02.htm.
4   Ibid., para. 202.

The theory and practice of rights frighten some politicians and professionals because they have the potential to expose flaws in their attitudes and behaviour on decision-making. In 2004, the Court of Session ruled that the impact of slopping out on Robert Napier in a Scottish prison breached Article 3 of the ECHR. Therefore, the Scottish Executive was wrong to repurpose the allocated funds to install toilets in every cell. In 2008, the Scottish Government was forced by the UK Supreme Court to change the law to give suspects the right to access a lawyer as soon as they were detained. The deprivation of the right had been controversial since the 1980s, but was endorsed in 2007 by a unanimous decision of seven judges at the Scottish Appeal Court. The Supreme Court unanimously voted that the Scottish judges had erred in law. However, these cases are well known because legal challenge is so rare.

Scotland does not have a vibrant history of human rights litigation. The latest figures show that 362 cases for Judicial Review were initiated in 2019–2020, a rise of 20 since 2010–2011, yet there were none on social security or the environment, and only 18 on housing matters (Scottish Government 2021). Driving up better human rights practice by litigants pursuing cases is not proving to be an effective strategy in Scotland.

Perhaps frustrated by slow progress, political attitudes have now shifted. The Scottish Parliament has a committee that explicitly includes Human Rights in its title, and in 2021 the First Minister's Taskforce on Human Rights Leadership recommended a new law to incorporate several UN treaties including the *International Covenant on Economic, Social and Cultural Rights* (ICESCR). Connecting legal rights with policy initiatives such as on 'Fairwork' will be the challenge. Public funding will help. Allocated in August 2021, £21 million over three years will be shared by 48 organisations to advance human rights, promote equality and tackle discrimination. It is time for optimism that duty bearers and right holders will realise that rights matter, preventing cases reaching court. New funding for strategic litigation to make enforcement feasible also has the potential to deter rights abuses. Scotland's human rights journey is loaded with challenges and opportunities.

Conclusion

Enforcement of human rights is a complex process – it is not a one-dimensional approach of judges deciding cases. Judicial and non-judicial remedies need to be developed and deployed. The prospect of access to justice will be a game changer, as the current rights complacency stems from the lack of top-down and bottom-up consequences. Explicit compliance with human rights law can be led and incentivised by politicians, and through health boards, councils and other publicly funded services, can put pressures on the rest. Publicly funded bodies need to deliver rights locally, trust people to know when their rights are abused and trust them with solutions. In services such as social care, the Feeley Review made human rights delivery central to the new system as a remedy for community concerns. Opportunities beckon not just to reimagine rights, but also accessible enforcement.

References

ACCC (2020) *Second Progress Review of the Implementation of Decision VI/8k on Compliance by the United Kingdom of Great Britain and Northern Ireland with Its Obligations under the Convention*, Brussels, Belgium: Aarhus Convention Compliance Committee.

Biggar, N. (2020) *What's Wrong with Rights?*, Oxford, UK: Oxford University Press.

Christman, B. (2019) 'New rules, old problems: The 2018 Protective Expenses Order regime and the Aarhus Convention', *Scottish Planning and Environmental Law*, 195: 106–108.

McMenemy, A., Johnson, C. and Koesters, N. (2021) *Mental Health and Deafness in Scotland: Exploring the Data*, Glasgow, UK: deafscotland and Queen Margaret University.

Pedersen, O. (2011) 'Price and participation: The UK before the Aarhus Convention's Compliance Committee', *Environmental Law Review*, 13/2: 115–121.

Scottish Government (2021) 'Table 25: Petitions for judicial review initiated and disposed of in the Petition Department of the Court of Session, 2010–11 to 2019–20', *Civil Justice Statistics in Scotland: 2019–2020*, 24 April, Edinburgh, UK: Scottish Government, www.gov.scot/publications/civil-justice-statistics-scotland-2019-20/.

Scottish Human Rights Commission (n.d.) *A Human Rights-based Approach: An Introduction*, Glasgow, UK: Scottish Human Rights Commission.

Totaljobs (2016) '1 in 4 deaf people have quit their job due to discrimination', *Totaljobs*, 22 August, www.totaljobs.com/media-centre/1-in-4-deaf-people-have-quit-their-job-due-to-discrimination.

Whitty, N., Murphy, T., and Livingstone, S. (2001) *Civil Liberties Law: The Human Rights Act Era*, Oxford, UK: Oxford University Press.

15

Towards Gender Justice: Enhancing Participation, Reimagining Economics and Ending Gender-based Violence

Kirsty Alexander and Jenny Morrison

Introduction

This chapter explains three inter-connected aspects of distributive gender injustice in Scotland and offers insights about what can be done to move towards and implement gender justice. The three aspects are: unequal gender representation and participation in public life, gendered divisions of paid and unpaid labour, and gender-based violence (GBV). These are amongst the most historically and structurally entrenched, and thus enduring, manifestations of unequal social relations in Scotland. As such, they deserve to be foregrounded in this chapter. We understand that experientially and socially, gender cannot be separated and abstracted from other forms of stratification and marginalisation, some of which are discussed elsewhere in this volume. In Scotland, as in other nations and states, gender, class, ethnicity, 'race' and disability 'intersect' (Crenshaw 2016), and we recognise the need to attend to the complexity of gendered inequalities in different spheres of life. Indeed, it is our view that a feminist lens ought to be considered within and across the perspectives, issues and policy proposals dealt with in this volume.

For the purposes of this chapter, 'gender' is understood as a social structure rather than a synonym for 'woman' or an expression of embodied identity (Carver 1996, Young 2002, Jackson 2006). Specifically, gender refers to the hierarchical relations between the social groups, men and women, and as a concept, allows us to identify and critique forms of regulation and stratification which create unequal power relations and constraints in individuals' lives. Indeed, in this approach, gender itself is regulated by what feminist sociologists call 'institutionalised heterosexuality' (Ingraham 1994). This refers to the normative social and cultural expectations about 'men' and 'women' which are (re)produced in law, public policy, cultural meanings and everyday social relations. Reading gender through the lens of institutionalised heterosexuality is useful here because it not only helps to explain cultural and social constraints with respect to embodied gender identity and expressions of sexuality, but it also shines a powerful light on the enduring but often normalised gendered divisions of labour and relations of violence which suffuse Scottish society. This chapter begins by explaining the three aspects of gender injustice before offering proposals for moving towards gender justice. We conclude with the view that gender justice would at least be within reach if Scotland's political institutions were to have increased governmental power.

Symptoms and Causes and Effects

The first form of gender injustice we highlight concerns unequal decision-making power and responsibility in Scotland's public political institutions. As we explain below, this has an impact on what is considered a social need and who has access to key resources. Ending the over-representation of men in decision-making has long been a high-profile area of equalities work in devolved Scotland. Stalled progress meant the once-record levels of women's representation in Holyrood were almost matched in Westminster – sitting respectively at 34.9% and 33.9% (Allen 2020). However, the 2021 election saw women's representation rise to a record 45% of MSPs. While the 50/50 Cabinet under Nicola Sturgeon is welcome, it remains to be seen whether this equality will become an embedded aspect of Scottish political life, and special advisers to the government remain two-thirds male (Scottish Government 2020b). Moreover, the high levels of women's representation in the early years of the Scottish Parliament were often also associated with a turn towards professional middle-class representation (Keating and Cairney 2006). As of 2021, only two women of colour have ever been elected to the Scottish Parliament, both gaining their seats in the 2021 election.

Parties of the left have generally achieved parity, with the Scottish Socialist Party achieving a 50/50 balance in its elected MSPs and the RISE (Respect, Independence, Socialism and Environmentalism) coalition fielding 54% women candidates (Engender 2016). Nonetheless, women on the left have faced resistance in promoting gender balance, and men often remain over-represented in social movement platforms (Alexander et al. 2019, Boyd and Morrison 2014). Meanwhile, there is the risk that a few high-profile women may mask the actual picture of representation in public and political life, with just 29% of local councillors being women, only a third of FTSE-350 board positions held by women, and less than 25% of judicial office holders and sheriffs being women (Scottish Government 2020). While women make up more than half of union members and 66% of representatives are women (TUC 2014), and although the STUC has been led by Rozanne Foyer from 2020, only 27% of STUC-affiliated unions were led by women in 2019 (Engender 2020).

For the problem of representation to clearly come to light, it matters where we look and who is visible. Often, disadvantaged social groups remain unseen and unheard in public discussion about representation. For instance, progress has been made in gender representation in the past decade, with a 50% increase in women on FTSE-350 boards and 50% of new appointees to public boards now women (Elliot 2019). At the same time, however, women's poverty and collective bargaining power have stagnated. This raises questions about the importance of the 'glass ceiling' relative to the 'sticky floor', which brings into sharp focus inter-connections between unequal participation and representation in public life and the second form of gender injustice we highlight here: gendered divisions of paid and unpaid labour. Indeed, feminist economists and organisations in Scotland have long drawn attention to the limits of formal equal opportunities when the 'sticky floor' is a major structural feature of the formal labour market in neo-liberal capitalism.

Dismantling barriers to job promotion and access to management roles for women are important factors in redistributing decision-making power among social groups, but this is only the tip of the iceberg in terms of establishing economic gender justice. The gender pay gap currently stands at 10% (Close the Gap 2021). Enduring gendered patterns in the labour market show that women are more likely than men to be employed part-time and in socially devalued sectors where low pay and precarious contractual arrangements are standard. Occupational gender segregation persists in Scotland, exposing deep-rooted cultural expectations – which are exploited in the labour market – regarding 'appropriate' social roles and responsibilities for men and women (Engender 2021a). Perpetuation of workplace discrimination, low pay and access to employment are shaped by racism, ageism and ableism (Close the Gap 2021), highlighting the importance of recognising the ways that structural, historical inequalities in power and resources shape labour market practices.

Feminist economists view these inequalities in the formal labour market through a lens which encompasses social relationships and activities that are excluded from neo-liberal and traditional socialist economics (Waring 1990, McKay and Bjørnholt 2014). People's experiences of labour market participation are not viewed in a bubble, divorced from activities and relationships in other spheres of life. On the contrary, activities in the formal and informal markets and in paid and unpaid labour patterns are foregrounded in this analysis. How we use our time, the caring activities we give and receive, and the quality of our lives also 'count' in feminist economics; activities that are invisible to mainstream economic approaches become visible in feminist economics (Engender 2021b, Nash 1995). This approach helps to illuminate the inter-connected gendered cycles of inequality between different spheres of life. With respect to labour market inequalities, these are recognised as being linked to the unequal distribution of responsibility for unpaid care work in Scotland. Childcare, elder care and care for people who experience disability is disproportionately borne by women. In turn, for those who care, gaining and maintaining secure paid employment or self-employment is a manifest and pressing challenge.

Having examined the gendered divisions of paid and unpaid labour, we turn now to the third form of injustice: gender-based violence. This remains a significant injustice for women which acts as a barrier to women's participation in the public sphere and re-embeds inequality in the labour market. According to recent data, globally 1 in 3 women have experienced some form of physical or sexual abuse from a male intimate partner (World Health Organisation 2021) and up to 71% of women in the UK have been sexually harassed in public spaces (UN Women UK 2021). Reported crime statistics show

60,641 incidents of domestic abuse for 2018–2019, 13,364 sex crimes for 2019–2020 (Scottish Government 2020a, 2019b) and 112 femicides in 2009–2018 (Long et al. 2020). Most of these crimes were perpetrated by men against women.

Nevertheless, these numbers offer only a partial view of the prevalence of GBV in Scotland because they focus upon incidents reported to the police. They do not account for forms of abuse which are not criminalised, such as all forms of sexual harassment and some types of online and digital technology-enabled abuse. Moreover, the statistics exclude important demographic information, such as the victim's race, immigration status, sexuality, religion and other protected characteristics. They do not reveal how other forms of GBV and discrimination may have combined with the abuse reported. Additionally, victim-survivors of GBV continue to face huge hurdles to access justice in Scotland. Many refrained from engaging with the criminal justice process due to fear of disbelief by authorities and the sheer complexity of the process, which is often described as re-traumatising. For cases that are reported, barriers remain due to legal requirements (e.g., corroboration), which make it harder for cases to reach court, let alone achieve conviction, particularly when it comes to rape.

What Can Be Done about It?

In order to transform the injustices discussed and for Scotland to become a democratic society, there is a need to redistribute power towards women. The Scottish Parliament currently lacks the power to legislate for gender quotas in parliament. This means that until electoral law is devolved or independence, political parties should be encouraged to adopt gender-balancing measures in candidate selection and formal gender quotas for elections (Engender 2020). The success of legislation for equality on public boards also points to a key strategy for the private and third-sector, given that mandatory quotas have been more successful than voluntary schemes globally (*Herald*, 4 May 2017).

Since women represent the majority of union members, removing the anti-democratic restrictions on union action, such as the Trade Union Act 2016 requiring a 50% threshold on ballots for strike action, would allow for women's democratic action and participation in the public sphere through protest. Whilst employment is reserved to Westminster, Scottish campaigning in this area speaks to a different form of women's participation not limited to a relative elite, but which nonetheless can wield power to change society.

Westminster also retains legislative powers with respect to employment law and overarching economic policy. Within the limits of devolved powers, the current SNP Scottish Government does recognise the need for a more holistic approach to economic gender justice. A stream of initiatives to close the income gap, address occupation segregation, and create childcare and social security infrastructure, among other issues, are set out in the report *A Fairer Scotland for Women* (Scottish Government 2019a).

The most recent Scottish Budget (2021–2022) includes an 'Equality and Fairer Scotland Budget' statement, outlining funding provision for initiatives to address a range of inter-connected inequalities, including those based on sex and gender. Importantly, this budget takes into account the impacts of the pandemic on disadvantaged groups of women and low-income households. In this sense, the advocacy of gender budgeting by organisations like Engender, Close the Gap and the Scottish Women's Budget Group has been notable, and represents an important step in cultural change with regard to imagining what the Scottish economy comprises.

Gender budgeting is one part of a broader, substantial re-conceptualisation of economics and economic recovery now happening in Scotland. Public discussions about the care and wellbeing economies, wherein inclusive growth and a revaluation of care are centred, are part of the political firmament (Engender and Close the Gap 2020). Feminist economists have long argued for the need to move away from standard measures of economic activity like Gross Domestic Product and the limited focus on formal labour market activity. Traditional national accounting approaches do not tell us much about the health of ourselves and our ecology (Waring 1990). Alternative feminist visions of economics foreground the democratic sharing of paid and unpaid labour not only as a privatised activity, but within the public sphere, the redistribution of care, respite and leisure time, and meeting human physical, emotional and social needs. These ideas are now part of the Scottish political firmament and government narrative about economics and distributive justice. Yet, whilst the National Performance Framework sets out a holistic approach to economics, it seems to be a forgotten aspect of policy. The Advisory Group on Economic Recovery (April 2020) explicitly calls for a 'wellbeing economy' in light of austerity and the pandemic, and at least in terms of the discourse of ideological change, echoes some key aspects of a feminist approach to economic gender justice. Yet this also sits alongside discussion of growth, such as in the Growth Commission, thus it remains to be seen how far such approaches will be implemented.

In terms of GBV, a fundamental transformation of the criminal and civil justice processes is necessary, including specialised courts for sexual crime trials, removing the 'Not Proven' verdict and improving civil justice processes. Currently, the joint Scottish Government and COSLA (Convention of Scottish Local Authorities) (2016) 'Equally Safe' strategy for action on all forms of abusive behaviour and violence directed at women and girls has led to important advances in the ways the criminal justice system operates for women. Laws against coercive control, stalking and image-based sexual abuse have been introduced in recent years. Additionally, the Scottish Government has committed funding for the provision of specialist legal support through the Scottish Women's Rights Centre, and created a joint protocol between Police Scotland and the Crown Office Procurator Fiscal Service to respond to dual and malicious reporting in domestic abuse cases. However, again, whilst these are welcome steps, deeper systemic changes are needed to increase women's confidence in the system. Some outstanding work includes: eliminating the 'Not Proven' verdict (a third verdict unique to Scotland), implementing Lady Dorrian's recommendation to introduce a specialist court for serious sexual offence cases (Scottish Courts and Tribunal Service 2021) and expanding specialist courts for other forms of GBV, addressing rape myths and stereotypes at all levels of the justice system and reforming criminal justice process in order to increase convictions. All of these efforts must centre the experiences of victims/survivors.

Additionally, deeper systemic changes are needed and carceral approaches to gender justice are limited. Gender inequality has structural causes, and is therefore preventable. Organisations like Zero Tolerance and Rape Crisis Scotland have led the prevention work in Scotland through nationwide research and training with early years' practitioners and parents, as well as workshops with children, teachers, university students and staff addressing sexual violence, consent and healthy relationships.

Whilst the Scottish Government has recognised the success of prevention and its importance in achieving gender equality aims, efforts in this area are ongoing. Recently, the First Minister's National Advisory Council on Women and Girls recommended high-level and far-reaching changes in education, leading to the establishment of the Gender Equality in Education and Learning (GETEL) group (Scottish Government 2021). It is expected that GETEL will propose actions to encourage engagement at all levels of the education sector in collaboration with violence against women organisations. If society in Scotland is serious about achieving gender justice, it must continue to have prevention at the heart of its policy and action.

We have argued that over the past two decades, Scottish Governments have taken steps towards reducing gender injustice, even if there are areas where feminists press for further policy change. Nonetheless, notable throughout are key areas outwith the current powers of the Scottish Government. Thus, there is also a need for increased governmental power to allow us to address the full inter-connected range of issues and realise distributive gender justice.

References

Alexander, K., Eschle, C., Morrison, J. and Turbine, M. (2019) 'Feminism and solidarity on the left: Rethinking the unhappy marriage', *Political Studies*, 64/4: 972–991.

Allen, G. (2020) *General Election 2019: How Many Women Were Elected?*, London: House of Commons Library.

Boyd, C. and Morrison, J. (2014) *Scottish Independence: A Feminist Response*, Edinburgh, UK: Word Power.

Carver, T. (1996) *Gender Is Not a Synonym for Woman*, Boulder, CO: Lynne Rienner.

Close the Gap (2021) *Close The Gap Briefing for Scottish Government Debate: International Women's Day*, Glasgow, UK: Close the Gap.

Crenshaw, K. (2016) 'The urgency of intersectionality', *TEDWomen*, www.ted.com/talks/kimberle_crenshaw_the_urgency_of_ intersectionality?language=en.

Elliot, C. (2019) *Female Representation on Public Boards Reaches 50%*, Glasgow, UK: Business for Scotland.

Engender (2016) *The Case for Gender Quotas in Scotland*, Edinburgh, UK: Engender.

Engender (2020) *Sex and Power in Scotland 2020*, Edinburgh, UK: Engender.

Engender (2021a) *Employment and Labour Market, Gender Matters Roadmap: Towards Women's Equality in Scotland*, Edinburgh, UK: Engender.

Engender (2021b) *Making Work Visible*, Edinburgh, UK: Engender.

Engender and Close the Gap (2020) *Gender and Economic Recovery*, Edinburgh, UK: Engender and Close the Gap.

Ingraham, C. (1994) 'The heterosexual imaginary: Feminist sociology and theories of gender', *Sociological Theory*, 12/2: 203–219.

Jackson, S. (2006) 'Gender, sexuality and heterosexuality: The complexity (and limits) of heteronormativity', *Feminist Theory*, 7/1: 105–121.

Keating, M. and Cairney, P. (2006) 'A new elite? Politicians and civil servants in Scotland after devolution', *Parliamentary Affairs*, 59/1: 1–17.

Long, J. et al. (2020) *UK Femicides 2009–2018*, London: Femicide Census.

McKay, A. and Bjørnholt, M. (2014) *Counting on Marilyn Waring: New Advances in Feminist Economics*, Bradford, Canada: Demeter Press.

Nash, T. (1995) *Who's Counting? Marilyn Waring on Sex, Lies and Global Economics*, Montreal, Canada: National Film Board of Canada.

Scottish Courts and Tribunal Service (2021) *Improving the Management of Sexual Offence Cases: Final Report from the Lord Justice Clerk's Review Group*, Edinburgh, UK: Scottish Courts and Tribunal Service.

Scottish Government (2019a) *A Fairer Scotland for Women: Gender Pay Gap Action Plan*, Edinburgh, UK: Scottish Government.

Scottish Government (2019b) *Domestic Abuse: Statistics Recorded by the Police in Scotland – 2018/19*, Edinburgh, UK: Scottish Government.

Scottish Government (2020a) *Recorded Crime in Scotland, 2019–2020*, Edinburgh, UK: Scottish Government.

Scottish Government (2020b) *Scotland's Gender Equality Index 2020*, Edinburgh, UK: Scottish Government.

Scottish Government (2021) *Gender Equality Task Force in Education and Learning*, Edinburgh, UK: Scottish Government.

Scottish Government and COSLA (2016) *Equally Safe: Scotland's Strategy for Preventing and Eradicating Violence against Women and Girls*, Edinburgh, UK: Scottish Government.

TUC (2014) *Women and Unions*, London: Trades Union Congress.

UN Women UK (2021) *Prevalence and Reporting of Sexual Harassment in UK Public Spaces*, London: All-Party Parliamentary Group for UN Women UK.

Waring, M. (1990) *If Women Counted: A New Feminist Economics*, London: HarperCollins.

World Health Organisation (2021) *Violence against Women Factsheet*, New York: World Health Organisation.

Young, I. (2002) 'Lived body vs. gender: Reflections on social structure and subjectivity', *Ratio*, 15/4: 410–428.

16

Race and Migration in Scotland

Gareth Mulvey, Talat Ahmed
and Colin Clark

Introduction

Although 'race'[1] and migration intersect in multiple ways, they are often discussed separately. Indeed, opposition to migration is now often used as a 'legitimate' proxy for racism. Scotland occupies an interesting space in this regard. It is a country with a limited history of anti-racist movements, and – apart from Irish migration and associated anti-Catholic discrimination – has had a limited history of migration until relatively recently. Scotland is also a country where matters of 'race' and migration, at a level of policy and practice, are currently situated in an uncomfortable devolution settlement. Taking issues of 'race' and racism first, there are few clear limitations on what Scotland can do under the constitutional settlement. As such, problems of – and with – racism in Scotland, as starkly illustrated by Davidson et al. (2018), are Scottish problems, fundamentally connected to an under-recognition of the country's past as well as present.

---

[1] We regard 'race' as a social/political construction that, fundamentally, does not exist. As such, we place the term in quotation marks in this chapter to signify its weakness as a term and concept.

The distribution of powers and policy-making becomes more complex when we look at migration and 'race' together. The polycentric nature of migration connects to questions of 'race' in profound ways. This is evident when considering the devolved settlement: we can observe distinct differences between immigration policy – which is currently reserved to the UK Government – and immigrant policy – which is currently devolved to Holyrood (Hammar 2006, Pietka-Nykaza et al. 2020). The UK Government maintains control over entry to the country and the conditions of entry, and the Scottish Government has control over how migrants, and people of colour, experience their lives once they are here. However, it is clearly not possible to disentangle these powers and where they sit. The various rights, including citizenship, remain determined by Westminster, and the politics of UK Government immigration policy casts a shadow north of the border in Scotland (Mulvey 2018).

Differences in terms of these 'hard' politics are also joined with variations in 'soft' politics. The largely civic nationalist language and rhetoric of the Scottish Government when compared to successive UK Governments has been perceived as considerably more 'migrant-friendly', and successive Scottish Governments have supported increased migration to Scotland, largely for demographic and economic reasons (Flynn and Kay 2017). This has been accompanied by some variations in terms of who is allowed rights associated with social citizenship. However, these expressions of welcome are rarely translated into actual material support, which is where we dovetail with issues of 'race'. Expressions of solidarity and a shared rejection of racism are just not enough for a progressive long-term strategy to be inclusive or for an anti-racist country choosing to embrace a radical, inclusive, civic nationalist agenda.

So this chapter first examines how we have historically (mis)understood 'race' and racism in Scotland before progressing to critically consider the legacy this has left for the present and future. In terms of contemporary analysis, we consider timely questions of racial equality and racialised violence in Scotland. A concluding section imagines some of the alternative futures if a more progressive Scotland can be realised where neo-liberalism is countered.

Historical Amnesia

To progress, we must retrace our steps. Questions of 'race' and racism in Scotland have for too long been pushed South – presented as an 'English' problem that has no place or presence this side of the border. Indeed, political rhetoric from public figures, including First Minister Nicola Sturgeon, tends to signal a message of an open and welcoming Scotland, a country that celebrates diversity, and when racism does appear, responses such as 'that is not who we are' are broadcast (see *Edinburgh Live*, 17 December 2020).

Such positivity is reinforced by a hospitable narrative around immigration epitomised in the 2014 independence referendum, whereby all those who had made Scotland their home, irrespective of birthplace or nationality, were entitled to vote (*BBC Scotland News online*, 8 January 2014). This marked a shift in official projections of Scottish civic and cultural identity, predicated upon shared understandings of a 'rainbow nation'. Nonetheless, current language and policy around migration is still largely couched in neo-liberal instrumentalist terms. Thus, it is the 'needs of' demographics and economy that are pivotal: Scotland has an ageing population, therefore Scotland needs immigration to ensure economic development and a future sustainable tax base.

While soft politics and warm words are welcome, there is also a question about the degree to which heritage is prioritised by the Scottish Government. Support for what it calls 'heritage languages' places an emphasis on those with a long lineage in the country, and it is striking that similar support is not available to speakers of other minority languages (Meer 2020). Viewing immigrants as only productive units of labour narrows migration policy to fit a highly instrumentalist agenda dictated by neo-liberal capitalist priorities rather than anti-racism, humanitarianism or even 'public good'. As such, we argue that a far more robust defence of a multi-racial, multi-cultural socialistic society is required.

Our central argument, viewed through a historical lens, is that a reductionist approach to migration tends to operate in tandem with a continued amnesia over Scotland's role in slavery and empire. We know Scots were actively involved at all levels of imperial industry: as owners, investors, overse-ers, doctors and slaving crews. As an example, in 1796, male Scots owned nearly 30% of the estates in Jamaica, and by 1817 a staggering 32% of the slaves (Black History Month 2015). While slavery was still legal on Scottish soil, adverts regularly appeared in newspapers for both the sale of enslaved people and enticing rewards for return of runaway slaves (*Edinburgh Evening Courant*, 13 February 1727).

As the 'second city' of Empire, Glasgow's wealth was built on the bloody fruits of slave labour in the colonies, evident in the sugar, cotton and tobacco plantations. Familiar names such as Scot Lyle, of Tate & Lyle fame, built their fortunes on chattel slavery (Chalmin 1990). James Ewing from Glasgow was the richest sugar producer in Jamaica (Cooke 2012). Tobacco from the Americas arrived from slave plantations into Leith in the seventeenth century, and James Gillespie profited via Virginia tobacco and snuff (*BBC Scotland News online*, 31 October 2018). The fortunes that slaves helped create kick-started the Industrial Revolution in Scotland and brought its merchants and traders great wealth. Many Scottish masters were also considered amongst the most brutal, with life expectancy on their plantations averaging a mere four years (Black History Month 2015).

The 1707 Anglo-Scottish Union created opportunities for more active Scottish involvement in the economic activities of the British Empire, particularly in India. Many Scotsmen found employment in government services, as missionaries, in commerce or in industry. Scotland's landed families gained access to the East India Company (EIC), and gradually became its dominant force, particularly when Henry Dundas both chaired and became President of the Board of Control of the EIC in 1784 (Bowen 2005). Under his leadership, as many as one-fifth of the EIC's writers in Calcutta and Madras were of Scottish origin by the 1790s. Indian imperial Scottish merchant firms include many names still known today: Andrew Yule, Forbes and Campbell, and Balmer Lawrie. Dundas's Indian adventure was surpassed only by his role in the Caribbean, where he brutally suppressed slave revolts in Grenada and Jamaica, using troops with dogs to hunt Jamaican Maroons down (*Open Democracy*, 30 July 2020).

In colonial India, at the political level, the first three governor-generals were all Scots. Indeed, by 1792 Scots made up 1 in 9 EIC civil servants, 6 in 11 common soldiers and 1 in 3 military officers. An even more prominent role was later played by Scots in the Indian military, with 8 out of the 38 Indian viceroys and governor-generals between 1774 and 1947 being of Scottish origin – the last being the Earl of Linlithgow. The riches of the East furnished a lavish lifestyle for Scottish elites. McGilvary (2011) estimated that in 1725–1833, around 3,500 Scotsmen worked in India and were remitting £500,000–750,000 p.a. back home. This was, as McGilvary (2011: 27) suggested, 'a colossal stimulus to life in Scotland'. It is evident that this troubling colonial and imperial past has helped shape present-day neo-liberal realities in Scotland in manifest ways.

The Past Helps Inform the Present

Failure to come to terms with this history is mirrored in Scotland's present, where the past helps inform the historical foundations for contemporary racism (Davidson and Virdee 2018). Issues of 'race' and racism continue to be a critical issue in the contemporary social and political landscape. Sheku Bayoh's death in 2015 while in police custody has still not found resolution (Akhtar 2020), and racist harassment and bullying in schools have increased, with more than 2,200 racist incidents reported in the last three years – the majority directed against children with a Muslim background (*Herald*, 6 January 2021). Racist attacks and violence have a long history in Scotland, such as events of 23 January 1919, when black sailors were attacked by a white mob with knives, batons and guns outside the offices of a mercantile marine depot in Glasgow (*Herald*, 23 January 2019). More recently, the murders of Axmed Abuukar Sheekh in 1989, Surjit Singh Chhokar and Imran Khan in 1998, Firsat Dag in 2000, Kunal Mohanty in 2009 and violent attacks on Syrian refugee Shabaz Ali in 2018 all need to be accounted for and recognised for what they were – racist murders demanding justice. In 2020, Police Scotland recorded 474 cases, marking a 50% increase on the previous year, with evidence suggesting the pandemic has triggered new waves of anti-Asian and Anti-Roma racism in particular (*BBC News Scotland online*, 15 March 2021; Clark 2021). To date, Scotland has no systematic way of monitoring racist incidents, and as such, the likelihood of 'race' being ignored or underplayed remains troubling across the criminal justice system. This evidence points to a long and continued history of racist attitudes and behaviours throughout society in Scotland.

In terms of broader policy and practice aspects to 'race' equality in Scotland, the long-standing strategic work of the Coalition for Racial Equality and Rights (CRER) is worth highlighting. Its activities have been crucial in holding the Scottish Government to account on matters of 'race' and racism, such as the relationship between poverty and ethnicity, the 'race' equality framework, human rights and public sector equality duties. CRER (2020a) has also responded to several Scottish Government consultations to ensure anti-racist approaches and concerns are noted, such as employment, hate crime, equal pay, social security and policing. In this context, we suggest that overt racism remains stubborn and persistent in society in Scotland – it exists alongside the everyday casual micro-aggressions that also impact on racialised minority communities. Structural racism, as CRER (2020b) found, continues to operate in areas such as employment, housing, health and education, as well the criminal justice system – and such matters have taken a turn for the worse due to the pandemic's impact.

Alternative Futures

How do we envisage an alternative future for Scotland, where fair immigration and racial justice are the norm? It is not, unfortunately, a straightforward task. Though we support 'no borders', we also understand that more 'moderate' forms of immigration policy and practice can improve what we currently have in place. Indeed, there were many positive elements in the Scottish Government's (2013) White Paper *Scotland's Future* concerning what a more humane refugee policy could look like in an independent Scotland. Following the New Scots advocacy work by the Coalition of Scottish

Local Authorities, the Scottish Refugee Council and the Scottish Government (2018), we believe Scotland needs to play a far greater role in processes of refugee resettlement, but it is for those going through the asylum process that we suggest more change is required. For example, all asylum claims should be determined by an independent agency, and not caught up in either government diktats or the 'control and protect' philosophies of government home or interior departments. Further, support during the asylum process should be provided by the general system of social security, which needs to be a living income. Once asylum claims are recognised, individuals should receive permanent status and a clear and timely means of accessing full citizenship rights, if desired. Additionally, newly recognised refugees require time, space and support to settle, and these aspects should be catered for.

In terms of non-refugee migration, a key post-Brexit principle must be the retention and defence of freedom of movement (Clark 2020), and with it a move away from migrants being characterised as either 'good' or 'bad', 'wanted' or 'unwanted', according to some dystopian policy algorithm or assumed economic value. Added to this, re-evaluating what constitute 'skills' would be constructive, as migration policy, outside of refugee-specific policies and family reunions, tends to use restrictive definitions of skills, essentially defining them in terms of low pay. However, much of this potential change depends upon Scotland becoming an independent nation state and possessing the appropriate levels of control. It also demands the political will and motivation to follow through on the public rhetoric of equality.

A 'no borders' approach would allow people to be able to move to Scotland – and to leave Scotland – as fits with their broader lives and livelihoods. Individuals' life chances should not be based on something they had no choice over, like the chance circumstance of where they were born. Scotland rejecting the confines of the Union might allow such a possibility, but it would also take a considerably more radical Scottish Government than has been witnessed so far under the SNP from 2007 onwards. Similarly, there is increasing evidence that a 'no borders' approach would have a beneficial impact on Gross Domestic Product (GDP) for both sending and receiving states, and whilst we do not believe GDP is an appropriate way to measure the wellbeing of a society, the more equal distribution of resources to emerge from no or open borders would be economically and ethically beneficial (Sagar 2020).

Crucially, whether concerning migrants, asylum-seekers, refugees or citizens, the Scottish Government must move beyond warm words and soft politics regarding minority ethnic communities. This demands a committed anti-racism agenda in policy and policy-making, within the levers that are currently available via devolution. Evidently, minority communities in Scotland still experience a racial penalty in terms of their rights; they are paid less, have poorer housing and are policed differently (Peterson 2020). A firm anti-racist stance must be taken to secure and guarantee the social, civic and human rights demanded. As such, this needs to be based on residence, rather than country of origin or state-constructed immigration status.

Moving beyond immigration policy and practice, one starting point is the mandatory teaching of Black and other minority ethnic histories in Scottish schools, as well as transparent and honest narratives around Scotland's role in empire and imperialism. An anti-racist education syllabus, from primary school to college and university levels, that begins to tell uncomfortable truths, about both past and present, would mark a radical departure and shift from where we are just now.

Likewise, moving the migration debate on from only questions of demography and economic contribution is essential.

To date, this tired and reductionist framing has led to highly instrumentalist approaches to immigration where it is seen only as a 'numbers game', and a subsequent framing of minorities' rights to be here as being contingent on 'contribution'. Clearer arguments need to be made about why a multi-racial, multi-ethnic, multi-cultural socialistic society is beneficial for all and why matters of culture, language and identity are just as important as economics. A shift here to narratives of inclusive communities, of social justice, of civic nationalism, would help change the framing and discussion.

Overall, we argue that a future anti-racist Scotland must be a socialistic country embracing a 'no borders' approach. It should be an independent nation state where settlement support is available for all who arrive and require it. People should have access to full social and economic citizenship at point of entry. Any restrictions on social and cultural rights, and disrupting access to full political citizenship, serve no one well. Scotland needs to reclaim control of its past and present in order to secure an alternative and more progressive future.

References

Akhtar, S. (2020) 'Containment, activism and state racism: The Sheku Bayoh justice campaign', *Identities: Global Studies in Culture and Power*, DOI: https://doi.org/10.1080/1070289X.2020.1813460.

Black History Month (2015) 'Scotland and slavery', 19 August, www.blackhistorymonth.org.uk/article/section/history-of-slavery/scotland-and-slavery/.

Bowen, H. (2005) *The Business of Empire: The East India Company and Imperial Britain 1756–1833*, Cambridge, UK: Cambridge University Press.

Chalmin, P. (1990) *The Making of a Sugar Giant: Tate and Lyle 1859–1989*, London: Harwood.

Clark, C. (2020) 'Stay or go? – Roma, Brexit and freedom of movement', *Scottish Affairs*, 29/3: 403–418.

Clark, C. (2021) 'One crisis after another: The impact of COVID-19 on Roma communities in Glasgow', Paisley, UK: Centre for Culture, Sports and Events, 14 January, http://ccse.uws.ac.uk/2021/01/14/one-crisis-after-another-the-impact-of-covid-19-on-roma-communities-in-glasgow/.

Coalition of Scottish Local Authorities, Scottish Refugee Council and Scottish Government (2018) *New Scots Refugee Integration Strategy 2018–2022*, Edinburgh, UK: Scottish Government.

Cooke, A. (2012) 'An elite revisited: Glasgow West India merchants, 1783–1877', *Journal of Scottish Historical Studies*, 32/2: 127–165.

CRER (2020a) *Hate Crime and Public Order (Scotland) Bill – Written Response from CRER, July 2020*, Glasgow, UK: Coalition for Racial Equality and Rights.

CRER (2020b) *Poverty and Ethnicity in Scotland: Analysis and Reflection on the Impact of COVID-19*, Glasgow, UK: Coalition for Racial Equality and Rights.

Davidson, N., Linnpää, M., McBride, M. and Virdee, S. (2018) (eds) *No Problem Here: Understanding Racism in Scotland*, Edinburgh, UK: Luath.

Davidson, N. and Virdee, S. (2018) 'Introduction: Understanding racism in Scotland', in Davidson, N., Linnpää, M., McBride, M. and Virdee, S. (eds) *No Problem Here: Understanding Racism in Scotland*, Edinburgh, UK: Luath, pp. 9–13.

Flynn, M. and Kay, R. (2017) 'Migrants' experiences of material and emotional security in rural Scotland: Implications for longer-term settlement', *Journal of Rural Studies*, 52/1: 56–65.

Hammar, T. (2006) 'European immigration policy: A comparative study', in Messina, A. and Lahav, G. (eds) *The Migration Reader: Exploring Politics and Policies*, Boulder, CO: Lynne Rienner, pp. 235–245.

McGilvary, G.K. (2011) 'The Scottish connection with India 1725–1833', *Études Écossaises*, 14: 13–31.

Meer, N. (2020). 'Race equality policy making in a devolved context: Assessing the opportunities and obstacles for a "Scottish Approach"', *Journal of Social Policy*, 49(2): 233–250.

Mulvey, G. (2018) 'Social citizenship, social policy and Refugee integration: A case of policy divergence in Scotland?', *Journal of Social Policy*, 47/1: 161–178.

Peterson, M. (2020) 'Micro aggressions and connections in the context of national multiculturalism: Everyday geographies of racialisation and resistance in contemporary Scotland', *Antipode*, 52/5: 1,393–1,412.

Pietka-Nykaza, E., Leith, M. and Clark, C. (2020) 'Scotland and Brexit: Citizenship, identity and belonging', *Scottish Affairs*, 29/3: 293–304.

Sagar, A. (2020) *Against Borders: Why the World Needs Free Movement of People*, London: Rowman & Littlefield.

Scottish Government (2013) *Scotland's Future*, Edinburgh, UK: Scottish Government.

17

Land Ownership and Community Development

Mike Danson and Craig Dalzell

Introduction

Compared with many European countries with small-scale and diversified land ownership, Scotland suffers from a disproportionate share of land held in the hands of a very few individuals and bodies. Some 1,125 owners hold 57% of Scotland's rural land, and just 432 individuals own 50% of Scotland's privately held land, while public bodies (including the national forest estate, Ministry of Defence and publicly owned crofting estates) account for 12.6% (Macleod 2021). The eight largest landowning charity and conservation bodies (including National Trust for Scotland, Royal Society for the Protection of Birds and John Muir Trust) together own just 2.6% of Scotland's land area. Community ownership has been growing since the early 1990s, but its 600,000 acres account for under 5% of the total land area of Scotland, compared with 750,000 acres being owned in tax havens, 'posing problems for law enforcement and tax authorities' (Wightman 2018).

There are important implications of such oligopolistic control for sustainable community development, economic and social opportunities (Danson 2020), and the Just Transition Commission (JTC 2021), alongside political parties and Citizen's Assemblies, recognises the need for further significant and substantial transfers of land to local people to promote a better, fairer, healthier and greener future. Scottish Land Commission (SLC 2019) and Community Land Scotland (CLS 2021) research has greatly improved our understanding of the impacts and effects of these high degrees of concentrated land ownership. While the main bodies representing the interest of the few – House of Lords, Scottish Land & Estates – always automatically respond to any such analyses with denial and distraction, the overwhelming evidence is of degradation of land, environment, communities and cultures through this aberration from the normal ownership of the commons elsewhere. It is important to recognise the differences between large-scale and concentrated ownership in understanding the implications of having control concentrated over decision-making locally, whether that be in the hands of a single person/trust, non-governmental organisation or state body. Scottish Land & Estates, representing large landowners, has consistently argued that how land is used and managed should focus on promoting effective and efficient economic development. Critically, others have prioritised fairness, equality and the fulfilment of human rights.

More recently, land ownership, use and management have been linked directly within the context of 'sustainable development', generating opportunities to strengthen transitioning to a more sustainable economy and society through broader and deeper relations between people and land. This deepening and broadening is consistent with both Scotland's National Performance Framework and the United Nations Sustainable Development Goals, which each emphasise the aims 'to reduce inequalities and gives equal importance to economic, environmental and social progress' (UN n.d.). As the UN (n.d.) argued:

Maintaining and restoring land resources can play a vital role in tackling climate change, securing biodiversity and maintaining crucial ecosystem services, while ensuring shared prosperity and well-being. Healthy and productive land can play an unparalleled role as an engine of economic growth and a source of livelihood for billions worldwide, including the most vulnerable populations.

The JTC (2021) embraced the potential offered in these objectives, along with the need for contributions to meet aspirations, targets and opportunities for all Scotland's people and communities.

STIFLED COMMUNITY DEVELOPMENT

Two centuries of clearances, emigration and degradation of communities, land and culture have created imbalanced landscapes, economies and populations. Sporting estates dominate much of the Highlands and Southern Uplands under the ownership and management of a small clutch of private interests. For decades, it has been recognised that these 'devastated terrains [have been] stripped of their natural forest cover, then … subjected to repeated burning, to intensive grazing, to overstocking and to other forms of maltreatment which had drained their soils of fertility and made them steadily less productive' (Fraser Darling 1995, cited in Danson 2020: 23). The cumulative effects of these structures and practices have generated exploited places which are underdeveloped in many senses, with supply chains distorted and truncated. Typically, the islands and landward areas suffer from limitations on breaking cycles of decline and dependency. These include, compared with the national average: below-average connectivity and incomes, slower economic convergence, poor job and career opportunities, and low-quality and high-cost services.

Without the capacity to create capital locally, the enterprising and entrepreneurial spirits of these communities, complementing their relatively high levels of secondary and tertiary skills and qualifications, are heavily constrained within their rural communities. Facing small local markets and high costs of creating and exporting goods and services, many leave. The centripetal pull of the core, especially university cities, sucks talents and energies away, trapping rural Scotland in persistent cycles of internal colonialism, poverty and deprivation. The other side of this pattern of restricted land ownership is that, unlike the position in Nordic countries and many other parts of Europe, there are but occasional possibilities for many in urban Scotland to (re)connect with their own natural heritage, with negative implications for mental and physical health and wellbeing, and for realising the economic potentials of buying from 'home'. This chapter will first examine and apply the economic concept of oligopoly in the context of land ownership, use and management; following this, an exploration of potential alternative visions for rural Scotland will be proposed, addressing the problems of concentrated land ownership; this will lead into offering strategies and policies for land reform as means to deliver to these better futures.

Oligopoly Ownership: Economics Perspectives and Practical Problems with Large Estates

Scottish Land & Estates argues that the focus in rural matters should be upon responsible use and management of the land rather than upon ownership as such. Its claim of responsible stewardship, based on efficient and effective estate practices, struggles to square with two centuries' evidence of unsustainable development and exploitation. Again, this contrasts with our northern neighbours' experiences and enjoyment of their own environments, leading to inevitable questions over the use and management of Scotland's land. Critically, these differences are essentially explained by the differences in ownership and the extremely high levels of large-scale and concentrated ownership, with power in the hands of very few (Danson 2020).

Private property rights underpin perverted land use and management regimes in Scotland, and though protected by law, these are not absolute. Generally, it is accepted that systems of land use planning and regulation are needed to ensure private interests are not at the cost of the wider interests. However, existing legislation and interventions are weak ways of controlling and overcoming the domination of private property rights in cases of concentrated land ownership. Significant concentrations of land ownership allow disproportionate power and control over communities and local economies, hindering inclusive growth and wider sustainable development objectives. Oligopoly control over land and related resources and activities are leading to market failures, in turn generating damaging economic and social outcomes for community, national interest and environment. And there are no countervailing benefits in the form of economies of scale and scope in land use and management which might balance these disadvantages of oligopoly control. Thus, it is difficult to identify, far less achieve, overall benefits to society or to the economy from concentrated land ownership.

OVERVIEW OF EXISTING LAND OWNERSHIP
AND LAND USE POLICY

Freed from the effective House of Lords veto over any significant attack on the power of the lairds, confronting the wasteful use and management of land by most of the large estates was quickly seen as a prime policy objective of the Scottish Parliament. In anticipation of being able to progress the land reform agenda, the Labour Westminster Government established an advisory group ready to inform public debate and strategies. Land reform subsequently has been an ongoing process to reverse two centuries of enclosures, clearances and concentration of land and power. Successive Scottish Parliament Acts have each represented important steps forwards in land reform. The initial 'Community Right to Buy' in crofting counties was progressively extended to cover the rest of Scotland, urban as well as rural areas, and 'Abandoned, Neglected and Detrimental' land which has adverse environmental impacts on the wellbeing of local communities, without the need for a willing seller. Within the national context of encouraging sustainable development, the Land Reform (Scotland) Act 2016 also introduced:

a Land Rights and Responsibilities Statement to help inform policy and practice around land issues in Scotland; a register of controlling interests in land; guidance on engaging communities in decisions relating to land which may affect them; a new Community Right to Buy land to further sustainable development, again without the need for a willing seller; and creation of a Scottish Land Commission. (MacLeod 2021: 176)

The SLC and CLS have been encouraging the mainstreaming of community ownership as a way of undertaking development and regeneration.

Alternative Visions and Green Recovery

Almost all of the issues identified with Scotland's dysfunctional relationship with its land are age-old, so they long pre-date the pandemic. However, the pandemic has shone a light on the vulnerabilities and inequalities in society and the need for reform across broad swathes of our economy, and highlighted the urgent need to make both economy and society resilient to future shocks – not least the impending climate emergency. There is not time to rebuild our COVID-disrupted economy back to something similar to its pre-2019 state and then transform everything again to meet our climate targets. Given the problems identified with that pre-pandemic world, it would not be wise to restore it anyway.

Thus, the only viable option is to consider the recovery from the pandemic and the preparations for the green transition to be one and the same. Once this realisation is made, the consequence is that the 'Green Recovery' cannot be achieved rationally or completely without substantial land reform (JTC 2021). Scotland has great potential to be one of Europe's 'carbon sinks' by restoring its peatlands and reforesting land currently razed flat and used for not much more than grazing and blood sports. Up to 50% of Scotland's land could be restored to a mosaic of rewilded land in the form of uplands, peat muir and Atlantic temperate rainforest. Rewilding is not as simple as merely abandoning land and allowing it to restore itself. Existing habitats are too fragmented and too small to allow for expansion on the timescales required, and in some areas they are absent entirely. Rewilding will therefore require an intensive programme of land management lasting decades and securing generations of employment on the land.

BENEFITS OF COMMUNITY OWNERSHIP AND RESILIENCE

The task of land reform, especially rewilding, demands that the people employed in carrying it out must work closely and directly on the land. This, apart from otherwise long commutes to remote rural areas, means it is imperative that local communities are employed as much as possible at all stages, and that, in many cases, will include ownership of the land itself. The direct link between community ownership and land stewardship will then run far deeper than that of an absentee landlord or, as is increasingly common, managers of their property portfolio. It will not run deeper if the local community are merely 'employed' to carry out tasks for others. In places where community ownership has been facilitated, supported and nurtured, it has resulted in greatly improved outcomes for the land and community. Many who take part in such schemes have experiences of such responsibility not being easy, but being both worthwhile and valued. Community ownership creates ties to the land that help build in resilience to the reforms. Absentee landlords or their portfolio managers either have little incentive to develop sustainably (beyond the public relations benefit) and even have incentives to asset-strip land for profit. Communities will respond poorly to any initiative done 'to them' rather than 'with them', so direct involvement is required wherever possible.

However, and even with the Land Reform (Scotland) Act 2016, for community ownership to become a major part of Scotland's land reform strategy, the process of gaining ownership of land must itself be radically enhanced. It is not good enough that communities must wait until local lairds deign to sell patches of their estates and then only at overinflated rates demanded by markets. Ironically, many estates are bought and sold not for their market valuation, but for the 'consumption of leisure', and so at real costs to the economy and society (Danson 2020). Even when the government steps in to offer financial banking and subsidy to such sales, this results in a transfer of wealth from the public purse to the landowner, who is in some cases a mere inheritor of land previously gained by the plunder or theft of the commons. If we continue with community ownership in this manner, it will result in communities owning small pockets of land deemed not very valuable to former landowners, and will not prove scalable to the requirements of climate and land reform commitments already made by the Scottish Government.

Land Reform Strategies and Policies

The key strategic consideration concerns how any proposed measures affect land ownership, use and management across the whole of Scotland. If solutions based on small, piecemeal community schemes do not scale up to the ambition of the intended reform, then the reform will not be achieved. It is easy to set grand-sounding targets, but it is harder to meet them. What is often not articulated is how much closer particular targets take Scotland to the final goal. If the sum of the pledges does not meet the overall target, then it matters relatively little if individual targets are all met. This is also the reason why a national strategy is required over and above the facilitation of local and community projects within it. Each of these comparatively small parts must add up to a greater whole. Subsidiarity and empowerment are essential throughout this process. Whether a particular project is being co-ordinated at a national level or is a purely local project, communities must be a part of them and must never have them imposed from above without their consent or participation. Statutory-based 'Regional Land Use Partnerships' (intended to offer a collaborative approach to land use decision-making in the public interest, and to prioritise and target delivery of public funding to achieve land use objectives) need to be complemented by a 'Public Interest Test' to regulate the purchase of oligopoly landholdings in order to address concentrated ownership (CLS 2021).

COMMUNITY OWNERSHIP, RESILIENCE AND EMPOWERMENT

Not every community will want to actively own the land around them, and certain areas of land may well benefit from wider public ownership (such as areas set aside as nature reserves or national parks, or significant parts of urban Scotland), but those communities which do wish to own land as part of a sustainability project must be enabled to do so, and they must be provided with the tools and support required to foster the skills to manage land effectively. Even, and especially, when outright ownership is not desired, communities must play the principal role in planning decisions. Doing this will almost certainly result in decisions being made with collective community consent and ensure the decisions reached will be the most resilient ones possible for that community. Without this sense of empowerment, communities may rebel against even the most well-meaning of projects, and the desired outcomes will not be achieved (see also Chapter 4).

FINANCING THE CHANGES

However empowered communities are, land reform is about much more than parcelling land down to a local community and telling them to 'get on with it'. Thus, national strategic planning frameworks must be drawn up to guide the entire country towards a more sustainable future. Some of the tools available to affect meaningful reform will therefore lie at national government level. Under the current limited system of reform, this often takes the form of finance and subsidies to allow communities to buy land at market rates. More radical proposals would involve a land value tax or property tax to reduce the speculated market land price and make it more expensive to simply hold land or to use it for unproductive purposes, supporting the plans of the Regional Land Use Partnerships. Environmental taxes like carbon or pollution taxes would also further broader national environmental targets (and could become a source of revenue for a landowner if the carbon tax is coupled with a carbon credit for activities absorbing CO_2 rather than emitting it).

POWERS DEVOLVED AND POWERS STILL NEEDED

Whenever radical reforms of this nature are raised, the limits of the powers of the devolved Scottish Government are often questioned. However, when it comes to land reform, most of the powers already lie with the Scottish Government – one notable exception being Inheritance Tax, which, whilst powerful, would act too slowly to be of use to avert the climate emergency. Policies such as completing and improving the Land Register would greatly increase the transparency of land ownership and allow communities to plan their next purchase of land, whilst compulsory sales/purchase orders would extend the 2016 Act across Scotland and allow communities to access land even if the current landowners were resistant. At the more intensive end of the strategic spectrum, the Scottish Government could introduce land value taxes aimed specifically at reducing the size of landholdings or an outright cap on the amount of land an individual or organisation may own. The Land Value Taxes and Regional Land Use Partnerships could be instruments to encourage better and more sustainable use of the land regardless of ownership. This said, the constitutional debate in Scotland still overshadows almost everything, and whilst independence or deepening devolution's scope would allow even more to be done, lack of ability to do everything should never be taken as an excuse for inaction now; such action would without doubt create a substantially different Scottish economic, cultural and environmental land-scape than the one we currently resign ourselves to.

References

CLS (2021) *Land for the Common Good: Community Land Scotland's Manifesto for a Sustainable Scotland*, Oban, UK: Community Land Scotland.

Danson, M. (2020) *Scoping the Classic Effects of Monopolies within Concentrated Patterns of Rural Land Ownership, Land and the Common Good*, discussion paper series, Oban, UK: Community Land Scotland.

JTC (2021) *Just Transition Commission: A National Mission for a Fairer, Greener Scotland*, Edinburgh, UK: Scottish Government.

Macleod, C. (2021) 'Community land ownership and sustaining Scotland's islands: Lessons from the Western Isles', in Burnett, K., Burnett, R. and Danson, M. (eds), *Scotland and Islandness: Explorations in Community, Economy and Culture, Studies in the History and Culture of Scotland*, vol. 13, Bern, Switzerland: Peter Lang, pp. 169–188.

SLC (2019) *Review of Scale and Concentration of Land Ownership: Report to Scottish Ministers*, Inverness, UK: Scottish Land Commission.

UN (n.d.) *Land and Sustainable Development Goals*, New York: United Nations.

Wightman, A. (2018) 'Open up the registers', *Land Matters … the blog and website of Andy Wightman*, 11 March, www.andywightman.com/archives/4568.

18

Confounding the Capitalist Car-centric Culture

*Caitlin Doyle Cottrill, Ellie Harrison
and David Spaven*

A developed country is not a place where the poor have cars. It's where the rich use public transportation.

(Gustavo Petro, Bogotá mayor 2012–2014)

Introduction

The first motor car to reach Scotland arrived at Leith Docks in 1895, and the following year an Act of Parliament permitted cars to travel faster than walking pace – and without being preceded by a man with a red flag (Ransom 2007: 116). Freed of these restrictions, car ownership multiplied quickly in the early years of the twentieth century, and has grown almost inexorably ever since. As the epitome of consumer capitalism, the car dominates Scotland's transport network. Accommodating motorists' demands – or needs, depending on one's perspective – for roads and parking, and planning new developments around the car, have been at the forefront of Scottish Office, Scottish Government and most local authority thinking since at least the 1950s.

Yet although 68% of commuters said they travelled to work by car or van in 2019, 12% walked, 10% went by bus, 5% took a train and 3% cycled (Transport Scotland 2021: 187–

188). And as of 2019, 28% of households in Scotland had no regular access to a car, with concentration in the largest cities: Edinburgh (41%) and Glasgow (47%) (Transport Scotland 2020c: 45). In Glasgow, one-third are 'simply being left behind', without access to a car or a rail or subway station, and are therefore completely dependent on a failing deregulated and privatised bus network (Begg 2019: 5), with fares rising well above inflation (Minchin 2021). Simultaneously, while walking is, in theory, at the top of the Sustainable Travel Hierarchy (Transport Scotland 2020a: 43), out on the street, pedestrians still languish at the bottom. The rise in car use has been facilitated and exacerbated by destruction – deliberate and consequential – of what were once world-class public transport networks. In Scotland today, many people have been forced to buy cars for want of other options, and it's those who can't afford to do this who have been disadvantaged the most.

Not only has transport policy in the post-war period exacerbated poverty and inequality, it has also been a climate disaster. Transport is now the biggest contributor to carbon and air pollution of all sectors in Scotland's economy, and the only one still increasing its share of greenhouse gas (GHG) emissions since the Climate Change (Scotland) Act 2009 (Scottish Government 2018). As of 2017, 40% of transport's GHG emissions came from private cars and 25% from road-based freight (Transport Scotland 2020b: chapter 13). Although there is now a push to electric vehicles, this will not address the many other negative side effects of car-centric culture. Electric vehicles still produce air pollution from brakes and tyres, perpetuate sedentary lifestyles contributing to obesity and diabetes epidemics, and require significant quantities of energy at a time when we need to rapidly reduce our consumption to address the climate emergency (Milovanoff 2020). Properly planned and co-ordinated public transport networks would be far more energy-efficient. And as the initial quote from Petro suggests, this is also how we help to build the more equal and better-integrated society which Scotland desperately needs.

We write this chapter from different perspectives and backgrounds – as activists, academics and practitioners. The future of Scotland's transport and infrastructure is such a vast and complex subject that it is only possible to provide a summary discussion. We have not been able to cover some areas (like the islands and international travel) in much detail. However, we hope to open dialogue on the opportunities and possibilities for transforming the Scottish transport network to become far more equitable and sustainable in the long term. We begin by defining the principles and objectives of a better transport system and how it can be delivered, then examine Scotland's crucial regional variations and freight, concluding on how we can 'build back better'.

Principles and Objectives

Although the Scottish Government took control of nearly all aspects of the country's transport system in 1999, the trajectory described above has continued apace. Traditional supply-side 'predict and provide' models have underpinned much road-building. Instead, the starting point should be to see transport as a function of demand: who is travelling, and what are their needs for access to opportunity? Addressing these – in each region – should be the initial task. In building a fair and sustainable Scotland, we should strive to localise jobs, opportunities, services and facilities so that demand for transport is dramatically reduced. Then, for travel further than walking, wheeling[1] or cycling distance, we should ensure – no matter where we live – reliable and affordable public transport options exist, so that sustainable travel choices become the

---

1 'Wheeling' refers to the use of wheelchairs or other mobility aids.

default. Following the Sustainable Urban Transport Project (2019), we propose an 'Avoid-Shift-Improve' (ASI) approach: (i) *Avoid* – reduce transport demand, (ii) *Shift* – promote and improve energy-efficient and sustainable transport modes, and (iii) *Improve* – improve the efficiency of the transport process. This simple hierarchy enables a more holistic approach to transport, which takes into consideration how non-transport decisions (like land use, development and housing costs) contribute to overall transport need. Three key principles underpin the delivery of ASI: (i) enshrine public transport standards in law – enabling everyone to live a good quality of life without needing to own a car, (ii) dramatically reduce the cost of using regional public transport – ideally made free at point of use (Sloman et al. 2018) or simple flat fares that give you access to all transport modes, and (iii) ensure transport modes pay their full environmental costs – with taxation and pricing which reflects their respective carbon impact; likewise, government funding for transport projects should be appraised on its contribution to the key objectives of decarbonisation and greater equity.

How to Deliver

REFORMING TRANSPORT GOVERNANCE

To deliver these principles and objectives, transport governance needs reforming. Given Scotland's geographic diversity, we should take a regional approach. In 2005, the Scottish Government set up seven Regional Transport Partnerships (RTPs) to cover distinct parts of the country. Whether these geographical areas are still too big is debatable, but the main issue is that they have neither the powers nor the funding necessary to do their jobs. To be able to deliver, RTPs should be transformed into 'total transport authorities' (Raikes et al. 2015), with power over whole transport networks in each area, including traffic/parking controls and public transport, as well as land use planning powers, so they can assist in the localisation of each economy and use the 'carrot' (of quality public transport) and the 'stick' (of car reduction measures) to help shift journeys onto sustainable modes.

Whether Scotland should reintroduce a new regional layer of government – like the regional councils abolished in 1996 – to oversee these new regional transport authorities is a significant question. Either way, the role of the new authorities would be to provide the 'guiding mind' for each region, to assess local needs, taking a holistic approach to planning and co-ordinating public transport to meet them. Different modes should not compete, and they should be treated as part of one fully integrated system – planned under the principle of 'one network, one timetable, one ticket', as in Munich City Region – to get people around as efficiently and sustainably as possible (Sloman and Taylor 2016: 19).

The role of the national transport authority, currently Transport Scotland, could then be simplified, with a focus upon facilitating collaboration for connections between regions, planning and managing the national networks such as railways and trunk roads, and ensuring that standards and decarbonisation targets are being met. Increased funding allocated to each of the regions, or raised through local taxes, could then be used for more context-sensitive regional transport planning.[2]

RAISING AMBITIONS

Although the travelling public may have become conditioned to the fragmented, unreliable and expensive public trans-

---

2 Scotland's public transport is currently chronically underfunded. For example, in London 20 times more per capita is spent on public transport than in Strathclyde.

port system deregulation and privatisation have created, it's important to remember that the UK is actually an anomaly in taking this approach (Alston et al. 2021). In raising ambitions, it's important that we learn from successes elsewhere. For example, Switzerland's basic service standards are enshrined in law, with even the smallest village guaranteed a bus service every hour, seven days a week from 6 a.m. to midnight, with frequencies increasing with settlement size. Everyone is connected, and routes are planned to perfectly co-ordinate with train timetables (Sloman and Hopkinson 2019: 5). Or public transport is free to use in the likes of Dunkirk, Calais, Tallinn and Luxembourg. When Dunkirk introduced free public transport in 2018, this proved the 'psychological shock' necessary to change behaviour (Dairaine 2020). Bus trips increased by 85% in the first year (with nearly half shifting from private cars).

Suggesting such transformational measures inevitably prompts questions about funding. There are many examples of progressive taxes which regional transport authorities should be empowered to implement (Sloman and Taylor 2016: 21). Businesses benefiting from getting employees to work quickly, efficiently and sustainably, thereby reducing their carbon impact, should contribute. Powers already exist for transport authorities in Scotland to introduce workplace parking levies and congestion charging, though none have yet used them holistically. It is vital that new taxes align with objectives of decarbonisation and greater equity, and that 'carrot' and 'stick' are balanced.

Transport for Quality of Life recommends an 'Eco levy on driving' – introduced simultaneously with free public transport to make it politically palatable and just, and to assist the 'psychological shock' necessary to change behaviour. This would charge drivers per mile, so would not penalise people for car ownership, but would encourage them not to use cars for journeys easily be made by other modes. It would be brought in first in urban areas which have good public transport connections, then eventually rolled out everywhere as a Swiss-style service is delivered (Sloman and Hopkinson 2019: 8). The ability to plan and co-ordinate the public transport network has been stymied by deregulation and privatisation of bus and rail systems. Fortunately, the Scottish Government agreed to bring ScotRail back into public ownership from 2022, and its Transport (Scotland) Act 2019 provides new powers to transport authorities to re-regulate buses for the first time since 1986.

Regional Variations – and Land Use Planning

Transport provision is highly dependent upon characteristics of the places and populations being served (Cottrill et al. 2020). With respect to place, density of activities and residents have a significant impact upon affordability and appropriateness of the transport service offer (Yigitcanlar et al. 2007: 30–37). In Scotland, areas classified as 'large urban' or 'other urban' account for around 35% of households each, with accessible small towns accounting for 9%, remote small towns 4%, accessible rural areas 11% and remote rural places 6% (Transport Scotland 2020c). This diversity of places indicates the need for a similarly diverse service offer. As noted above, urban areas generally demonstrate higher proportions of households without a car, largely reflective of public transport accessibility and walking, wheeling and cycling being more realistic transport options (Gray et al. 2001: 113–125). In suburban and rural areas, however, lower population densities make traditional fixed-route, fixed-schedule public transport services less efficient. Island areas present further complexity, as connection to the mainland and other islands for key services is dependent upon a narrow set of transport options including bridges, ferries and air travel.

New regional transport authorities will enable tailored approaches to addressing these varying transport needs, based upon local populations and geographies. This could include shifting demand from private cars by providing support for flexible and demand-responsive public transport in areas where demand is not sufficient to support fixed-route services. To *Avoid* travel, initiatives such as the '20-minute neighbour-hood' (Scottish Government 2020), combining consideration of land use, transport and activities, should be further sup-ported, with associated investment in wider pavements, cycle paths, lighting, benches etcetera to ensure walking, wheeling and cycling are safe and viable alternatives for everyone.

A recent report by the Urban Transport Group (Linton and Bray 2019) highlights the wider policies necessary for such measures to be effective, including: a national land use planning framework favouring public transport-oriented developments rather than car-based low-density sprawl; a national funding framework with more options for ensuring that 'value uplift' from new developments is used to improve transport connectivity; and measures to improve the planning capacity of local authorities in order to respond effectively, rapidly and imaginatively to opportunities for high-quality public transport-oriented development.

Travel between Regions

The regional approach is critical to efforts to *Avoid* travel – encouraging people to travel within their regions for work and leisure – rather than excessive travel beyond. It is the opposite of that taken by the Scottish Government since devolution, which has favoured investment in expanding the national road network, facilitating longer, less sustainable commutes.

Despite declaring a 'climate emergency' in 2019, it is persisting with its £9 billion investment at 2010 prices (but now approaching £15 billion) in its road-building programme. Although some of Scotland's national rail network has been substantially upgraded, notably electrifying all routes between Edinburgh and Glasgow, this is not on the scale necessary to *Shift* many more people out of cars. North of the Central Belt, progress on enhancing the rail routes parallel to key trunk roads has been woeful. The Scottish Government plans to electrify all the inter-city rail routes linking Glasgow and Edinburgh and Aberdeen and Inverness by 2035, but this must be accelerated. To reduce private road traffic and secure a substantial modal shift (of passengers and freight) to train and bus/coach, the Scottish Government's transport priorities must change drastically so that carbon reduction is at the top. The money currently spent on road-building should be slashed – focusing primarily on improving safety with proven measures such as average speed cameras and maintaining existing roads to a higher standard. Financial savings should be diverted to capital and revenue funding of sustainable transport systems as we move towards a society which seeks to *Avoid* increasingly longer journeys.

Freight

Freight transport rarely makes headlines, but plays a fundamental role in Scotland's economy. For 2012, the last year for which the Scottish Government published full data on modal split, road haulage's share of freight was 42%, coastwise shipping 30%, pipeline 19%, rail 9% and inland waterways 1% (Transport Scotland 2020b).[3] Road haulage, with its inherent

---

3   Statistics on rail freight are incomplete within Scottish Transport Statistics 'due to difficulties obtaining updates to the data covering all the rail freight companies' (Transport Scotland 2020b).

flexibility and low barriers to entry, operates in a highly competitive marketplace and generally delivers very high levels of service quality to its customers. But the downside – illustrating 'market failure' – is that its external costs are substantially greater than competitive modes such as rail and sea. For example, heavy lorries are disproportionately involved in fatal accidents, and typically generate three to four times the GHG emissions produced by rail freight (Network Rail 2013). The sheer ubiquity of the road network and the flexibility of the lorry means that rail can never hope to capture a majority of Scotland's freight, but up to a quarter should be feasible with the right government support. For the remaining road freight, environmental and safety impacts must be addressed. One innovation is to create urban distribution centres where multiple consignments from full lorry loads are broken down into local delivery rounds for smaller electric vans better suited to the city environment, with local collection/consolidation points for multiple van deliveries (Taylor et al. 2020: 2). Such an approach reflects not just the ASI principles of *Shift* and *Improve*, but also that a sustainable Scotland needs to reduce – and not just for transport reasons – overall demand for consumption of goods.

Building Back Better

The pandemic has had significant consequences for transport. While all travel has been affected, public transport's recovery rate has been slower than for private cars, reflecting concerns with travelling in shared spaces. What this means in the longer term is uncertain. But the lull in public transport use provides an opportunity to radically re-think, re-build and re-launch world-class regional public transport networks that are safe, reliable, affordable and sustainable. Emission reductions resulting from the initial lockdowns also provide cause for optimism, based as they are on reduced car use and local-ising lifestyles. The measures suggested in this chapter aim to ensure that this optimism is realised. Almost all the required power levers to transform transport already lie with the Scottish Government.[4] In terms of further devolution, what is most urgent is for the Scottish Government to reverse its long-standing policy of centralisation and devolve some of these powers down to the regional level so that Scotland's new regional transport authorities can deliver.

References

Alston, P., Khawaja, B. and Riddell, R. (2021) *Public Transport, Private Profit: The Human Cost of Privatising Buses in the United Kingdom*, New York: Center for Human Rights & Global Justice, New York University.

Begg, D. (2019) *Connecting Glasgow: Creating an Inclusive, Thriving, Liveable City*, Glasgow, UK: Glasgow City Council.

Cottrill, C.D., Brooke, S., Mulley, C., Nelson, J.D. and Wright, S. (2020) 'Can multi-modal integration provide enhanced public transport service provision to address the needs of vulnerable populations?', *Research in Transportation Economics*, 83: C231–C245.

Dairaine, X. (2020) *Imagine if Buses Were Free ...*, Glasgow, UK: Free Our City, Glasgow.

Gray, D., Farrington, J., Shaw, J., Martin, S. and Roberts, D. (2001) 'Car dependence in rural Scotland: Transport policy, devolution and the impact of the fuel duty escalator', *Journal of Rural Studies*, 17/1: 113–125.

Linton, C. and Bray, J. (2019) *The Place to Be: How Transit-oriented Development Can Support Good Growth in the City Region*, Leeds, UK: Urban Transport Group.

Milovanoff, A. (2020) 'The myth of electric cars: Why we also need to focus on buses and trains', *The Conversation*, 21 October.

---

4   One of the few exceptions being national demand management (as opposed to local authority schemes), and the railway maintenance powers retained by Network Rail.

Minchin, J. (2021) 'Transport Scotland statistics show a decline in ridership before pandemic', *Intelligent Transport*, 24 February.

Network Rail (2013) *Value and Importance of Rail Freight*, London: Network Rail.

Raikes, L., Straw, W. and Linton, C. (2015) *Total Transport Authorities: A New Deal for Town and Rural Bus Services*, London: Institute for Public Policy Research.

Ransom, P. (2007) *Iron Road: The Railway in Scotland*, Edinburgh, UK: Birlinn.

Scottish Government (2018) *Scottish Greenhouse Gas Emissions 2016*, Edinburgh, UK: Scottish Government.

Scottish Government (2020) *Protecting Scotland, Renewing Scotland*, Edinburgh, UK: Scottish Government.

Sloman, L. and Hopkinson, L. (2019) *A Radical Transport Response to the Climate Emergency*, Machynlleth, UK: Transport for Quality of Life.

Sloman, L. and Taylor, I. (2016) *Building a World-class Bus System for Britain*, Machynlleth, UK: Transport for Quality of Life.

Sloman, L., Hopkinson, L., Cairns, S., Stewart, J., Newson, C. and Goodwin, P. (2018) *We Need Fare-free Buses! It's Time to Raise Our Sights*, Machynlleth, UK: Transport for Quality of Life.

Sustainable Urban Transport Project (2019) *Sustainable Urban Transport: Avoid-Shift-Improve (A-S-I)*, New Urban Agenda 9, Eschborn, Germany: Deutsche Gesellschaft für Internationale Zusammenarbeit.

Taylor, I., Goodman, A., Goodwin, P., Hiblin, B., Hopkinson, L., Stewart, J. and Sloman, L. (2020) *The Short-haul Response to Covid and the Climate Emergency*, Machynlleth, UK: Transport for Quality of Life.

Transport Scotland (2020a) *National Transport Strategy: Protecting Our Climate and Improving Lives*, Glasgow, UK: Transport Scotland, www.transport.gov.scot/our-approach/national-transport-strategy/.

Transport Scotland (2020b) *Scottish Transport Statistics: No. 38, 2019 Edition*, Glasgow, UK: Transport Scotland, www.transport.gov.scot/publication/scottish-transport-statistics-no-38-2019-edition/.

Transport Scotland (2020c) *Transport and Travel in Scotland 2019: Results from the Scottish Household Survey*, Glasgow, UK: Transport

Scotland, www.transport.gov.scot/publication/transport-and-travel-in-scotland-2019-results-from-the-scottish-household-survey/.

Transport Scotland (2021) *Scottish Transport Statistics: No. 39, 2020 Edition*, Glasgow, UK: Transport Scotland, www.transport.gov.scot/publication/scottish-transport-statistics-no-39-2020-edition/.

Yigitcanlar, T., Sipe, N., Evans, R. and Pitot, M. (2007) 'A GIS-based land use and public transport accessibility indexing model', *Australian Planner*, 44/3: 30–37.

PART III

Political Practice

19
Leisure and Culture

Kathryn A. Burnett and Douglas Chalmers

Introduction

What constitutes Scotland's leisure, or 'non-work', and the complex landscape of arts and culture underpinned by ideological positions, cultural histories of policy and varying ethos of practice? This chapter considers this question in order to assesses 'what's wrong' with the current state of leisure and culture, and to ask why certain issues and realities remain problematic and challenging for Scotland. It then turns to considering alternative futures and focuses with concluding remarks as to how these might be realised.

Scotland's Leisure and Cultural Landscape

What might be understood as 'leisure' and 'culture' in regard to work, labour and the economy is often sidelined within discussions of policy and economy as either mere descriptors of economic sectors or as social add-ons – that is, not necessarily being essential requirements for an economy, polity or a functioning future-proofed society. For example, leisure, culture and arts do not feature at all in Common Weal's blueprint for 'starting a new country' (see McAlpine 2018). Scotland, notwithstanding complex and complicit histories of denial, eradication, and defamation, has nonetheless collectively positioned culture as an inherently national identifier, highly valued in both general and specific terms, although subject to shifting narratives of purpose and endeavour. The 2017–2019 National Culture Strategy for Scotland public consultation offers a recent illustration, where:

> a number of respondents noted that they were pleased to see culture taking its place in the National Performance Framework with a new dedicated National Outcome for culture ... recognition that culture is not about 'additional benefit' but is essential to our lives and wellbeing.
>
> (Scottish Government 2019: 10)

Furthermore, perhaps, there is a common belief that, although complex, cultural change pre-figured political change, such as the move towards devolution (Hames 2020). Scotland as a national collective increasingly positions itself ontologically – the essence of being – if not politically, as independent. It is important to look at how long-standing and more emergent issues and debates configure Scottish leisure and culture in these general terms.

Culture and leisure constitute significant parts of the labour market and important drivers of economic growth, and figure prominently in narratives of political challenge, cultural resilience and social inequalities (sustainability, climate emergency, social justice, wellbeing and personal health) (Creative Scotland 2014). Scotland's communities have witnessed an expansion of post-devolution policy and consultation with regard to culture. This is not without criticism. Complexities related to any 'national' approach, suggestive of McIlvanney's 'mongrel nation' notion (Hassan 2016), include varying local and regional experiences and shifting terrains of inclusion, diversity and individuality (Culture Counts 2021). Nevertheless, the National Cultural Strategy outlined the Scottish Government's (2020) future vision. Core ambitions include 'opening up' the potential of culture as 'a transformative opportunity across society', placing culture as a 'central consideration across all policy areas including health and wellbeing, economy, education, reducing inequality and realising a greener and more innovative future' (Scottish Government 2020: 30). Furthermore, the strategy, in line with broader devolved government policy since 1999, foregrounds the empowerment of individuals, communities, and the organisations with regard to cultural growth and facilitation.

But What's Wrong?

What and who constitute culture and leisure are questions Scotland has long contended with. Differences of opportunity, access and experience, particularly by class, gender, language, ethnicity, age, residence and assumed ability, have all deeply underscored how culture and leisure are differently enjoyed and valued. National public funding for them is competitive and limited despite the devolved status of these sectors. Deliverables are often funded and managed at local authority levels, and invariably squeezed.

Modern mass twentieth-century leisure was understood to be activity which was not paid work. Workers were employed to facilitate leisure, yet access and assets were divided along class, gender and ethnicity lines. Leisure's purpose was seen as to occupy and, indeed, discipline the masses. 'Free' time was to be undertaken productively for individual and collective (social) improvement and civic health, yet some activities like gardening and cooking were often undertaken more by necessity than choice. Cultural deficit models informed policy contexts of cultural participation with narratives of who, why and how people could and should 'do' leisure and culture. Scotland's museums and collections protect and promote the lived experience of 'ordinary' people's culture and leisure.¹ More presciently, once-alternative visions and activism progressing decolonisation of cultural and leisure are now welcomed, but continuing this will necessitate sustained focus and unflinching debate, not least with regard to the current hegemonic control of assets, ownership and cultural sponsorship. Identity and resources unquestionably interface with narratives and actualities of inclusion, value and success.

Today, Scotland experiences a varied landscape of leisure and cultural production and consumption across its urban and rural communities, configuring variously within and outwith its homes and workplaces. What is available and experienced has been especially signified during the pandemic. Realities of affordability, of built ecologies and accessibility were brought sharply into relief, addressing pressing concerns and desires, only to dissipate as political narratives of 'the country's' thirst for a 'return to normal' ensued. In this regard, the collective strength of workplace experience and practice through unions and professional bodies articulating and defending Scottish

---

1 Scotland's national civic and public museums, galleries and libraries have played an important role here in retaining and promoting the history and contemporary experience of arts, leisure and cultural life across Scotland's communities, with local history societies, community trusts crucial to documenting arts, life and leisure within local and regional spaces. Glasgow has the largest civic collection of art in Europe, with much of the everyday 'cultural life' of ordinary people celebrated in collections such as Glasgow's St Mungo's Museum, the People's Palace or Riverside Museum. The National Museum of Scotland, as a flagship project, signified both a new millennium and a newly 'devolved' parliamentary identity. Local historical societies and Comunn Eachdraidh, regional collections such as Shetland Museum and Archives, gendered ones such as Glasgow Women's Library or 'creative' interfacing such as the Scottish Storytelling Centre or enhanced collaborative digital archives such as Tobar an Dualchais/ Kiste of Riches are further examples of Scotland's collective wealth of cultural commons.

labour rights, as well as cultural and leisure worker conditions for 'good' work, must not be underestimated (see also Chapter 13). The leisure and cultural sectors, including entertainment, sport, media, tourism and heritage, collectively generate significant Gross Domestic Product. Yet despite employment- and income-generation, these sectors are less visible within wider labour market narratives. The nature of work in the arts, entertainment and creative industries is certainly quite singularly defined as often self-employed, part-time and freelance. The leisure and entertainment sectors encompass sports, fitness, gambling, wellbeing and hospitality. Such cross-overs, along with arts, culture and events, form a complex matrix of both public sector and private capital spaces, operations, employment and experience that requires active support for workers' conditions and wellbeing, as well as addressing the consumption inequities and implications that may prevail. Scottish education plays a key role in framing and delivering on sport's transformative potential. Sport, pastimes and related tourism, as well as doing and engaging with the arts, are deemed to be cultural pursuits, leisure and play. Yet with what, by whom, where or when this can and should take place remain conditioned by class, gender, ethnicity and other embodied norms. Everyday aspects of finding space or opportunity to 'play' encounter restrictions for children and adults alike. Our national conversations are sometimes conflicted in their messaging – enjoying our 'empty countryside' – but access to outdoor space remains conditioned by asset access and ownership (e.g., affordability and availability of accommodation and transport) that, despite land reform and community empowerment legislation, remains a landscape of commercial and capital privilege.

By the late twentieth century, the practice and success indicators of leisure had shifted. Post-industrial economic drivers fostered leisure business opportunities and regional development with regard to arts and culture growth and commodification. Neo-liberal narratives of flexible creative economies engendered an expanding creative class and cultural quarter ethos dominating Scotland's urban millennium regeneration policy. Sharing experiences with European cities such as Bilbao or Gdansk, Glasgow and Dundee showcased and pioneered cultural and leisure trends that included critical re-imagining. Scotland's national economic policy, before and following the 2014 Commonwealth Games, embraced flagship developments regarding sport and events complementing the long history of Scotland's commercial expansion of tourism and heritage sectors.

The industrial model of leisure and culture maps in turn onto arts, culture and events venues, forming a complex matrix of public sector and private capital spaces, operations and employment that is underpinned by profit margins and measurable impact indicators. Looking at who and what we are culturally, nationally, demands ongoing wellbeing assessment, but this is not always easily 'measurable' (Oman 2020). Creative Scotland (2014: 26) requires organisations it funds to 'mainstream equalities in their planning, programming, and audience development through the Promoting Equalities Programme'. Seeing our arts, leisure and culture as communities of experience is arguably a strength. We can build on this. The complex nurturing required for community cohesion is no simple fix, however, whether that be sports funding, language policy or heritage privilege.[2]

Digital and social media arguably offer accessible democratic platforms. Issues, concerns and alternatives can be raised and questioned, solutions found and shared. But this communication landscape is itself conditioned regarding equality of

---

2   Recently, de-colonising debates have gained more traction reasserting diversity, inclusion and access concerns.

access, control of assets, policy and normalising trends where agencies (individual and institutional) can be particularly expert, resourced and able to manage and monitor debates. Digital and media literacy is itself a national concern requiring promotion, facilitation and ongoing critique. Creative Scotland's (2014: 27) digital strategy for arts was especially advanced throughout the pandemic, but how future legacies will be realised as fully inclusive is yet to be tested. Media is a sector operating within ideological frames. It is subject to neo-liberal economics and rarely outspoken or challenging of either the institutional cultural *status quo* or the deep structural realities of leisure access and experience. Scotland operates within a global media marketplace, and although the public state broadcast model still dominates in the collective psyche (including Scotland's Gaelic-language BBC Alba and the BBC Scotland digital channels), future media production, distribution and consumption are worthy of ongoing review. Digital media play significant roles in collective, alternative and disrupted channels of communication and asserting of a shared sense of Scotland's public sphere of our arts, language, leisure and sport. How media 'mediates' (i.e., what it presents and privileges and how it portrays Scotland's cultural and leisure spaces and activities) is powerful. It frames expectations, norms and cultivating ambitions and desires. Our media – what we make, support and share – serve a key purpose in platforming discussion, debate and correction where the complexities and ambiguities of what is 'working' for Scotland's culture and leisure may be examined and critiqued. In short, reporting and debating in critically measurable terms via 'good journalism' – a once globally significant Scottish trade and profession – remains core to future collective ambitions, whether undertaken via broadsheet, broad Scots, Twitter or TikTok.

Our collective understanding about how integrated Scotland's leisure, arts and cultural work is to global labour required a pandemic to bring it to broader attention. What work is and how it correlates to leisure and culture is an important research field, offering useful insight and debate. Arts and culture as work raise issues about precariousness and the precarity 'risk' for artists, creative and media freelancers and cultural workers generally. Union agreements, advice and support offer crucial frames of reference for artists and creative freelancers to recognise and counter discriminatory practice (The Lines Between 2019, STUC 2016). The arts and cultural industries sectors are rewarding, exciting environments. Work can and should have significant meaningful value. Culture and leisure work is symbolically, but not necessarily, practically accounted for as having 'added value', however. This was recognised inherently by the STUC being the first labour movement body to employ an arts officer. Nonetheless, levels of working pay, security of contract and tenure, and a fusion and overlap of boundaries of work and non-work practice and lived experience take their toll. This is often assumed to be a largely urban problem (tied to the creative sector/cultural class as an urban phenomenon), but cultural and leisure work are undertaken across the whole of Scotland – a significantly rural nation – with arts, culture, heritage, sport, tourism and events activities deeply embedded within rural and remote rural economies and communities. These sectors interface with other key production sectors such as food and drink, life sciences, textiles and crafts. The Scottish education sector informs and underpins Scotland's sustainability agenda, health and wellbeing as well as its culture and leisure economies. Yet how differing cultural, artistic and leisure activity are valued in practice remains a concern.

Who does leisure and cultural work, and how? The gendered, ethnic and age nature of much hospitality and tourism employment with its substantial reliance on global labour markets is recognised by unions, research and some professional bodies. Pandemic restrictions exposed the acute sense of social (as well as financial) loss with regard to arts, cultural venues, but also leisure, sport and tourism. Emerging longer-term from Scotland's lockdown will be a varied experience, and there are significant concerns that despite demand, the actual ongoing working conditions and job security realities for many across these sectors will be inadequate. Other issues arising from the 'necessity' (and risk) of global movements of cultural goods and services have been exposed with Brexit and the expansion of digital and artificial intelligence technologies impacting upon Scotland's cultural and leisure sectors. Finally, in terms of who contributes to the success of culture and leisure, the under-recognised free labour delivered by volunteers realising national and local ambitions of culture and leisure requires much greater attention. The STUC Youth Committee's examination of youth employment (STUC 2019) raised issues of wage exploitation and discrimination across leisure, tourism, hospitality and entertainment. Education (see Chapter 9) offers further cause for concern when much of Scotland's college and university diversity and inclusion take-up – despite state payment of tuition fees – is only just possible for many students by virtue of their part-time work. This inequity is compounded for many in arts and leisure-related studies, where relatively low-paid and work precarity norms await graduates (The Lines Between 2019).

Conclusion

Scotland's future perspectives, as well as comparative small state success and ambition, can and will be drawn from various arenas. These include minority language,[3] performativity of arts and culture for social wellbeing, mediatisation of cultural wealth, and lifelong learning, health and inclusive reference frame arts and culture. These hold transformative societal potential, especially in an independent future. The erosion of boundaries between work and leisure and how cultural and artistic activity 'is leisure' is a complex landscape of 'self-branding' commodification. Pressures of the 'overblown reflexive' (Fleming 2009) individualisation required to secure earning power in cultural and creative sectors require redress. In terms of future focus, Culture Counts (2021) set out a manifesto for government cross-party group culture after the 2021 Scottish Parliament elections, including diversity, climate and environment, health, as well as education, procurement and place. Both Brexit and COVID place Scotland at a particular juncture for this sixth Scottish Parliament, and leisure and culture will be impacted by both. Creating a Culture Act for Scotland would address much of our commentary here, but so too does the need to evidence the conditions of labour required to produce art, culture and leisure and to challenge norms and narratives of success and inclusion. Research on young people's education and training contexts of 'play' is powerfully suggestive of what adults need too, where 'play mentalities' and leisure futures speak to the infinite variability of enjoyment and irreducible value of 'non-productive' time. Ambition is welcome, attainment is to be supported, and access 'for all' to be celebrated. Necessary steps to be legally and morally 'fit for purpose' in realising these visions is a national

---

3   So, for example, although there are no monolingual Gaels in Scotland, provision for Gaelic arts and culture and leisure activities in Gaelic remains limited overall, and this despite improvements in some areas such as GlasgowLife's activity, the production of Gaelic novels, the reflection of Gaelic culture through the BBC Alba channel and the significant contribution that Gaelic makes to Scotland's economy.

project of deep focus, evidence-building, transparency and debate. Our cultural and leisure futures will nevertheless continue to be shaped by our 'hopeful travelling', curiosity, and our connections to people and place.

References

Creative Scotland (2014) *Unlocking Potential, Embracing Ambition: A Shared Plan for the Arts, Screen and Creative Industries (2014–2024)*, Glasgow, UK: Creative Scotland.

Culture Counts (2021) 'A Cultural Manifesto for 2021', *Culture Counts*, https://culturecounts.scot/cultural-manifesto-2021.

Fleming, P. (2009) *Authenticity and the Cultural Politics of Work: New Forms of Informal Control*, Oxford, UK: Oxford University Press.

Hames, S. (2020) *The Literary Politics of Scottish Devolution: Voice, Class, Nation*, Edinburgh, UK: Edinburgh University Press.

Hassan, G. (2016) *Scotland the Bold*, Glasgow, UK: Freight Books.

McAlpine, R. (2018). *How to Start a New Country: A Practical Guide for Scotland*, Glasgow, UK: Commonprint.

Oman, S. (2020) 'Leisure pursuits: Uncovering the "selective tradition" in culture and well-being evidence for policy', *Leisure Studies*, 39/1: 11–25.

Scottish Government (2019) *A Culture Strategy for Scotland: Analysis of Responses to the Public Consultation – Key Themes Report*, Edinburgh, UK: Scottish Government.

Scottish Government (2020) *A Culture Strategy for Scotland*, Edinburgh, UK: Scottish Government.

STUC (2016) *Challenges Experienced by Women Working in Music and the Performing Arts Sectors*, Glasgow, UK: STUC.

STUC (2019) *W/Age Rage Report: The Minimum Wage and Young Workers*, Glasgow, UK: STUC.

The Lines Between (2019) *Scottish Artists Union's Membership Survey Results 2018*, Edinburgh, UK: The Lines Between.

20

Radical Scotland

Rory Scothorne and Ewan Gibbs

Introduction

In 1979, Marxist historian Gwyn Alf Williams published a book on Welsh history titled *When Was Wales?* The point of his provocative question was that 'Wales' meant different things to different people over time. The same can be said of Scotland, and it can also be said of 'Radical Scotland'. When was 'Radical Scotland'? There was a magazine of that name during the 1980s, which sought to unite 'Home Rulers' in Labour and left-wingers in the SNP behind a campaign for self-government. It was in the previous two decades, however, that people in Scotland first began to think seriously and methodically about the links between radicalism and Scottish identity. They formed societies to commemorate events like the 1820 'Radical Rising' and figures like John Maclean and James Connolly. They wrote, and read, books like T.C. Smout's *History of the Scottish People* (1969), James D. Young's *The Rousing of the Scottish Working Class* (1979), Jim Hunter's *The Making of the Crofting Community* (1976), Tom Nairn's *The Break-up of Britain* (1977) and Gordon Brown's edited collection *The Red Paper on Scotland* (1975). That male-dominated print-culture also involved a range of left-wing magazines, predecessors to *Radical Scotland* such as *Scottish International* (1968–1974), *Calgacus* (1975–1976) and *Crann-Tàra* (1978–1982). Women, too, began to make their own claims on (and criticisms of) a distinctive Scottish radicalism, fighting against abortion and divorce restrictions, establishing institutions like Scottish Women's Aid, and forming their own magazines like *MsPrint* (1978–1981). They, too, began exploring in unprecedented detail specific obstacles and opportunities Scotland presented for radical action. The same goes for the gay rights activists who formed the Scottish Minorities Group in 1969, and the environmentalists who set up the Scottish Campaign to Resist the Atomic Menace in 1978.

This action and thought forged dense networks between activists and intellectuals across the radical left, many of whom joined together in campaigns for a Scottish Parliament during the late 1970s and 1980s. The idea of 'Radical Scotland' – whatever its many possible meanings – emerged from this period, reflecting a manifest and diverse tradition, produced and reproduced through the collective work of several generations of people in Scotland. However, by the new millennium, atomisation of culture and identity and a yawning generation gap in media consumption had broken down some of the vital transmission belts keeping these traditions alive. The decline of many traditional beliefs has been good. But the tradition of Scottish radicalism has suffered too. Retracing its development and breadth is this chapter's purpose, so that today's radicals can understand where they've come from in order to better think about where they're going. It starts by exploring changes in radical thinking about sovereignty and geo-politics, followed by the related decline of a critique of Scottish political economy within the world system. This is followed by a consideration of radical ideas about the relationship between state and people in the context of devolution, and changing understandings of Scotland's social structure. Questions about organisation of radical politics are then explored, followed by an overview of the enduring importance of cultural radicalism.

Sovereignty and Global Scotland

Contemporary Scottish nationalism is decisively post-sovereign. Its idea of independence is not the vision of total autonomy and self-sufficiency that inspired nationalist movements and nation-building projects for much of the twentieth century. This is in some ways a relatively recent transformation. In the 1975 referendum on British membership of the European Economic Community, the SNP's official stance was against. Some members opposed membership on London's terms, whilst others opposed it outright. Other voices of the left like Jim Sillars – then a Labour MP – were against, as were unions led from the left such as the National Union of Mineworkers Scottish Area. During the 1970s, assessments of Scotland's political economy were informed by the flourishing discipline of developmentalist economics, adopting the cutting-edge criticisms of an emerging neo-colonialism that were at the heart of Immanuel Wallerstein's 'World Systems Theory'. Proponents of the 'branch plant' (Firn 1975) thesis on Scotland's economy argued that the increasing ownership of Scottish assembly lines by US multinationals was de-skilling the Scottish workforce and making the country dependent upon foreign control. Entrepreneurial innovation and the capacity for research and development were leaking out of a formerly autonomous industrial nation. The Fife miners' leader Lawrence Daly (1962) summed this up when he argued that Scotland was losing its independent nationhood through its domination by centralised London government and decisions made in distant boardrooms, just as a wide host of countries were taking their place on the world stage following decolonisation.

Daly's concerns and those of economists such as Firn (1975), who first put forward the 'branch plant' thesis in the 1975 *Red Paper on Scotland*, were given a more popular expression in John McGrath's play *The Cheviot, the Stag and the Black, Black Oil* (1973). It is perhaps the landmark cultural production associated with Radical Scotland, combining humour with an emotive appeal to Scotland's democratic spirit, demonstrating how clan chiefs, Lowland lawyers, English aristocrats and American oilmen conspired to ravage the Highlands, displace its people, destroy Gaelic culture and exploit the landscape and natural resources. Perhaps, the most uncomfortable scene is McGrath's depiction of Gaels in North America finding common affinity with First Nation peoples. This massages the reality of Scotland's leading role in British settler-colonialism and the complex position of Highlanders in the new world. But the idea of Radical Scotland was not simplistically informed by victimhood either. In 'Freedom Come All Ye', the closest thing Radical Scotland has to an alternative national anthem, Hamish Henderson famously hoped that 'Broken faimlies in lands we've herriet / Will curse Scotland the Brave nae mair, nae mair.'

When Scots played an important role in supporting the anti-Apartheid struggle or made common cause with resistance to American imperialism in Vietnam, they did not necessarily do so on the pretence of similarity. This often challenged the popular rhetoric of grievance politics, which blamed 'Westminster', 'England' or 'the union' for problems whose causes were often closer to home or further afield. Many radicals recognised that it was Scotland's connections to the history and contemporary legacies of British imperialism that created a moral responsibility to act. This also provided a practical basis for solidarity activities, such as targeting British banks operating in South Africa. There is a lot to learn here, for there is a tendency to look for similarities with other countries in Scottish discussions of international relations, downplaying Scotland's continued support for a global hierarchy which gains benefit at the expense of the Global South. International solidarity, especially amongst the nationalist left, is increasingly focused upon causes that can be seen to parallel Scotland's situation, like Catalonia, though claims to similarity are questionable. The environmental movement is a more hopeful prospect in this respect. There is widespread recognition that Scotland's status as a rich nation comes from over two centuries of carbon burning and energy extraction, which continues in the North Sea.

Who Owns Scotland?

Radical Scotland's past strengths in political economy have been mostly abandoned, especially in the common sense of left-wing activists. Past understandings of locally anchored industries and powerful unions helped radicals to link the national question – and politics more generally – to people's everyday experiences of exploitation. These traditions were largely sustained by the Communist Party and its allies in the Labour left and STUC. Contemporary manifestations of this tradition include the Red Paper Collective and Campaign for Socialism within Scottish Labour, but these are increasingly marginal political forces. The old opposition to monopoly capitalism, focused on the role of multi-nationals in Scotland's industrial economy and the oil sector, has been replaced by a much vaguer and less coherent analysis drawing upon different strands of international left-wing thinking with less specific placement in a unique national situation. Nevertheless, there is now broad agreement across union and social movements, and amongst the left of Scottish Labour, the SNP and Scottish Greens, that the effects of deindustrialisation and the entrenchment of market liberalisation are still having negative impacts in the forms of rising inequality and precariousness. A more penetrating assessment of the structure of the ownership of Scotland's economy – mirroring the one that has been developed around land ownership (see Chapter 17) – would help to develop a more grounded case for structural reforms. It could also help to identify choke points for activists to target.

Re-establishing a Scottish tradition of radical political economy would mean critiquing and criticising the Scottish Government's (2014) 'reindustrialisation' agenda, which was first announced in the run-up to the 2014 independence referendum. This prospectus promised huge increases in exports and 100,000 new manufacturing jobs. There is some potential to expand Scottish industrial employment in sectors such as renewable energy engineering, but a more level-headed assessment is required. Scotland will not become a twenty-first-century version of an old industrial nation, and its labour market will continue to be heavily weighted towards services. The SNP's 'sustainable growth' vision of Scottish independence goes too far in accepting the decline of domestic control, however, ceding monetary power to the Bank of England and industrial control to multinationals. North Ayrshire Council's recent moves towards Community Wealth Building provide a more realistic model for constructing sustainable and more equitable local economies. Any vision for a more democratic Scottish economy has to have at its heart former coalfield localities that have increasingly become dormitories for larger settlements. Areas such as these lie across Scotland's central belt. They require initiatives that restore distinctive local profiles and offer economic opportunities in close proximity. Radicalism must learn to embrace, rather than overlook, the 'foundation economy' of essential services and goods distribution provided by the public sector and helped by locally owned small businesses. Work on this has begun through Scotland's limited infrastructure of left-leaning think tanks, but popularising such a critique requires an agenda that focuses less on influencing government and more on shaping public attitudes.

State and Society

Building that future will require major changes to the behaviour and structure of the state in Scotland. Radical Scotland was historically associated with a form of republicanism which is now more muted. Discontent over the Crown Estate's role in wind farm licensing, which includes royalty payments to the monarch, is an indication of the important overlap between economic and political radicalism. Older Euroscepticism has largely been displaced by opposition to Brexit, a reactionary British nationalist project with far-right leanings, though some on the radical left have sought to re-state a critique of the EU based on its lack of democracy, market fundamentalism and treatment of smaller nations. A more developed assessment of the constraints and opportunities of an independent Scotland's prospective EU membership is required, and on terms recognising the dominant role of liberal market orthodoxies and big business interests in the European project.

Any such discussion also demands a more reflexive consideration of contemporary Scotland's social structure. A more nuanced assessment of class is required which recognises that old binaries between manual and non-manual employees are not necessarily the defining feature of contemporary Scotland. The long-term ideological and cultural effects of social mobility have to be contended with alongside a more recent and drastic rise in precarious work. The same goes for the rise in home ownership since the 1970s, and the more recent countervailing fall in the proportion of owner-occupiers among Scotland's households. Radical Scotland's infatuation with male industrial workers can become a stultifying caricature, even where it offers a politically convenient binary between a

Scottish 'proletarian nation' and patrician Anglo-Britishness. Instead, the radical left must reckon with Scotland's social structure resembling the UK's more than at any point in recent history. Relinquishing the 'proletarian nation' (Foster 1992) can inspire a sober assessment of the new class alliance sustaining the SNP, grouped around public sector employment, services and the welfare state.

Organising Radicalism

Scottish radicalism has experimented with a wide range of organisational forms. This has encompassed everything from historical societies to old and new media and political parties, and all of these have a role to play in sustaining and renewing the radical tradition. Certain problems frequently recur, especially with perennial questions about 'horizontality' versus hierarchy, centralisation and decentralisation, as well as newer questions about effective representation of diverse political identities. For a tradition to live, it needs to be loose and undogmatic; to be effective, however, it sometimes needs a degree of discipline and focus. Such contradictions are inescapable features of radical politics everywhere, and the Scottish radical tradition is replete with examples of success and failure to assess. Today, Scottish radicals are particularly inspired by the Living Rent tenants' union, whose careful balance of democracy and top-down discipline has been sustained by the momentum that comes from relative success. Yet there are questions about how far radical organisations can reach into politics. In the 1970s and 1980s, radicals could claim to speak 'for' Scotland, leaning on national identity for support in the absence of any higher representative body. Today, however, Scotland is represented by a parliament that more accurately reflects the small-c conservatism of the Scottish public. As a result, radical parties and movements are often left fighting for space at the margins of devolved politics, which often absorbs their ideas but jettisons the urgent, transformative spirit behind them. Examples of this include the Scottish Government's rhetorical embrace of a 'Just Transition' agenda for the fossil fuels sector, and its commitment to a more diverse and inclusive political system that focuses on representation over empowerment or emancipation.

If there is one big story of Scottish radicalism's organisational development, it is what Lang (2013) calls 'NGO-isation' (see also Chapter 12 on the professional-managerial class). As social movements have gained profile and influence, they have often been tempted to place themselves on a more secure and respectable footing by turning into non-governmental organisations (NGOs), departing from an active extra-parliamentary political base and becoming more streamlined and policy-focused. Or, where movements force issues onto the political agenda, it is often less conflict-oriented NGOs which move in to influence policy. These movements and their causes thus become absorbed into the apparatus of government via 'consultation', and lose the ability – or the desire – to transform the system as a whole. This process is so powerful because it is double-sided: NGOs in Scotland have been vital to some of the country's most progressive policy achievements, but this has come at a cost. There are few forces left in the country which are genuinely challenging the political and economic system overall. The 'corporate capture' in the neo-liberal age of Scotland's political parties and government is thus mirrored in the 'third sector capture' of much of Scotland's radical energy, as the precarity and exhaustion of left-wing activism draws people towards a more professionalised and consensus-building approach to politics, increasingly bypassing the harder work of transforming public attitudes by involving the people in politics. One alternative to this dynamic for radicals is to pay closer attention to a thorough renewal of Scotland's union movement, directing attention back towards organising workers on their own terms rather than performing the roles of advocacy and service provision on their behalf. These efforts have already begun through STUC-backed projects like Better Than Zero, Workers' Reunion and the Workers' Observatory.

Cultural Revolution?

The most likely source of renewal for Scottish radicalism is, perhaps, in culture. Where devolved politics tends to trap radicalism in bureaucratic and partisan forms, or subordinate it to constitutional goals, a more liberated, imaginative and avant-garde radicalism can be pursued in cultural realms. In its bracing, raucous encounter between culture and politics, McGrath's *The Cheviot, the Stag and the Black, Black Oil* allowed Scottish radicals to articulate their concerns about multinational capitalism, nationalist complacency and their fragile cultural inheritance simultaneously.

But how might new radical concerns suitably be brought together in collectivised cultural forms in our post-modern landscape? Fortunately, cultural production neither has to win elections nor appeal to the lowest common denominator. It is driven forwards by experimentation and critical distance. It is only by making a virtue of these that Scottish radicalism can reach a more productive understanding of its present marginalised state. This means greater radical engagement not only in the production of art, but also in the analysis and criticism of popular culture and identity, understanding these things not just as forms of elite propaganda, but as insights into the everyday attitudes from which radicalism has become estranged. Standing back from Scottish society can allow radicals to get a better impression of what that society actually looks like as a whole, and where the most effective entry points are. While

Scotland's print media is hamstrung by asset-stripping foreign ownership and a reliance on advertising revenue, online grass-roots media like *Bella Caledonia* can help to encourage these efforts. One positive example from recent years may be 'The World Transformed', a portable festival of politics, education and culture – from training sessions to club nights – shadowing Labour conferences.

Conclusion

Essentially, Radical Scotland is the idea that there's something distinctively radical about Scotland. Often, the radical reputation rests upon the sense Scotland is profoundly working-class (Foster 1992). This reading points to the importance of industrial labour and public sector employment to the Scottish economy in the second half of the twentieth century. Alternatively, Radical Scotland rests on Scotland being distinctively left-wing, or at least consistently voting in a more leftward direction than its larger southward neighbour. The accuracy of these definitions can be contested through contrary readings (see, for instance, Gall 2005). However, the key point is that we should therefore understand Radical Scotland as an intellectual tradition, and one that is the product of an unequal class alliance. The predominantly university-educated middle-class intellectuals who produced and popularised the idea leant heavily on working-class history and were, in the post-war decades, inspired by contemporary workplace and community activism. Yet the unbalanced nature of this alliance, especially during devolution, is revealed in the uneven distribution of benefits from a devolved settlement that owes much to the ethos and personnel of Radical Scotland. A nation's people with a parliament and a First Minister that both enjoy growing public authority are less willing to grant legitimacy to peripheral voices, claiming the nation for themselves. At the same time, Radical Scotland's version of history provides a reforming *élan* and credibility for technocratic national governance. The consensus-building approach of the devolved government counteracts the construction of oppositional coalitions to its left. Forces acting to make change 'from below' in Scotland retain an interest in making a claim on the nation's history to gain representative legitimacy. They should aim to do so in an esoteric and unorthodox manner, shaping usable pasts fit for an era of rampant landlordism, tech capitalism, urgent decarbonisation and resistance to the new bureaucratic forces of an NGO-ised third sector–state nexus.

References

Daly, L., (1962) 'Scotland on the dole', *New Left Review*, 17: 17–23.

Firn, J. (1975) 'External control and regional policy', in Brown, G. (ed.) *The Red Paper on Scotland*, Edinburgh, UK: Edinburgh University Student Publication Board, pp. 153–169.

Foster, J. (1992) 'A proletarian nation? Occupation and class since 1914', in Dickson, A. and Treble J. (eds) *People and Society in Scotland, Volume III: 1914–1990*, Edinburgh, UK: John Donald, pp. 201–240.

Gall, G. (2005) *The Political Economy of Scotland: Red Scotland? Radical Scotland?* Cardiff, UK: University of Wales Press.

Lang, S. (2013) *NGOs, Civil Society, and the Public Sphere*, Cambridge, UK: Cambridge University Press.

Scottish Government (2014) *Reindustrialising Scotland for the 21st Century: A Sustainable Industrial Strategy for a Modern, Independent Nation*, Edinburgh, UK: Scottish Government.

21

Social Democracy
and Labourism

Alex Law and Kenny MacAskill

Introduction

In this chapter, we consider the potential for labourism and social democracy to roll back neo-liberalism in Scotland. This requires some clarification of what 'labourism' and 'social democracy' mean in the context of neo-liberal Scotland. Labourism is an ideology founded on the capacity of the industrial working class to effect ameliorative political change. The chief ends of post-war social democracy were full employment, progressive redistribution of income and wealth, and a 'cradle to grave' welfare state. Social democracy would be delivered by the Labour Party in parliament, buttressed by the union movement, as the organic representatives of working-class interests. Until relatively recently, British labourism helped to naturalise the UK state as the taken-for-granted institutional framework for reforming capitalism and alleviating social suffering.

This chapter then asks whether labourism continues to have any relevance for an aspiring social democratic Scotland in the greatly changed context of a reconstituted working class and a highly constrained union movement contending with the crisis-ridden rapids of neo-liberalism. As the local fraction of 'the planetary neoliberal vulgate' identified two decades ago by Bourdieu and Wacquant (2001), Scotland is governed by a highly educated, socially unrepresentative professional-managerial class (PMC) which has banished all talk of 'capitalism', 'class' and 'exploitation' as obsolete (see Chapter 12). This takes on additional significance for a small, inter-connected polity like Scotland where neo-liberal prescriptions are advanced alongside social democratic verities in the form of competitive nationalism. An independent Scottish state, it was (and continues to be) hoped, would undo the iniquities inflicted on society and economy by neo-liberalism. Yet the competitive nationalism advanced in some quarters of the independence movement suggests otherwise.

First, we briefly outline the vicissitudes of social democracy and labourism in Scotland. Second, any discussion of neo-liberalism in Scotland needs to address the class basis of competitive nationalism. Finally, we argue for 'progressive neo-liberalism' to be supplanted by egalitarian democracy in post-pandemic Scotland.

Social Democracy and Neo-liberalism in Scotland

Labourism gave way to civic nationalism in Scotland as the best way to preserve what was left of social democracy and to progressively extend social protection and greater equality. As is well known, working-class support for Labour collapsed after 2014 while the SNP made historic incursions deep into the ranks of the young working class and well-educated professional-managerial class, especially in new towns and suburbs, but also resonating with the old working-class heartlands of Dundee and Glasgow. Scottish nationalism appeared to decisively supplant British labourism, substituting the social harmony of civic nationalism for class division as its motivating ideology. New Labour's 'third way' foundered in Scotland on the back of its aggressive commitment to neo-liberal political economy at the expense of welfare nationalism (Law 2005). Some of the worst of these practices were revoked by SNP Scottish Government reforms, including the removal of charges for medical prescriptions, university fees and care for the elderly, enabling Scottish nationalism to effectively claim for itself the mantle of social democracy in Scotland.

People in Scotland are not inherently more radical than elsewhere (Gall 2005), although survey data consistently suggest that they feel themselves to be slightly more socially democratic in their social attitudes than England (Yarde and Wishart 2020). A huge majority (81%) of people in Scotland feel society falls well short of the ideal image they have for it and that the UK government has been singularly unsuccessful at tackling inequalities, a feeling especially acute among supporters of independence (Yarde and Wishart 2020: 10). Support for parties identified as social democratic (Labour, Liberal Democrats and SNP) has also been consistently higher in Scotland since the Scottish Parliament was formed more than two decades ago. While a large majority of people in both Scotland and England perceive income distribution to be unfair, Scots are more likely to feel strongly that inequalities are 'very unfair', to object that higher incomes are able to buy better health care and education, and more marginally, that higher earners ought to pay more tax (Yarde and Wishart 2020: 13). SNP supporters are more likely to be dissatisfied with the lack of political will to address inequalities (Yarde and Wishart 2020: 15).

In any case, post-war social democracy was never the exclusive preserve of British Labour. Social democracy formed an ideological consensus amongst ruling elites for three decades until the mid-1970s. A need for the state reform of capitalism was shared by ruling Conservative and Labour governments alike. Social democracy developed as part of a pragmatic adaptation imposed on political elites by a combative labour movement reshaped by the experience of total war and conditions of post-war economic boom. A long-term process of democratisation across British society eroded traditional ideals of deference to a natural hierarchical order. With the promise of non-market social reforms, nationalisation of economic assets and institutionalised class conflict, the British state hoped to stabilise threats to the social order posed by democratisation processes, post-imperial retreat and ailing British capitalism.

By undermining the disciplining of workers via market-based coercion, which was no longer accepted by workers as a self-evident 'law of nature', post-war social democracy thus created an apparently intractable problem for capital. Thatcherism and Blairism forged a practical neo-liberal political economy that imposed greater market dependency on labour as atomised individuals. In this process, social democracy mutated into social liberalism as the ideological adjunct of economic neo-liberalism. Labourism wilted in the face of the twin demands of social liberalism and electoral calculation. With the left increasingly marginalised by this hostile environment, union leaders and party conferences abandoned what they viewed as the superannuated positions of social democracy and succumbed more or less willingly to the terrain of social liberalism.

Whatever Happened to Labourism?

Ralph Miliband (1961) long ago argued that the ideology of labourism ensnared socialism in a trap, caught between state power and civic power. On the one hand parliament, and on the other hand the labour movement. Despite his critique of the Labour Party, Miliband came to argue there was no alternative but to grudgingly accept that Labour is the principal agency of social democratic reforms. Until the 1980s, the view could be entertained by Miliband and many others that militant grassroots trade unionism could impose a more radical programme of social justice on the parliamentary Labour Party.

A central problem for labourism was that it rested on an unchanging conception of class relations premised on large industrial workplaces that were the masculine preserve of the manual working class. Class can all too easily be frozen in time and space, fixed to particular lifestyles, or abandoned altogether as historically obsolete. This problem is accentuated when 'white' male industrial manual labour is taken as the prototype for 'the working class', with the implication that highly qualified, non-manual labour somehow forms a class apart or one that transcends class-bound realities.

Deindustrialisation in Scotland acted like an acid to dissolve the class assumptions of labourism. In many ways, the survival of more or less stable class inter-dependencies between 1945 and 1970 was contingent upon the long economic boom, assertive workplace unions and welfare state. This state of exception cannot be taken as a datum to assess class relations in Scotland today. In Scotland, the traditional classes on which political support depended – landowners, industrial bourgeoisie and organised labour – have undergone radical transformation. In the process, classes correspond even less neatly to political alignments than at any time since the 1920s.

Fractions of the PMC in the public sector – health, education, civil service, local government – and in the service sector more broadly have been shifting their political allegiance from labourism to nationalism, attracted perhaps by the prospects of an independent nation-state needing to fill high-level state functions. Such functions demand advanced levels of education acquired over long periods of unwaged study. Extensive preparation outside the workplace and the feeble investment in research and development of private capital in Scotland help explain the PMC's authority in Scotland. Through long years of austerity, however, public sector professions became far less secure, as many grades of staff experienced cuts, officious managerialism and task overload.

The disappearance of the working class as a supposedly homogenous collective subject in Scotland, as elsewhere, compliments the self-image of the PMC as a universal ideal. For some, the working class is a zombie category, artificially kept alive by devouring the energies of political activists and misguided intellectuals, requiring little evidence beyond ritualistic invocation from a revered liturgy. We are all 'middle-class' now, except, that is, for a few malingerers on the margins of society. By dismissing all talk about the working class as an empty ideological slogan, politicians endlessly propound the neo-liberal project of individual self-improvement to develop more resilient, flexible and marketable forms of 'human capital'.

Class and Democracy

Devolution was premised upon the need to restore democracy and accountability to 'the regions' in response to the crisis of democratic legitimacy of the unitary UK state. People fought for independence in 2014 as part of a long tradition of democratic struggles for the right of self-rule by the people in the pursuit of 'autonomy, dignity, civic rights and egalitarian socio-economic change' (Therborn 2020: 23).

While the unreformed UK state remains resistant to democratic accountability, in Scotland small circles of enclosed political and civic elites orbit around Holyrood. Democracy is reduced to a sport managed by an inter-connected layer of the PMC: career politicians, advisors, officials, lobbyists, researchers, think tanks, consultants, public relations specialists and media journalists. MSPs are overwhelmingly drawn from formative occupations in middle-class professions, including lawyers, teachers and lecturers, or as functionaries in 'politics-facilitating roles' (Cairney et al. 2016). Both groups tend to be educated at select schools and universities. Very few elected politicians in Scotland are drawn from a background in working-class occupations.

An unrepresentative and unelected Scottish state represents a major barrier to achieving a more egalitarian and democratic Scotland. The unelected state in Scotland has a long history stretching back to the Scottish Office in the nineteenth century and corporatist forms of governance in the twentieth century. In the latter case, organised labour was incorporated by the governing bodies of a semi-autonomous civil society. In the shadow of deindustrialisation, neo-liberalism and devolution, the incorporated power of labourism has been replaced by a shallow pluralism and a hardening centralisation of unelected power.

Hopes the Scottish Parliament would revitalise social democracy came up against the limits of parliamentary democracy to accommodate the kind of deep-seated structural change required for even minimal forms of distributive justice and the rolling back of neo-liberalism. To simplify considerably, the first phase from 1999 to 2007 involved a parliamentary alliance between Labour and the Liberal Democrats. This political species was largely continuous with 'third way' 'new' Labour UK governments, whose central purpose was to consolidate and deepen neo-liberal political economy initiated by Thatcherism in the 1980s.

Since 2007, a second phase saw SNP governments enact popular measures to curtail the most gratuitous forms of 'the enclosure of the commons' and the commodification of public services in Scotland. Even here, however, this was social democracy-lite at best, hemmed in by neo-liberal nostrums about small nations like Scotland being agile and flexible enough to exact competitive advantage at the interstices of neo-liberal globalisation. First Minister Alex Salmond (2008) claimed that Scotland could become a 'Celtic Lion' in emulation of the 'Celtic Tiger' of neo-liberal Ireland, nimbly taking competitive advantage of the pre-crisis banking sector: 'With RBS and HBOS – two of the world's biggest banks – Scotland has global leaders today, tomorrow and for the long term' (Salmond 2008). If even an astute politician and experienced economist could be taken in by such hyperbole, then sober analysis is required of the prospects for social democracy in Scotland, whether inside or outside the Union.

Many activists look to a vibrant grassroots independence movement to press the ultra-cautious SNP leadership for more daring policies that begin to equalise the starting conditions of life chances across Scottish society. Grassroots mobilisations always threaten to push beyond the controlled prescriptions of the SNP. When a humanitarian protest in the Pollokshields area of Glasgow prevented the Home Office from forcibly removing immigrants in May 2021, it momentarily threw into relief the tension between images of the coercive UK state and a more benign 'progressive' Scottish sub-state. Scothorne (2021: 8) noted that disruptive protests like Pollokshields suggested 'the gap between Scottish and British politics has a radicalising potential that goes beyond the question of independence'. Yet the political gap also has the potential to serve flattering self-images of social democratic Scotland in defiance of stubborn socio-economic realities.

Egalitarian Democracy or Progressive Neo-liberalism?

Just as labourism was readily incorporated into state institutions, so the symbolic capital of new social movements is available to be sequestrated by neo-liberalism. What Fraser (2019) termed 'progressive neo-liberalism' formed a hegemonic bloc out of the symbolic capital of the new social movements – feminism, multi-culturalism, anti-racism, gay and trans rights, environmentalism – allied to a deeply regressive political economy. Progressive motifs are routinely mobilised by leaders of public sector organisations, and high-tech, corporate, financial and rentier capital. Individuals with the required types of social, economic and especially cultural capital are the principal beneficiaries of progressive neo-liberalism.

A variant of progressive neo-liberalism was incorporated into the devolved state through the social intimacy of elite networks in a small nation. The same faces appear year-in, year-out, with a select few, including erstwhile radicals, exercising disproportionate influence. The field of governance now orbits around an unelected and unaccountable but highly influential civic elite that reproduces itself, often supported by public patronage. Indeed, the Scottish state actively regulates 'civic Scotland' through its patronage networks, particularly in relation to the voluntary sector and arts, and even organised labour through the STUC.

The politics of class is essential to egalitarian democracy in Scotland. Today, the social fact of worker self-organisation is routinely dismissed as anachronistic, 'workerist' or 'class reductionist'. Classes are not made according to some preconceived plan. Class is always in process as a relationship to, first, other classes and, second, within the same class. Although classes are functionally and dynamically inter-dependent, they also develop at a social distance from each other. Mobilising the language of class gives expression to antagonistic social interests. In this sense, labourism helped constitute the working class and identified its interests with Labour. However, static labourist conceptions of class proved a fateful weakness when class relations were reconstituted with the dissolution of social collectivities in workplaces and communities into disposable, market-dependent individuals.

Scotland is not anywhere closer to becoming a classless society. Class advantages and disadvantages are being remorselessly passed on inter-generationally. Despite democratic efforts to equalise opportunities through widening educational access in Scotland, cultural conditioning is a game at which even the squeezed PMC will always manage to keep their children's noses out in front.

Attachment to class is not simply a matter of instrumental necessity. It is also a matter of cognitive perception and emotional solidarity. Profound class distinctions structure an everyday consciousness of social reality, not least through hierarchies of social evaluation and demonisation. Here the re-introduction of the lexicon of class into the Scottish public sphere, unburdened by labourist assumptions, might break the spell that we somehow all mingle freely in a fluid society of individuals, made flesh by viral networks and creative juices released by the 'knowledge economy', rewarding personalised human capital of resilience, expertise and creativity, and let the devil take the hindmost.

The labourist conception of social democracy depended on capturing the centralised power of the UK state for socially progressive ends amenable to national capitalism. Until the pandemic, it was argued that nation-states could no longer defy the forces of neo-liberal global markets, neglecting, of course, the constitutive role of the state in forming neo-liberal orders. States were circumscribed in their scope for large-scale public spending, and any progressive redistribution of resources was unthinkable lest cosmopolitan elite leaders and managers deprive the UK of their handsomely renumerated talents. Unable to contest neo-liberalism by wielding state authority, the best that could be hoped for were decentralised struggles and local campaigns.

Austerity compounded the maldistribution of income and wealth and intensified social suffering. Drastically regressive tax and benefit reforms further impoverished wider layers of British society as the price of the sovereign debt crisis, which, in turn, is the price of profligate financial capital. Yet, in response to the pandemic, the UK state embarked on a colossal programme of public borrowing and spending after imposing austerity for more than a decade. In this state of exception, the centralised nation-state revealed its capacity for society-wide planning, co-ordination and resource allocation, albeit under a dysfunctional Tory Government that sought to enrich its own elite group and prop up a reactionary neo-liberal variant of capitalism. So, clearly, there were a multitude of problems with how this was done, not least the stench of endemic corruption at the level of state and business elites, as well as the dilapidated state of the NHS and public sector after decades of privatisation, marketisation and managerialism. But, nevertheless, it was done.

With the re-legitimisation of state action, the Scottish state could become a pole of attraction for extending the claims of social democracy by yoking the redistributive politics of material equality to the inclusive politics of social equality. If inequalities of wealth and power are understood primarily through the prism of class division and agency, then this will have definite social and political effects. Its effect will be to more adequately organise cognition of social and economic relations and exert a rival political diagnosis over rather less compelling dogmas about competitive nationalism and progressive neo-liberalism currently doing the rounds in Scotland.

References

Bourdieu, P. and Wacquant, L. (2001) 'Neoliberal newspeak: Notes on the new planetary vulgate', *Radical Philosophy*, 105: 1–6.

Cairney P., Keating, M. and Wilson, A. (2016) 'Solving the problem of social background in the UK "political class": Do parties do things differently in Westminster, devolved, and European elections?', *British Politics*, 11/2: 142–163.

Fraser, N. (2019) *The Old Is Dying and the New Cannot Be Born: From Progressive Neo-liberalism to Trump and Beyond*, London: Verso.

Gall, G. (2005) *The Political Economy of Scotland: Red Scotland? Radical Scotland?*, Cardiff, UK: University of Wales Press.

Law, A. (2005) 'Welfare nationalism: Social justice and/or entrepreneurial Scotland?', in Mooney, G. and Scott, G. (eds) *Exploring Social Policy In the 'New' Scotland*, Bristol, UK: Policy Press, pp. 53–84.

Miliband, R. (1961) *Parliamentary Socialism: A Study of the Politics of Labour*, London: Merlin.

Salmond, A. (2008) 'Free to prosper: Creating the Celtic Lion economy', speech delivered at Harvard University, 31 March, http://web.archive.org/web/20081010163026/http://www.scotland.gov.uk/News/This-Week/Speeches/First-Minister/harvard-university/.

Scothorne, R. (2021) 'Not all Scots', *London Review of Books*, 43/11: 8.

Therborn, G. (2020) *Inequality and the Labyrinths of Democracy*, London: Verso.

Yarde, J. and Wishart, R. (2020) 'An unequal union? Attitudes towards social inequality in England and Scotland', in Curtice, J., Hudson, N. and Montagu, I. (eds) *British Social Attitudes: The 37th Report*, London: National Centre for Social Research, www.bsa.natcen.ac.uk/media/39400/bsa37_social-inequality-in-england-and-scotland.pdf.

22

'The People's Parliament', Political Classes and 'the Missing Scotland'

Gerry Hassan and Hannah Graham

Introduction

The Scottish Parliament is many things. One is a living institution embodying the idea of democracy. It has changed how politics and public life are perceived in Scotland. It is even possible to argue that, returning after three centuries, it has changed the notion of 'Scotland'. Although the idea of a parliament has been a success in filling a democratic deficit, its actions have often fallen short. Its mixed record, containing successes and failures, tells us much about participation and connectedness, power and the politics of the political classes. The parliament also has diverse meanings for different constituencies and communities, whether by class, gender, ethnic, generational or insider/outsider axes. It is not seen in neutral terms for people come to it with their own preconceptions, expectations, hopes and fears.

This contextualisation of how it sits and interacts with surrounding networks should come as no surprise. Yet the nature of the public sphere in Scotland, sitting within a fragile eco-system of partial autonomy intersected with influential London-centric media and other voices, is seldom contextualised and critically examined. For example, BBC Scotland often receives criticism, sometimes referenced to overall BBC power dynamics, but these are rarely placed in context of the wider public sphere in Scotland or discussed with awareness of power and relationships in Scotland and across Britain (Hassan 2014b, Ponsonby 2015). This absence of understanding power relationships has, since 1999, reinforced privileging of existing voices and interests, maintained marginalisation of other voices testifying to their being seen as 'silently silenced' (Mathieson 2005) and exposed the failure of public discourse to value the idea of 'relational space' (Barr 2008, Hassan 2014a). This chapter reflects on whether Holyrood has lived up to the 'People's Parliament' rhetoric. And what of those voices that were previously peripheral – 'the missing Scotland' of 'the People's Parliament'? To do so, we consider the nature of the Scottish political classes and official notions of engagement and inclusion, and explore what this means for power and inequalities, concluding with an assessment of what this means for Scotland and social justice.

The Scottish Political Classes

Who curates and narrates Holyrood's stories? Well-kent faces and voices of the Scottish political classes, mostly. Predominantly, party leaders and prominent MSPs, enabled by briefings and the ghost writing of staffers and special advisers, and a relatively small circle of political journalists and commentators. Behind the scenes, communication managers and corporate lobbyists seek influence, amongst them figures well connected as 'ex'-politicians or staffers. The world of media commentary, journalism and newspaper editorship is similarly homogeneous (Engender 2020). The community around Holyrood and professional politics is defined by the privileged white, middle-class, male gaze (see also Chapter 12 on the professional-managerial class).

One perspective on the Scottish Parliament is to celebrate its creation and existence. Kerri Friel, an anti-poverty campaigner from Glenrothes, captured this sentiment by describing Holyrood as 'its very existence is a light in the dark' (Hassan 2019: 10). Equalities campaigner and 'Pass the Mic' (showcasing women of colour) founder Talat Yaqoob (2019: 127) viewed it as 'an exclusive and elite group' of insiders and influencers in a modern parliament that merely talks the language of inclusion. Chief Executive of the Scottish Council for Voluntary Organisations Anna Fowlie judged: 'What interests me is that it hasn't trickled down ... devolution to local councils and then to communities .... Actual power still rests with the wealthy, with men and with big, global business' (Hassan, 2019: 10). For all the talk of inclusivity and empowerment, one dimension the Scottish Parliament has mostly kept away from is a discussion about who holds power in society and how they can be held accountable. The Ferret's 'Who runs Scotland?' investigation in 2021 highlighted this, being one of the very few investigations to do so (see especially Mann 2021).

Scottish Parliament committee evidence sessions tend to hear from the same CEOs, directors and spokespeople. Similar to other elites and influencers of the Scottish political classes, these people are not overly diverse (Halpin et al. 2012, Engender 2020). Legitimately given a place at the committee table, they often develop expertise in interpreting political and civil service speak, fashioning their part in choreographies of consultation, giving evidence, framing policy issues and scrutinising efforts. They may also be members of relevant parliamentary cross-party groups, and in a small nation, such proximity, relationships and commonly called upon expertise are not unexpected. Throughout two decades, only modest progress has been made in committees seeking evidence from beyond 'the usual suspects' to try to reduce a proximity gap. Much remains to be done to further diversify the voices and make lived experiences heard; realistically, change will only come when those with institutional authority are challenged and forced to change (Bochel and Berthier 2021).

Beyond the political classes, public perceptions of Holyrood's influence and accessibility have grown more favourable. Since 1999, the Scottish Social Attitudes Survey has asked, 'Do you think that having a Scottish Parliament is giving ordinary people more say, less say, or makes no difference in how Scotland is governed?' Since 2005, there has been a gradual upward trend of people thinking Holyrood gives ordinary Scots more say, with a majority of 56% believing this in 2019, and 36% perceiving it to make no difference to how much say ordinary people have (Reid et al. 2020: 25). Such attitudes differ in strength, with age, income and education demographics implicated in how much credence is given to Holyrood's influence and political engagement.

A different assessment would note limitations hardwired not just into the devolution settlement, but the conservative tendencies within the main player which brought the parliament into being: Scottish Labour. Although it formed the first Scottish Executive with the Liberal Democrats, it had little constructive or visionary notion about what the Scottish Parliament was meant to positively do and the kind of different Scotland it wanted to embody. Former civil servant Jim Gallagher said of it: 'Holyrood has proved better at being than doing' (Hassan 2019: 10). Journalist and lawyer Michael Gray believes the problem is inherent in the project of devolution as it was devised by Labour, the Liberal Democrats and other forces: 'The "Dream" of creating devolution aspired to a forum for a Scottish democratic voice … at the expense of a detailed political programme' (Gray 2020: 90).

Such tendencies are also emerging within the SNP in light of its four successive election victories. It is now patently the dominant party, but this has changed it as much as it has Scotland, revealing a policy agenda which, while celebrating its so-called social democratic characteristics, is threadbare in places. Beyond the independence question, the striking feature of parliament and politics is the degree of continuity from Labour to SNP, and a conservative politics of not substantively shifting power, resources or voice to those previously without it. Instead, insider groups and interests that know how to work the networks and avenues of the system have been rewarded. Instances of listening to lived experience in the sense of engaging with activist advocates or small groups of community representatives are evident, yet substantive radical shifts following this are not evident.

Redressing this necessitates recalibrating power, influence and proximity, and requires clarity on who is and is not invited, consulted and asked to speak. If the Scottish Parliament and politics in Scotland wish to open themselves up to missing voices and perspectives, they will have to reflect on power dynamics in society, and acknowledge the entrenched conservatism and hegemonic stability which underpins the dynamics of the main players in Scotland's political system. That brings forth the question of realistically how the system and its entrenched interests can be challenged, and issues of agency.

When Has Holyrood Listened and Led?

Two examples illuminate success in listening, grappling with complexity and plurality, and leading. First, the Section 28 (Clause 2a) debate on the Thatcher legislative banning 'promotion' of homosexuality in schools in the early days of the Scottish Parliament was a watershed moment. It was the first major public debate about homosexuality in Scotland, unveiling various anxieties and sensitivities – from virulent homophobia via the 'Keep the Clause' campaign to the nervousness of a near-entire generation of mostly male politicians such as Donald Dewar. The resulting debate brought diverse voices to the fore in the public domain: from social conservatives and those who believed in traditional values in education and the family to a nascent LGBTQ+ equality network, and a union movement that had already begun to address such issues. The result was a near 'cultural war', a public wobble in the then Scottish Executive, the passing of abolition, and the defeat of homophobic views. Its aftermath produced a decade-plus of continuous LGBTQ+ progress in advancing rights and equality, aided by leading LGBTQ+ parliamentarians, including some party leaders.

Second is the example of 'people-powered politics' in how the Scottish Parliament and Scottish Government responded to experiences of children and young people in care through their activism, the Independent Care Review (Duncan 2019) and the Children and Young People (Scotland) Act 2014. There has since been cross-party consensus-building and MSPs giving time and attention, making fiscal and policy commitments towards ensuring more caring corporate parenting, to addressing inequalities and adversities experienced by this group, and vocal activism on keeping 'the promise' of Scotland's ambition that children grow up loved, safe, respected and able to flourish (Independent Care Review 2020). Care-experienced young people have influenced how political parties, public institutions and charity groups across Scottish society have been, and continue to be, held to account.

Beyond important domestic issues, the Scottish Parliament has been pivotal to Scotland's emergence on the global stage, and our nation's part in high-profile, high-stakes international events and interventions. Enduringly memorable is the Iraq

War parliamentary debate of January 2003, when MSPs voted to support the war 67–51. What many recall was the passion and elegance of debate on both sides, particularly from those of differing parties, such as the SNP's George Reid and Labour's John McAllion, who opposed military action. This was an illuminating moment for Scottish politics on many levels: a devolved parliament debating global reserved issues and taking sides on the issue of what the British state did in the Scottish people's name – and defining for some that they wanted to take such decisions fully in Scotland – a sentiment which would feed into the 2014 independence referendum.

What Would a Different Politics Look Like?

Rapper and social commentator Darren McGarvey spoke at the Scottish Parliament's *Festival of Politics* in 2018. He was asked, 'How did you become so articulate?' He offered two answers, starting with personal reflections on growing up in Pollok and then moving to challenge an underlying assumption: 'Why wouldn't I be articulate?' The questioner responded: 'Yes, um, but you are exceptionally so,' being met with,'Aye, compared to who, though?'(Scottish Parliament 2018). McGarvey's problematisation of who is enabled to speak in and on Scottish public life, what is expected of people based on their voice, class and story, and how politicians and media often frame him as 'some kind of success story' are issues about inequalities that resonate.

If Holyrood is inclusive, representative and accessible, what is it inclusive, representative and accessible compared to? Westminster? In further diversifying shortlists for elections, committee witness invitations, parliamentary events and public engagement, what do parliamentarians and parliamentary staff expect of those with whom they engage? It should not be surprising that diverse voices can articulate their own experiences and communities. What would it take to go beyond 'passing the mic' and instead to address power imbalances and exclusions which the parliament and politics reinforce, and that, in over 20 years, have done too little to challenge and change?

Participative politics cannot just be about the parliament and being consulted on already well- developed legislative programmes, important though this is. Rather, the Scottish Parliament and political classes must be stopped from just talking to and about themselves and their place in Scotland and their processes, structures and powers. Diverse others are not simply visitors or guests, or one-time constituent queries on topical issues. Power has to be understood in its multi-layered, relational and contingent nature, as fluid and continually being made and remade, while at the same time being embedded with inequality and privilege. Powers to initiate and frame, rather than just respond, are critical here.

Two examples illustrate the potential for how more diverse arrays of citizens might engage with the Scottish Parliament, by 'doing politics differently' in a consensus-driven approach principally determined by participants (not politicians and policy-makers) (see also Chapter 12). Established in 2019 and concluding in 2021, the Citizens' Assembly of Scotland gathered 100 people broadly representative of the population in Scotland to explore three focal questions: what kind of country are we seeking to build, how best can we overcome the challenges Scotland and the world face, and what further work should be carried out to give us the information we need to make informed choices about the future of our country (Citizens' Assembly of Scotland 2021)? This Citizens' Assembly was established with a legislative basis and orchestrated independent of the Scottish Government and Parliament, but reported to both, with non-partisan convenors, facilitators and researchers enabling conversations and voting, informed by expert evidence sessions. Scotland's Climate Assembly (2021), established through the Climate Change Act 2019, was orchestrated using a similar method, but with a more defined focus. The vision and recommendations developed by citizens who participated are testament to pressing issues that people care about.

Fundamentally, the Scottish Parliament's processes may be enlightened enough to recognise the importance of inclusivity and participation, but how does this develop to address unequal power dynamics in an unequal society? Ranging from issues of economic and social exclusion, to drug deaths, fairer work and land reform, the widespread assumption of some in the early days of the parliament was that any competing interests could be brought together, reason could prevail and compromise be found, this being the view of the official Civic Forum in the Section 28 episode. The clarion call 'Nothing about us without us is for us' is a powerful one, but often with conflicting interests, as the powerful may be willing to listen, but not act in a way that cedes power. This is not enough, and more is required: leadership charting a direction, values, and the art of communication and persuasion.

Post-devolution Scotland

The relationship between idea and practice, where the intentions, processes and outcomes are not just about the parties and how they act, but also about the context of Scottish society and the nature of the devolution project itself, have been charted. All have consequences for inclusivity, transparency, and listening to and respecting the voices of 'missing Scotland'.

Over the past century, society in Scotland was a managed democracy which gave credence and privilege to professional groups, hegemonic interests and experts. They safeguarded and gained from Scotland's negotiated autonomy within the

Union. As the scale of government intervention expanded after 1945, a kind of 'planned freedom' became a defining mission of these groups: making the lives of citizens better through state intervention. This was the world of 'Labour Scotland'. It came at the cost of atrophying Labour as a radical party and aiding the transformation of social democracy into a politics centred on administration and pragmatism. From the 1970s onwards, British politics shifted rightward, and in Scotland turned into a profound defensiveness, positioning itself in opposition to first Thatcherism, then 'new' Labour. This worked pre-devolution to the advantage of Scottish Labour, but with the Scottish Parliament's re-establishment, increasingly to the SNP. A sense of managed democracy has been enhanced by the limited politics of devolution – namely, a political project initially established not to overturn existing arrangements in Scotland, but to validate and, at best, modernise them. More than 20 years on, we are still living in the shadow of that politics, and have still to fully flesh out what post-devolution politics – whether independent or within the Union – should look like.

Talking about more open processes and structures matters, but ultimately power, voice and inequality are what are critical alongside agency. They require that 'We need to learn, or relearn, how to build comradeship and solidarity instead of doing capital's work for it by condemning and abusing each other' (Fisher 2013). This includes nurturing a politics which understands the landscape in which it is situated, including domestically and in relation to the British state, which thinks about power dynamics and relationships, and grasps that only an explicitly post-devolution politics can bring about fundamental change. That entails thinking beyond traditional political perspectives of mainstream Scotland – and challenging some of the most cherished shibboleths in its society and politics. Only in this context, can we truly aspire to and live up to a politics of inclusivity and openness which listens to the sounds of the silenced of 'the missing Scotland'.

References

Barr, J. (2008) *The Stranger Within: On the Idea of an Educated Public*, Rotterdam, the Netherlands: Sense Publishers.

Bochel, H. and Berthier, A. (2021) 'Committees and witnesses in the Scottish Parliament: Beyond the "usual suspects"?', *Scottish Affairs*, 30/3: 337–354.

Citizens' Assembly of Scotland (2021) *Doing Politics Differently: The Report of the Citizens' Assembly of Scotland*, Edinburgh, UK: Citizens' Assembly of Scotland.

Duncan, F. (2019) 'People-powered Politics', in Johnston, J. and Mitchell, J. (eds) *The Scottish Parliament at Twenty*, Edinburgh, UK: Luath, pp. 77–88.

Engender (2020) *Sex and Power in Scotland 2020*, Edinburgh, UK: Engender.

Fisher, M. (2013) 'Exiting the Vampire Castle', *OpenDemocracy*, 24 November, www.opendemocracy.net/en/opendemocracyuk/exiting-vampire-castle/.

Halpin, D., MacLeod, I. and McLaverty, P. (2012) 'Committee hearings of the Scottish Parliament: Evidence giving and policy learning', *Journal of Legislative Studies*, 18/1: 1–20.

Gray, M. (2020) 'People and politics: Reshaping how we debate, discuss and listen', in Hassan, G. and Barrow, S. (eds) *Scotland after the Virus*, Edinburgh, UK: Luath, pp. 88–94.

Hassan, G. (2014a) *Caledonian Dreaming: The Quest for a Different Scotland*, Edinburgh, UK: Luath.

Hassan, G. (2014b) *Independence of the Scottish Mind: Elite Narratives, Public Spaces and the Making of a Modern Nation*, Basingstoke, UK: Palgrave Macmillan.

Hassan, G. (2019) 'Back to the future: Exploring twenty years of Scotland's journey, politics and stories', in Hassan, G. (ed.). *The Story of the Scottish Parliament: The First Two Decades Explained*, Edinburgh, UK: Edinburgh University Press, pp. 1–27.

Independent Care Review (2020) *The Promise*, Glasgow, UK: Independent Care Review.

Mann, J. (2021), 'The influence industry: Meet the lobbyists with most access to political power in Scotland', *The Ferret*, 12 July, https://theferret.scot/meet-professional-lobbyists/.

Mathieson, T. (2005) *Silently Silenced: Essays on the Creation of Acquiescence in Modern Society*, Hook, UK: Waterside Press.

Ponsonby, G. (2015) *London Calling: How the BBC Stole the Referendum*, Delhi, India: NNS Media.

Reid, S., Montagu, I. and Scholes, A. (2020) *Scottish Social Attitudes Survey 2019: Attitudes to Government, the Economy and the Health Service, and Political Engagement in Scotland*, Edinburgh, UK: Scottish Government.

Scotland's Climate Assembly (2021) *Doing Politics Differently: Scotland's Climate Assembly Interim Report*, Edinburgh, UK: Scotland's Climate Assembly.

Scottish Parliament (2018) 'Festival of Politics 2018: In conversation with Darren McGarvey (aka Loki)', *YouTube*, www.youtube.com/watch?v=ENn8kVsWlSI.

Yaqoob, T. (2019) 'Twenty years of devolution: Small steps towards equality, but we need big leaps', in Johnston, J. and Mitchell, J. (eds) *The Scottish Parliament at Twenty*, Edinburgh, UK: Luath, pp. 127–135.

23

Community Campaigns – the Power to Change

Willie Sullivan, Lynn Henderson,
Linda Somerville and Ruth Lightbody

Introduction

Institutional power no longer delivers for citizens. It always struggled to do so, but did so much better before. Consequently, new sources of citizens' power must be organised and new institutions created or old ones remade. Prime amongst turning to popular power are representatives of workers, community campaigns and using the organs of the existing state. So this chapter begins by examining why the people have been failed by existing democracy and why institutions are failing to work for people (see also Chapter 12). It then moves to consider three issues: (i) whether new, vibrant muscles can be developed on the body of existing unions; (ii) whether communities can create their own new institutions of power situated within themselves; and (iii) how the state can facilitate and support the potential pockets of worker and community power.

Failing States and States of Failing

States are powerful institutions and actors, directing huge resources, holding the legitimacy of hegemony and being lawfully violent. They should act in citizens' interests, and representative democratic governments should help ensure this. Yet representative systems, especially the Westminster model, throw up a range of challenges here (Lijphart 2012). Majoritarian political systems (as in the UK and US) encourage division and discord. Losing parties and voters accept being out of office and influence on the understanding that they will get a chance next time around. That acceptance of the legitimacy of competing political interests has now declined into highly divisive delegitimisation of political opponents. This is largely fed by online propaganda run and funded by extreme elements supporting particular political ideologies (see, for example, Klarman 2020). In Britain, the state has mostly failed to represent the interests of large groups of its citizens, particularly when these interests came into conflict with those of ruling elites (*Economist*, 1 August 2020). There are periods of surges in popular power when policies have better served wider interests, but these are exceptions, not the rule. The 'golden age' of representative democracy in Britain was probably the post-war consensus, one brought about by recognising sacrifices made by millions of working-class people in war, their unwillingness to accept the *status quo* while the USSR had, at least in theory, planned to create workers' power across the globe. The British state bent to popular interests. Since then, the state and political parties have broken almost all ties with the citizens. The structures that connected them – mass political parties, responsive local government, civil society, unions and so on – have declined or been dismantled to such an extent that the political classes float free of the electorate, connected only very loosely and distantly by an electoral system failing to equate votes cast with representation.

Where stands Scotland here? Scotland is different, in that the current and long-standing governing party has been part of a social movement in the shape of the independence campaign (Thiec 2015). As power and influence hardly ever enjoy being fettered, there are ongoing attempts by SNP politicians to shake off the 'Yes' movement and party democracy despite these being the main connections back into the lives of the people they should be acting for. What can be gleaned from this is that the constraints and counter-balances that social movements place upon political parties are vital in ensuring parties cannot be overly influenced by elite groups – such as the 'corporate lobby' or professional-managerial class (PMC) – seeking to access state power to protect and advance their own narrow interests, which often conflict with those of the wider population.

Add to this the most profound revolution in how information is communicated, so that institutions of government find it hard to evolve anywhere near rapidly enough to keep up. This would be true even if they were not largely conservative in defence of hierarchy and privilege connected with the British state. One approach to these pressures on the proper functioning of democracy is to 'reinforce the citadel' – to re-focus power back to the centre by dint of Boris Johnson's authoritarian populism. The Scottish Government is at least trying to open up an alternative route with a flirtation with citizens' assemblies. Although we need the state on our side, we cannot become dependent upon it. Consequently, we need a movement built upon the interests of local causes and communities linked together by unions, insider activism within the state, local and national, and community campaigns and organising. This would be the beginning of a means to claim the state for its citizens and to institutionalise new forms of democratic control.

A Different Kind of Unionism

It's over a hundred years since 'Red Clydeside', and 2021 marked 50 years on from the Upper Clyde Shipbuilders work-in. Today, the union movement looks very different compared to then. Union power has been in decline for more than 30 years, often being attributed to shrunken manufacturing capacity, neo-liberal hegemony and the growth of the service economy. Yet trade unionism in Scotland has transformed over this period from being predominantly skilled, male and industrial to one in which public sector women workers delivering essential services are winning victories utilising both industrial power and widespread community and service-user support (which were also used during 'Red Clydeside'). Levels of union membership have now stabilised across Britain in the last few years up to 2020, and union density in Scotland remains higher than the UK average (Department for Business, Energy & Industrial Strategy 2021).

Even before the pandemic increased homeworking, union struggles were fought and won with the backing of communities. And while the workplace remains the unit of most union organising, the practice of the community of solidarity is of increased importance where a more feminised workforce in care work, health and teaching extends across all of society. And as the presence of homeworking emphasises, links of workers to the communities in which they live and work could not be stronger. McAlevey (2016) described the forging of broad, powerful strategic alliances aspect of her theory of union organising as workers, through their unions, connecting the dots to their many community contacts, systematising deep ties enabling workers to win more in a process of 'whole worker organising'. This theorised method is not unique to North America. Through the STUC, a cadre of mostly young, Scottish trade unionists spent time studying her work, taking part in bespoke training delivered by her in Glasgow in 2017 and 2018, and more recently as part of the Rosa Luxemburg Foundation's sponsored digital 'Strike Schools', linking with thousands of union organisers around the world.

So it is not surprising that key elements of 'whole worker organising' appeared in recent Scottish union actions and successes, including the Glasgow equal pay strike in 2018 (see McCarey and Smith 2019), janitors' strikes in 2017, and teachers' pay dispute in 2018 (see Flanagan 2019). Linking workers' power in the workplace directly to the communities they serve as well as getting them active in their communities as parents, carers, members of churches, political parties and community organisations means every worker can find solidarity in their community and build power in their community to bring about change.

Small-scale campaigns by unions can be fought and won within communities. When the Westminster Government sought in 2011 to close the tax office in Wick in the far north of Scotland, the Public and Commercial Services (PCS) union mounted a campaign to save the 19 revenue jobs and keep the office open. The workers would otherwise have had to commute to Inverness. PCS set up the 'Wick Wants Work' campaign group, and it considered the strategic importance of keeping high-quality jobs in its community. With the Dounreay nuclear plant decommissioning, the Caithness community was in danger of being stripped of work. The campaign set out to build support, not just approaching the local trades union council, but also reaching out to local businesses, gaining the support of the local chamber of commerce. By building up the ties to the community to raise voices in support of these workers, the union campaign successfully postponed the office closure by two years. Whilst the office did eventually close, the local jobs stayed in the community for another five years, as Her Majesty's Revenue & Customs (HMRC) trialled homeworking. It was not until 2016 that voluntary redundancy was offered to the Wick staff as part of an overall HMRC plan to reduce staff and centralise the majority of its operation throughout Britain around a small number of massive hub sites. Although these campaigns are largely reactive, they offer the prospect of building worker and community influence in a way that is a considerable advance on what was practised before, which was largely only in the form of industrial action.

Local Democracy in Action

Popular participation in local representative democracy is essentially limited to voting in periodic elections. For most, that is the beginning and end of their encounter with local democracy. The next five years see the small band of elected representatives agree budgets, set priorities and decide the political direction in our winner-takes-all democratic marketplace. The model is transactional: a vote is traded for a promise. There is no collaborative decision-making, no participatory process and no transfer of power to communities. Disempowerment follows as decisions about key public services are taken without recourse to those who voted and rely on these services. Yet the Scottish Government (2019) review of local democracy tells a different story:

> The clear evidence from the submissions is that people do want to have more control of decisions on issues that matter to them. This is particularly the case for control of decisions that are seen to directly affect communities, which should apply more locally. The vast majority of submissions expressed views that demonstrate a desire for a change to the status quo.

The absence of formal structures and resources – in the form of institutions – to facilitate challenging decisions and initiate positive changes has not prohibited communities taking action. Across Scotland, local people have acted collectively to stop school closures, defend community centres, halt demolitions, demand better bus services and take ownership of local buildings no one else wants. The commitment and tenacity required to succeed cannot be underestimated, as communities have to navigate opaque bureaucratic processes without formal training, knowledge or support. The measure of successful campaigns is not entirely objective, for the process of engagement, building capacity, knowledge, confidence and agency of those involved is a powerful legacy even when campaign aims are not fully achieved. And the power created when individuals work collectively, and ideally with other working-class organisations, to make change can resonate beyond local boundaries.

In 2012, Edinburgh City Council was forced to abandon plans to privatise over 2,000 jobs after 'Save Our Services', a community campaign led by groups of local women combined with UNISON's local government union branch. The decision also halted the council's ambitious project to sell its outsourcing model, developed at a cost of £4 million, to other local authorities. This highlighted what Ganz (2010) outlined as strategy of turning the resources possessed into the power required to achieve goals. This model of leadership and community organising focuses upon creating a shared commitment, story and structure to distribute power and develop leaders.

So, when faced with a proposal to demolish a much-loved red sandstone building on Leith Walk, Edinburgh and build six storeys of mixed accommodation, mainly student flats, the local community responded with anger and hostility. Careful campaign management ensured that from day one the opportunity to build power to make change was central. The usual format of 'listen and leave' meetings was replaced with network-building sessions to agree shared objectives, examine where power lay, identify skills and agree tactics (Somerville

2018). There were no committees or rigid structures, and the inevitable rise of an informal hierarchy was acknowledged and kept in check. Closely watched by planners, council officials and developers, the 'Save Leith Walk' campaign successfully stopped the demolition and forced the developer back to the drawing board. Over the course of two years, the group utilised community organising tools, consensus decision-making and distributed responsibility to develop the capacity, agency and ambition of local citizens, resulting in a crowdsourced alternative plan for the site and a bid for a community buy-out.

Communities have the ability to create institutions of power that can influence outcomes and deliver positive change. Yet such campaigns are usually temporary and in response to outside agents which have objectives contrary to local needs. Creating a fairer Scotland which represents the aspirations of local communities requires new institutions and methods to shift structural power and devolve decision-making to those most familiar with impacted services, place and space. Community organising as both a method and movement is key to this. It is a challenge to local authorities and national government to replace the talk of community empowerment and invest in a sustainable community organising movement that creates networks of trained community organisers. Local democracy thrives when people can see a strategy for transformation in their communities, and their central place within that process.

Democratising Local Politics

This penultimate section examines how the local politics can be reconfigured to allow for this empowerment. We already have in Scotland an impressive narrative surrounding community empowerment and engagement (Lightbody and Escobar 2021; see also Chapter 12 in this volume), and the pandemic highlighted the value of community responses as well as the need for networked approaches to tackling the crisis (South et al. 2020). But to generate resilience and wellbeing, engagement and participation need to be 'built into the bones' of how we do politics in Scotland.

Innovative practices such as citizens' assemblies and participatory budgeting have been readily adopted by the Scottish Government. Participatory budgeting is now being institutionalised by all local authorities in Scotland. This offers citizens the chance to decide how local funding should be spent, which has the potential to change the relationship between communities and institutions (Escobar et al. 2018). The Scottish Government hosted two citizens' assemblies, on the future of Scotland and on climate change. The former made 60 recommendations to the Scottish Government, most of which received over 75% support and many of which received over 90% support among those taking part (Citizens' Assembly of Scotland 2021), highlighting the ability of random citizens to reach agreement. Instead of polarisation and conflict-generation, these processes managed to facilitate consensus from differing ideological perspectives on issues of social justice, tackling poverty, and health and wellbeing. The Assembly on Climate Change met for the first time in early 2021, and has since made 81 policy recommendations from its over 100 members (Scotland's Climate Assembly 2021). It is worth considering how the Scottish Government will implement so many policy recommendations, given the danger of cherry-picking those which suit its agenda whilst appearing to take the recommendations seriously.

These innovations require committed actors, participants, organisers, facilitators and experts to enter into a laborious and time-consuming process. Citizens' assemblies and participatory budgeting moved online during COVID, which was daunting given the previously perceived importance of face-to-face interaction. Yet this move appears to have been successful, allowing organisers and practitioners to flex their muscles using digital innovations and change the face of democratic innovations for the future (Chwalisz 2021).

From this, we can see that beyond electoral politics, the desire of citizens to engage exists and decision-making can be made legitimate. Similar attention has been paid to community engagement by the likes of the *National Standards for Community Engagement* (What Works Scotland and Scottish Community Development Centre 2016). In addition, people can be offered a greater stake in their community through community ownership and development trusts (Henderson et al. 2018; see also Chapter 17 in this volume). Asset transfer is a key component of the Community Empowerment (Scotland) Act 2015, and the Scottish Government further supports this venture with the Community Ownership Support Service. Ownership of assets can help empower communities by making them stakeholders and decision-makers (Henderson et al. 2020). We are at an early stage, so it would be wrong to prejudge the outcomes of these various initiatives and innovations. But at least a course is being set out upon.

Conclusion

For democratic and participative innovation to penetrate local levels and connect the local to the national, we have to think more carefully about embedding and institutionalising these initiatives and innovations into a dense network of inter-linkages that take many forms, involving people as workers and as citizens. This would include issues of form and shape like utilising referendums or our upskilled citizens to become advocates for activism in their local areas. Whatever form this takes, it will require investment in the lives of communities and people. If citizens are struggling to live, political participation is not a priority for them. Good practice must be linked beyond standalone processes and one-off innovations. Innovative practices such as citizens' assemblies and participatory budgeting need to be linked with local initiatives. The media also have a role to play in publicising participatory processes and reporting their outcomes. Public engagement must be built into the decision making-process beyond consultation and deliberation so that it includes the implementation and evaluation stages of the policy process.

References

Chwalisz, C. (2021) 'The pandemic has pushed citizen panels online', *Nature*, 589: 171.

Department for Business, Energy & Industrial Strategy (2021) *Trade Union Statistics 2020*, London: House of Commons Library.

Citizens' Assembly of Scotland (2021) *Doing Politics Differently: The Report of the Citizens' Assembly of Scotland*, Edinburgh, UK: Citizens' Assembly of Scotland.

Escobar, O., Garven, F., Harkins, C., Glazik, K., Cameron, S. and Stoddart, A. (2018) 'Participatory budgeting in Scotland: The interplay of public service reform, community empowerment and social justice', in Dias, N. (ed.) *Hope for Democracy: 30 Years of Participatory Budgeting Worldwide*, Faro, Portugal: Epopeia and Oficina, pp. 311–336.

Flanagan, L. (2019) '"Value Education, Value Teachers" campaign marches on', *Scottish Left Review*, 109: 18.

Ganz, M. (2010) *Why David Sometimes Wins: Leadership, Organization, and Strategy in the California Farm Worker*, New York: Oxford University Press.

Henderson, J., Revell, P. and Escobar, O. (2018) *Transforming Communities? Exploring the Roles of Community Anchor Organisations in Engaging with, Leading and Challenging Public Service Reform*, Edinburgh, UK: What Works Scotland.

Henderson, J., Escobar, O. and Revell, P. (2020) 'Public value governance meets social commons: Community anchor organisations as catalysts for public service reform and social change?', *Local*

Government Studies, www.tandfonline.com/doi/full/10.1080/030 03930.2020.1787164.

Klarman, M. (2020) 'The degradation of American democracy', *Harvard Law Review*, 134/1: 4–262.

Lightbody, R. and Escobar, O. (2021) 'Equality in community engagement: A scoping review of evidence from research and practice in Scotland', *Scottish Affairs*, 30/3: 355–380.

Lijphart, A. (2012) *Patterns of Democracy: Government Forms and Performance in Thirty-six Countries*, second edition, London: Yale University Press.

McAlevey, J. (2016) *No Shortcuts: Organizing for Power in the New Gilded Age*, New York: Oxford University Press.

McCarey, J. and Smith, B. (2019) 'Equal pay victory – how Weegie women won', *Scottish Left Review*, 110: 6–7.

Scotland's Climate Assembly (2021) *Recommendations for Action*, Edinburgh, UK: Scotland's Climate Assembly, www.climateassembly. scot/sites/default/files/inline-files/Scotland%27s%20Climate %20Assembly%20Recommendations%20for%20Action.Web Version%20%282%29%20%282%29.pdf.

Scottish Government (2019) *Local Governance Review: Analysis of Responses to Democracy Matters*, Edinburgh, UK: Scottish Government, www.gov.scot/publications/local-governance-review-analysis-responses-democracy-matters/.

Somerville, L. (2018) 'Scotland needs a community organising movement', *Scottish Left Review*, 109: 22.

South, J., Stansfield, J., Amlôt, R. and Weston D. (2020) 'Sustaining and strengthening community resilience throughout the COVID-19 pandemic and beyond', *Perspectives in Public Health*, 140/6: 305–308.

Thiec, A. (2015) '"Yes Scotland": More than a party political campaign, a national movement fostering a new active citizenship', *French Journal of British Studies*, XX/2: 1–15.

What Works Scotland and Scottish Community Development Centre (2016) *National Standards for Community Engagement*, https:// static1.squarespace.com/static/60b74b3ad7fb3972cfe271b0/t/6 12ce339dff85a247d7864fd/1630331714162/NSfCE+online_ October.pdf.

24

Constitutional Conundrums:
Is There Still a Third Way?

Michael Keating

Introduction

This chapter examines whether there is still a constitutional 'third way' between Scottish independence and the Union. It has been the preferred choice of the largest group of Scots, but it has never been formulated as a clearly defined option. Since the 2014 referendum, opinion has polarised between independence and the Union. Brexit increased this, as supporters of independence are likely to favour rejoining the EU, whilst pro-EU voters lean towards independence as the way of achieving it. Yet, in the modern world, absolute sovereignty is an illusion. Whatever constitutional path is taken, Scotland will remain embedded in a complex web or relationships across these islands, Europe and the world.

Political opinion in Scotland on the constitutional question for most of the twentieth century divided three ways. Unionists supported the *status quo* of direct rule from Westminster, nationalists supported independence, and 'Home Rulers' (to use the old term) favoured a Scottish Parliament or Assembly within the UK. Devolution in 1999 appeared to simplify matters. Unionists rapidly accepted devolution, which became the new *status quo*, and 'Unionism' came to be associated only with opposition to independence. Nationalists, previously divided between 'fundamentalists' who wanted immediate independence and 'gradualists' who accepted devolution as a first step, united on the next step to full independence. It was not long, however, before a new middle ground opened up in the form of enhanced devolution or 'devo-max'. The arrival of the first SNP Scottish Government in 2007 provoked new interest in the concept as a way of staving off the first ever serious independence challenge.

Polls since devolution have consistently given credence to the idea of the 'third way', as they have regularly shown that voters want devolution to go further. In a three-way choice with independence and the *status quo*, the 'more powers' option usually gained most support. It was also likely to be the second choice of most of those preferring either of the other two. There was support for a second option in the 2014 independence referendum, but the Westminster Government was against it, and no organised movement arose to formulate such a question. The referendum itself polarised opinion and the campaign saw a substantial 'No' to 'Yes' move, but both sides knew the crucial votes were in the middle. That is why both sought to gain that middle ground. The 'No' campaign came up with the famous 'Vow' that defeat for the nationalists would not mean the *status quo*, but more devolved powers. The 'Yes' campaign insisted that Scotland was in six unions with the rest of the UK (political, monetary, monarchical, defence, European and social) and would only come out of the political one. Surveys showed that a substantial number of 'Yes' voters still favoured something less than complete independence.

Scotland is not alone here. Surveys in comparable cases of Quebec, Catalonia and the Basque Country also showed strong preferences for the middle ground. Although Welsh devolution was approved only narrowly in the referendum of 2017, opinion there has also favoured more powers. Academics have argued that independence in the modern world is not a single thing to be grasped once and for all. In a global era, the key ideas are inter-dependence and the ability of a nation to manage its relationships at multiple levels. Formal sovereignty is not a guarantor that a nation will be able to control its fate; that depends more on its resources, capacities and relationships with others. Even sovereignty itself has been questioned, as in a 'post-sovereign' world, authority is divided and shared. Indeed, by sharing sovereignty, nations may be able to enhance their capacity, as the Irish have discovered with Europe.

None of this, however, means there is a coherent third way or that devo-max or other formulas really have much substance to them. In one sense, the idea of a third way is trivial, since with any two political propositions, there is always some empty ground between them. Similarly, survey respondents are easily tempted to plump for the intermediary choice when faced with two difficult and risky alternatives. Canadian federalists in the 1990s used to tease Quebec nationalists by showing how 'Yes' voters expected impossible things like keeping Quebec's MPs in the Canadian Parliament or being defended by the Canadian military. In any case, devolution was itself supposed to provide a third way, attracting soft Unionists and soft nationalists as well as satisfying those who always supported it. In order to assess whether any devo-max formula is viable, three critical issues must be addressed: constitutional formulas, competences over policy fields, and the relationship with Europe.

Constitutional Formulas

The devolution settlements of 1999 in Scotland and Wales are based on the principle that nothing in them affects the sovereignty and supremacy of the Westminster Parliament, which can override the devolved legislatures, change their powers or even abolish them. As right-wing Tory MP Enoch Powell famously put it in 1973: 'Power devolved is power retained.' The only safeguard is the legislative consent (Sewel) convention, to the effect that Westminster will not 'normally' do any of these without the consent of the devolved legislatures themselves. It was generally felt, like other conventions, that this would become part of the UK's uncodified constitution, and thus politically binding, especially after it had been enshrined in legislation after the 2014 Scottish independence referendum in respective Scotland and Wales Acts. In practice, the legislative consent convention did not survive its first real test, which arose over its application to the EU Withdrawal Bill. Not content to rule that the situation was not normal or that EU membership was a reserved matter, the Supreme Court dismissed the convention as not having any force whatever, being merely a 'political' arrangement.

There has long been a competing view of the constitution, to the effect that the UK is not a unitary state, but a plurinational union dependent on consent. The issue of sovereignty in Scotland was not resolved in the Union of 1707, but left in abeyance. The devolution settlements of 1999 were not the gift of a sovereign parliament, but the product of an act of self-determination in the referendums that preceded them. Labour has signed onto such an interpretation in endorsing the 1988 *Claim of Right*, however much it has subsequently tried to reinterpret it. There have been various efforts to give substance to this more robust understanding of the Union by moving away from the language of devolution, with its historic implications. Some people have revived the term 'Home Rule' as an alternative, as this conjures up ideas of national self-determination. In fact, as used in the late nineteenth and early twentieth centuries, the term faced exactly the same ambiguities. For Irish nationalists it meant self-determination, while for Prime Minister William Gladstone it would not affect the absolute power of Westminster.

There has been much talk of federalism. This is another old standby, described by historian Alvin Jackson as the 'wonder drug' of constitutional reformers. In itself, it does not address the sovereignty question. Joseph Chamberlain, who left Gladstone's Cabinet because of his opposition to Home Rule, eventually embraced federalism, but in a form that retained Westminster sovereignty. Now proposals for federalising reforms, from the Constitution Reform Group, Scottish Fabians and others like the Red Paper Collective, shy away from this issue. The Welsh 'radical federalism' proposal stipulates minimum standards for services, a rolling back of the existing devolution settlement. A paper commissioned for then Labour leader Jeremy Corbyn did challenge Westminster sovereignty, but shared it with English local government as well as the UK's constituent nations, suggesting this might not be the most serious way to address the issue.

For federalism to be meaningful, two things are necessary. First, it must provide that the Westminster Parliament as well as the devolved bodies be subject to binding limitations on their powers which are judicially enforceable. It might be useful here to make a distinction between sovereignty and supremacy, which are often confounded in the UK debate. Sovereignty is a property of the state as a whole, and resides, in the conventional view, with the Monarch-in-Parliament. This in itself says nothing about the relationship amongst these, which nowadays means between government and legislature. So we might have a view of sovereignty as something intrinsic in the UK constitution, including the devolved nations, without having to accept that the Westminster Parliament can always have the last word. In other words, Westminster does not have automatic supremacy. Something like this exists in the constitutional order of the European Union, whose law has supremacy only in defined fields and which has never claimed sovereignty.

The second condition for federalism is that something will have to be done about England. A state in which over 80% of the population comes directly under the central government does not qualify as a federation. There is not a meaningful demand in England to constitute itself as a unit within a federation. This is hardly surprising when it is the English vote that usually determines the parliamentary majority and government for the UK, whilst only a confederal situation might avoid this. Nor is regional government for England, however desirable in its own right, a way of federalising the UK. Nobody has even suggested that English regions could have their own legal systems, education systems, police systems or independent health services.

There are equally problems with the idea of a fully codified constitution for the UK or that of a citizens' assembly to produce one. The UK is a contested idea, understood very differently in its constituent parts. The Northern Ireland settlement explicitly accepts it, with its open-ended nature and encouragement for Unionists and nationalists to retain their own ideas and aspirations. In a less divisive way, the same is true in Scotland, with its different understandings of authority and sovereignty. Sometimes, leaving these matters in abeyance is a better recipe for harmony than forcing them.

If federalism is not going to happen, this does not mean the devolution settlement cannot be read in a federalising spirit. This would entail abandoning the idea that devolution is a gift from the centre, and returning to the idea of Union by consent. The issue of consent in Scotland is symbolised by the Sewel Convention. In fact, there are now multiple consent provisions added to the original ones, including changing devolved powers through Section 30 orders, changing powers through primary legislation, transferring powers under the EU Withdrawal Act, and approving changes in Internal Market regulations. None of these is binding on Westminster, but it would be a simple matter to make them so. The sovereignty issue could be sidestepped by vesting it in our constitution as a whole, while Westminster supremacy would be curtailed.

Competences

The division of powers in the Scotland Act 1998 largely followed the competences assigned to the Scottish Office in pre-devolution times. So it devolved most of domestic policy, with the exceptions of taxation and cash welfare payments of all kinds. Since then, there have been two important transfers of powers. Both of them responded to political shocks, respectively the narrow SNP victory in 2007 and the surprisingly strong 2014 referendum 'Yes' vote. The first transfers followed the recommendations of the Calman Commission of 2008–2009, which sought to clarify the principles for division of competences. Heavily influenced by the ideas of fiscal and welfare federalism, it argued for a large role for the UK Government in social welfare and redistribution. This heavily constrained the amount of devolution recommended in welfare, and to a large degree in taxation. The second transfers followed the Smith Commission of 2014 and were based on inter-party negotiations in which the SNP demanded as much as it could get and Labour offered as little as possible. An overarching philosophy such as that deployed by Calman was absent. In both cases, Whitehall departments offered as little as possible, and when pressed, came up with piecemeal items like licensing of air guns, speed limits and drink-driving limits rather than whole policy fields like arms control and road traffic. Smith resulted in some more devolution of welfare powers, including a power to top up UK benefits. A major concession was transfer of rates of tax on earned income, but again, this did not represent devolution of the whole field.

The outcome is a complex division of competences, which has lost much of the clarity of the original scheme without necessarily giving much more scope for Scotland to make its own strategic choices. Welfare policy in the UK has undergone a major shift in recent decades. The concept of social citizenship which underpinned the post-war settlement has gradually given way to a selective and punitive regime reverting back to ideas of the deserving and undeserving poor. The idea that getting people into work is usually the best form of welfare has been distorted into the idea that benefit sanctions will do the trick, there being plenty of work available. With continuous centre-left majorities in the Scottish Parliament, attitudes have been rather different. The term 'social security' has been revived to cover new devolved benefits, and there is more use of universal rather than selective entitlements. At the same time, control of personal taxation could open up new ways of linking the tax and benefit systems. Yet, at the time of the Smith Commission, Universal Credit was off the table as a matter for negotiation (apart from some housing elements). An opportunity was missed to design a distinctly Scottish welfare system in the way that Quebec managed within Canada.

Two other fields could complement this. One is labour market regulation, where Conservative laws since the 1980s have driven down union membership and eroded workers' rights (see Chapter 13). Another is the partly devolved field of economic development, including spatial development policy and urban renewal (see Chapters 5 and 11). Taking the three fields together, there would be potential for constructing a distinct Scottish social model and social compromise, with more emphasis upon inclusion and tackling inequalities, rather than making minor modifications to UK regulations. It is no longer enough, as in the original settlement and in theories of fiscal federalism, to leave all the redistributive functions to the higher level of government. Distributive issues arise in all taxation and public service matters, as well as in economic development strategies which may benefit some people and areas at the expense of others. The current UK Government's 'levelling up' agenda applies largely in England, although it has involved some encroachment into devolved matters, and seems driven more by political and electoral considerations than by a serious analysis of spatial disparities. This is a field in which Scotland can take a distinct direction. Of course, there will also be difficult questions over the boundary between reserved and devolved competences and the interaction between reserved and devolved benefits, which means wider devolution of welfare would need detailed work and modelling. Such work has not yet been done.

Brexit

EU membership provided a vital external support system for the 1999 devolution settlements. By providing overall frameworks for regulation in economic and environmental matters, it permitted greater flexibility within the UK. The EU Internal Market was particularly important, allowing a considerably greater degree of devolution in economic policy within the broad European framework. Following Brexit, the Westminster Government created the Internal Market Act 2020, which takes these European powers back to Westminster in a much more constraining form. Goods and professional services which are approved for sale in any part of the UK must be allowed for sale in any other part. This undermines Scotland's capacity to regulate on a range of safety, environmental and social grounds, because while it can pass regulations, they would apply only to Scottish producers, and possibly put them at a disadvantage.

Brexit has also undermined both the independence and devo-max options. Independence in Europe is now more difficult because it would create a hard border between Scotland and England (where Northern Ireland is more complicated). A 'third way' solution would have to resolve the question of whether Scotland is to be in or out of the EU, or at least the EU Internal Market. It is striking that so many of the recent federal proposals ignore this question, seemingly taking Brexit for granted. Yet opposition to Brexit and support for independence have become increasingly connected.

The Northern Ireland Protocol provides a way for Northern Ireland to be in both the EU and the UK internal markets, but this is a unique mechanism. The EU allows some sub-state territories of member states to opt out of membership (Greenland, Azores) or out of some of its regulations (Azores, Canaries). It has never hitherto allowed a part of a non-member state to opt in. The Northern Ireland Protocol was an exception achieved because of the insistence of a member state, Ireland, and in consideration of the delicate political and security situation there. The Scottish Government's proposal of 2016 to remain within the European Internal Market using the machinery of the European Economic Area (the 'Norway' model) received short shrift from the UK Government. This meant it never got on the negotiating agenda, but there is little reason to think the EU would have entertained it either. If the problems with the Northern Ireland Protocol can be resolved, it might be possible to revisit this issue. In the mean time, the Scottish Government has sought to stay close to the EU via the Legal Continuity Act, which gives ministers powers to maintain dynamic alignment with EU regulations.

Looking Forward

Following Brexit and the 2019 general election, the Westminster Government has doubled down on parliamentary sovereignty. The legislative consent convention is effectively dead, and Westminster has shown no compunction about using its powers to the full. There are new spending powers in devolved fields, a strengthened presence of UK departments on the ground, and a lot of Union flag-waving. The Internal Market Act massively constrains the regulatory capacity of devolved governments. All this means that constitutional change might be required just to defend the existing settlement, let alone extend it. Opposition parties talk the empty talk of federalism with little attention to exactly what it means and which powers might appropriately be exercised at which level. Yet the peoples of these islands do need to find a better way to live together. Outdated ideas about sovereignty and control have been exposed by the Brexit saga. It seems likely that Scotland will muddle through to some version of devo-max or independence-lite. It is just to be hoped that, in doing so, attention will be paid to the need for effective capacity to deal with the major social and economic problems it faces.

Recommended Reading

Jackson, B. (2020) *The Case for Scottish Independence*, Cambridge, UK: Cambridge University Press.

Keating, M. (2021) *State and Nation in the United Kingdom: The Fractured Union*, Oxford, UK: Oxford University Press.

Mitchell, J. (2020) *The Return of the Scottish Question – Constitutional Options for Scotland*, Glasgow, UK: Jimmy Reid Foundation.

Afterword:
From National to Local

Dave Watson

Several themes may strike readers of this book. The first for me is the breadth of the factors that make up the wealth of the nation. When I first studied economics, we were taught a range of formulas that calculated everything from a nation's output to the money supply. In this book, the contributors demonstrate that the wealth of a nation depends on much more than mathematical calculations. And so, perhaps more than anything else, it is inequality that holds back our economy. At the outset, we are reminded that more equal societies do better on almost every measurement. Then we have arguably the most significant challenge facing our society: environmental and climate justice. Successive governments' nudge and leverage approach has failed to push markets into the gear change we need to achieve the scale of action required. It also reminds us we live in an interconnected world, which involves action beyond our borders.

Several chapters cover subjects that are not traditional economic concerns, yet are essential to a functioning economy. These include housing, education, transport, land, health and decent work. Housing, in particular, has become a key commodity in an inflated and financialised global market, increasing both the cost of home ownership and renting. Transport policy has exacerbated poverty and inequality, and it has also been a climate disaster. Transport is now the biggest contributor to carbon and air pollution of all sectors in Scotland's economy. Land ownership is a particularly Scottish concern, with a disproportionate share held in the hands of very few individuals and bodies.

Then there are chapters on the structural factors that undermine our economy. These include the need for economic democracy that challenges the elite domination of wealth and economic decision-making. As well as addressing the weak forms of political governance, several contributors highlight the development of a highly educated, socially unrepresentative professional-managerial class, which has banished all talk of 'capitalism', 'class' and 'exploitation' as obsolete – leaving little appetite amongst the political elites for change. Chapters on culture, human rights, race and gender also point to complacency in what we like to think of as 'Radical Scotland'.

The second big theme that comes through all the contributions is that a better Scotland is possible. If the analysis might depress us, the possibilities are plentiful: from a new approach to bottom-up public ownership and investment in worker-owned businesses to individual economic rights, public participation and deliberation of the economy itself; a healthier Scotland that can achieve a substantial reduction in health inequalities and raise life expectancy improvements again; an education plan that starts with play and a statutory early years provision moving through to active and interdisciplinary learning in our schools, and then colleges and universities that collaborate rather than compete; devolving power with new approaches to engagement and participation and practical measures to improve gender representation, tackle racism and strengthen human rights; and a new approach to leisure and culture, which is not about 'additional benefit', but is seen as essential to our lives and wellbeing. There are also solutions to the difficult decisions on taxation that move away from simply safeguarding the interests of the rentier class.

This collection has been prepared during a pandemic that has not only had fatal health consequences for so many, but will also have a long-term economic impact. Scotland has suffered a higher percentage of job losses regionally than anywhere else in the UK, and the second highest degree of job disruption. Most contributors show how the pandemic highlighted the underlying weaknesses of Scotland's economy and public services, not least in the social care sector, as well as how we can genuinely and radically 'build back better'.

Finally, this collection would not be a book about Scotland without mention of our national obsession: constitutional change. Many contributors highlight what can be achieved with the existing powers, further devolved powers or independence. Others argue for a rival political diagnosis over the rather less compelling dogmas about competitive nationalism and progressive neo-liberalism currently doing the rounds in Scotland. The final chapter examines the challenges in finding a third way and the UK Government's post-Brexit efforts to constrain devolved administrations. However, it also reminds us that in the modern world, absolute sovereignty is an illusion. Whatever constitutional path is taken, Scotland will remain embedded in a complex web of relationships across these islands, Europe and the world.

The most pleasing theme in the chapters for me is the emphasis upon local solutions to Scotland's economy, the particular focus of my contribution in this Afterword. Scotland has one of the democratic world's most centralised forms of government and one of the least 'local' local democracies. The neo-liberal approach to economic development in Scotland has focused upon attracting inward investment, resulting in the wealth generated by workers, local people and businesses being extracted by often distant shareholders. Large amounts of public money have also been poured into some areas, hoping that it will trickle down to the people who live there –

when in practice much of that money did not stay there. These firms are often the first to flee when the economic cycle shifts. Community wealth-building (Centre for Local Economic Strategies 2019) seeks to address this by encouraging plural ownership of the local economy, increasing investment using fair employment, progressive procurement and the socially just use of land and property. This includes directly managing services previously outsourced to large companies remote from the community.

In Britain, the 'Preston Model' (Manley and Whyman 2021) has pioneered this approach. Preston Council has worked with local anchor institutions such as universities and hospitals and through its procurement practices to ensure a greater share of the money it spends stays in the local economy. In Scotland, North Ayrshire Council (2020) has led the way with its strategy which sets out its ambition to become a 'Community Wealth Building Council'. The strategy argues that the answer is no longer traditional economic growth: 'We need a new approach to our economy, centred on well-being and inclusion. A fair local economy must be central to our aims of tackling poverty and inequality' (North Ayrshire Council 2020: 2).

The economics of place is also finding its place in the discourse on economic democracy. Kelly and Howard (2019) include community and place in their principles of a democratic economy, in contrast to the extractive economy that has devastated too many communities. They highlight how anchor institutions like councils, colleges and the NHS built a new economy of place – less inclined to abandon their community to profit as maximising corporations did. Ownership is vital in all these examples, including municipal, co-operatives, social enterprises and private companies. Providing new forms of finance is also critical. The Scottish National Investment Bank could play an important role, together with the development of local and regional banks. There are European and US examples of how this is working in practice.

One such ownership model is municipal socialism (Watson 2018). Outsourcing of public services has fragmented delivery and extracted wealth from communities. Municipal socialism makes a case for the collective provision of a wide range of local services based on plural forms of democratised and decentralised common ownership. The pandemic has highlighted the tragic consequences of relying upon large-scale private care providers whose business model is based on fragile and high-risk investment models designed to maximise short-term financial returns. The co-operative movement and other forms of community ownership could also play a much larger role in regenerating local economies, providing an alternative to private ownership. Initiatives like Inclusive Economy Liverpool are renewing the co-operative model in the city. The community-owned pub is another example of community ownership that has been growing in recent years. They can enhance the experience of being part of a community that works together for the common good.

Councils can facilitate local initiatives by creating spaces to encourage participative economic development. Barking and Dagenham's 'Every One, Every Day' has opened 'maker spaces' equipped with tools and equipment for new businesses. Ninety per cent of participants are women, not least because the centres include affordable childcare. Doncaster Council is buying shops in town-centre locations, carefully thinking about the kind of businesses that will set a new tone – locally owned, independent and more artisan-based. The Stove Network in Dumfries town centre is a Scottish example of this trend. The regeneration of the Gorbals in Glasgow has created a model '20-minute neighbourhood' where almost all of what is required by residents can be reached within a short walk or cycle. The Green New Deal (What Works Centre for

Local Economic Growth 2021), with the development of a circular economy, sharing initiatives and the local production of food with markets and food halls, has a vital role to play in this.

The problems facing our high streets and town centres will not go away after pandemic measures are relaxed and economic support ends. There will still be excess retail capacity in many high streets, and many consumers may regard online shopping as safer and more convenient. Consequently, we need to rethink our town centres as places where people live and work, not just shop. Scotland's Towns Partnership has done some excellent work in piloting projects, but it now needs the funding to step up a gear, rather than yet another government review (see Scottish Government 2020). Our high streets need a regeneration programme that redevelops redundant retail spaces and car parks into homes, workplaces, community hubs and social areas.

Supporting participatory economics in our communities requires not just economic solutions (Watson 2020). A comprehensive programme of measures here includes investing in the social infrastructure that enables communities to flourish through fair funding for local authorities, leading to integrating public services around community hubs, improving health and wellbeing, creating a sharing economy and good public transport, and enabling active travel. Most importantly, there needs to be a decentralisation of power to local government and communities, which includes developing appropriate public engagement strategies for each community, focusing on overcoming inequalities of power and influence.

A New Scotland: Building an Equal, Fair and Sustainable Society highlights some challenges for traditional thinking on the left in Scotland. We should be proud of our radical history while applying the lessons to a Scotland in thrall to a neoliberal economic orthodoxy with weak governance systems.

The solutions cannot be dictated from the top. Instead, they must be developed and organised from communities of interest and place. *A New Scotland: Building an Equal, Fair and Sustainable Society* offers a different vision for Scotland and signposts new approaches to our enduring challenges.

References

Centre for Local Economic Strategies (2019) *Community Wealth Building: Theory, Practice and Next Steps*, Manchester, UK: CLES, https://cles.org.uk/wp-content/uploads/2019/09/CWB2019 FINAL-web.pdf.

Kelly, M. and Howard, T. (2019) *The Making of a Democratic Economy*, Oakland, CA: Berrett-Koehler.

Manley, J. and Whyman, P. (2021) (eds) *The Preston Model and Community Wealth Building: Creating a Socio-economic Democracy for the Future*, London: Routledge.

North Ayrshire Council (2020) *Community Wealth Building Strategy 2020–2025: An Action Plan for a Community Wealth Building Council*, Irvine, UK: North Ayrshire Council, www.north-ayrshire. gov.uk/Documents/nac-cwb-strategy-brochure.pdf.

Scottish Government (2020) 'Healthier, greener town centres', 1 July, Edinburgh, UK: Scottish Government, www.gov.scot/news/ healthier-greener-town-centres/.

Watson, D. (2018) *Municipal Socialism for Modern Scotland*, Glasgow, UK: Jimmy Reid Foundation, http://reidfoundation.org/2018/05/ new-policy-paper-municipal-socialism-for-modern-scotland-local-public-enterprise-for-the-common-good/.

Watson, D. (2020) *Building Stronger Communities*, Glasgow, UK: Jimmy Reid Foundation, https://reidfoundation.scot/2020/08/ building-stronger-communities/.

What Works Centre for Local Economic Growth (2021) *Local Green Investments*, London: What Works Centre for Local Economic Growth, https://whatworksgrowth.org/resources/ local-green-investments.

Contributors' Biographies

Dr Talat Ahmed is Senior Lecturer in South Asian History at the University of Edinburgh. She is the author of *Mohandas Gandhi: Experiments in Civil Disobedience* (2019) and *Literature and Politics in the Age of Nationalism: The Progressive Episode in South Asia, 1932–56* (2009). She is Co-Director of the Centre for South Asian Studies at the University of Edinburgh and a Fellow of the Royal Asiatic Society.

Kirsty Alexander has worked as a social researcher and taught Politics and Applied Gender Studies in higher education for a number of years, most recently at the University of Strathclyde.

Brian Boyd is Emeritus Professor of Education at the University of Strathclyde. A former headteacher of two comprehensive schools, he has written extensively on Scottish Education and was editor of the Hodder Gibson series *Continuing Professional Development in Education*.

John Bratton divides his time between Canada and Scotland. He has more than 30 years' experience of university teaching, mainly in Britain and Canada. His research interests traverse the sociology of work and management. He has authored eight books, including *Capitalism and Classical Social Theory* (with David Denham, 2019) and *Work and Organizational Behaviour* (2021), and edited *Organizational Leadership* (2020).

Dr Kathryn A. Burnett is a Senior Lecturer at the University of the West of Scotland. With a background in social anthropology, sociology and cultural studies, her research interests include mediatisation and representation of remote and island spaces; identity, place and 'commons' narratives of Scotland; arts policy, cultural work and Scottish cultural heritage contexts; and the sustainability ecologies and enterprise cultures of small island and 'remote rural' contexts. She is Co-Director of the Scottish Centre for Island Studies.

Dr Claire Bynner is a Research Fellow at the University of Glasgow. She combines research expertise on urban policy, neighbourhoods and community cohesion with a professional background in the field of public participation and local governance. She leads the research team for Children's Neighbourhoods Scotland, a place-based approach to reducing child poverty in Scotland. Her recent research examines family wellbeing, service responses and collaboration during the COVID-19 pandemic.

Jane Carolan co-ordinates the work of the Institute of Employment Rights Scotland. For 30 years until 2017, she held various leadership positions within UNISON.

Douglas Chalmers is a Senior Lecturer at Glasgow Caledonian University, where his research concerns the economics of Gaelic-language arts and culture. Previously, he played different roles in Scottish politics, serving variously as Secretary of the Campaign for a Scottish Parliament, Scottish Secretary of the Communist Party and Convenor of Democratic Left Scotland. Most recently, he finished a secondment as the President of the University and College Union (UCU), having previously been UCU Scotland president.

Mary Church is Head of Campaigns at Friends of the Earth Scotland (FoES). Working with communities on the front line of the fracking industry in Scotland, she led FoES's campaign to stop onshore unconventional oil and gas extraction. She currently works on issues including climate justice and just transition. She helped found the Environmental Rights Centre for Scotland, sits on the board of Stop Climate Chaos Scotland, and is an active founder member of the COP26 Coalition and the Just Transition Partnership.

Colin Clark is Professor of Sociology and Social Policy at the University of the West of Scotland. He is co-author of *Here to Stay: The Gypsies and Travellers of Britain* (2006) and co-editor of the academic journal *Romani Studies*. He is also a Director of the Coalition for Racial Equality and Rights and a Trustee of Romano Lav (Roma Voice). He also acts as research advisor to the Traveller Movement, the Scottish Human Rights Commission and the Advisory Council for the Education of Romanies and other Travellers.

Andrew Cumbers is Professor of Regional Political Economy at the University of Glasgow. He is the author of *Reclaiming Public Ownership: Making Space for Economic Democracy* (2012) and *The Case for Economic Democracy* (2020). He is also a Managing Editor for the journal *Urban Studies*.

Dr Jim Cuthbert joined the UK Civil Service after taking his PhD at the University of Sussex, and after lecturing in statistics at the University of Glasgow. He worked in the Treasury and the Scottish Office, and before retiring was Scottish Office Chief Statistician. He has written extensively on the Scottish public finances, often in conjunction with his wife, Margaret Cuthbert. His other research interests include utility pricing, purchasing power parities and investment theory.

Craig Dalzell is the Head of Policy and Research at the Scottish 'Think and Do' Tank, the Common Weal. There, he has written multiple policy papers on subjects such as land reform, energy, housing, banking and social security. He lives in rural Clydesdale.

Mike Danson is Emeritus Professor of Enterprise Policy at Heriot-Watt University. He has published widely on rural, regional and island economies, micro-breweries, minority languages, and many other areas of Scottish economic policy and social development. He is Chair of the Basic Income Network Scotland, Depute Convenor of the Jimmy Reid Foundation Project Board and a Trustee of

Nordic Horizons and Community Renewal. He has advised national and international organisations and is Co-director of the Scottish Centre for Island Studies. He lives in the Monadhliath Mountains.

Alex de Ruyter is a Professor at Birmingham City University and serves as Director of its Centre for Brexit Studies. He brings wide-ranging research experience in the areas of labour markets, globalisation and social exclusion, having published numerous articles in leading national and international journals. He is also a regular contributor to various media outlets on Brexit and related issues.

Dr Caitlin Doyle Cottrill is Senior Lecturer and Director of Centre for Transport Research at the University of Aberdeen. Her research spans the inter-related topics of transport, individual behaviour, technology and data, linked by an underlying commitment to encouraging inclusive, sustainable and efficient mobility. Her work has a strong focus in support of public and active transport modes, especially for vulnerable and under-served users. In addition, she has developed work in facilitating data sharing between transport service providers and travellers in a privacy-preserving manner in order to encourage better decision-making.

Ruth Dukes is Professor of Labour Law at the University of Glasgow and has recently led the 'Work on Demand' research project examining contracting for work in a changing economy (such as in the 'gig' and platform economies). She works closely with the Institute of Employment on formulating pro-worker policies for changes in labour law.

Dr David Erdal has spent his working life leading businesses towards economic democracy. He has experience of teaching in China during the Cultural Revolution, studied business at Harvard, and in 1985 took over running his family's paper mill, Tullis Russell. There he moved it towards democratically governed employee ownership, completing the buy-out in 1994. Since then, he has helped many businesses become employee-owned. He has a PhD from St Andrews University in the psychology of sharing from an evolutionary perspective, and is the author of two books on employee ownership, *Local Heroes* (2009) and *Beyond the Corporation: Humanity Working* (2011).

Carole Ewart is a public policy and human rights consultant working with civil society to build organisational capacity, share knowledge and develop skills, with degrees in Modern History and Politics and in Human Rights Law. She is Convener of the Campaign for Freedom of Information in Scotland, and serves on the Project Board of the Jimmy Reid Foundation and the Editorial Committee of the *Scottish Left Review*.

Iain Ferguson is Honorary Professor of Social Work and Social Policy at the University of the West of Scotland. He is the co-author of *Global Social Work in a Political Context: Radical Perspectives* (2018) and author of *Politics of the Mind: Marxism and Mental Distress* (2017) as well as contributing to the collection *Breaking Up the British State: Scotland, Independence and Socialism* (2021). He is Advisory Editor of *Critical and Radical Social Work*, and is a member of the *International Socialism Journal* Editorial Board.

Larry Flanagan is General Secretary of the Educational Institute of Scotland and a member of both the General Councils of the Scottish Trades Union Congress and Trades Union Congress. He was recently elected President of the European Trade Union Committee for Education, the European region of Education International.

Rozanne Foyer has been the General Secretary of the STUC since 2020, having over 25 years' experience in the union movement. Beginning as a workplace activist in the Benefits Agency, where she led a successful campaign against support services privatisation, she became a union organiser and then STUC Assistant Secretary,

National Officer with the Transport and General Workers' Union and its successor, UNITE.

Gregor Gall holds a number of visiting professorships and is an Affiliate Research Associate at the University of Glasgow. He is the author and editor of over 20 books, mainly on industrial relations. He is editor of the *Scottish Left Review* and Director of the Jimmy Reid Foundation.

Ewan Gibbs lectures in Economic and Social History at the University of Glasgow. He published *Coal Country: The Meaning and Memory of Deindustrialization in Post-war Scotland* (2020) and is now completing a BA-Wolfson fellowship for the 'Decarbonising the Economy and Society: Policy, Labour and Community in Energy Transitions' project. He is widely published in journals of labour history and industrial relations.

Dr Hannah Graham is a Senior Lecturer in Criminology at the University of Stirling. She has written or edited four books, is an Editor of the European Journal of Probation, and is a member of the Scottish Sentencing Council, an independent advisory body. She lives in Glasgow, watches a lot of Scottish Parliament TV, and tweets as @DrHannahGraham.

Ellie Harrison is an artist, activist and author of *The Glasgow Effect: A Tale of Class, Capitalism & Carbon Footprint* (2019). She has campaigned for better public transport, founding the national Bring Back British Rail campaign in 2009 and helping to popularise the policy of rail re-nationalisation. In 2016, she helped to establish the Get Glasgow Moving campaign to demand a world-class, fully integrated and affordable public transport network for Greater Glasgow under public ownership and control. She continues to work on both campaigns on a voluntary basis, alongside other local community projects, freelance work and lecturing part-time at Duncan of Jordanstone College of Art & Design in Dundee.

Gerry Hassan is Professor of Social Change at Glasgow Caledonian University and has written and edited over two dozen books on Scottish and UK politics, including *The Strange Death of Labour Scotland* (2012), *Caledonian Dreaming: The Quest for a Different Scotland* (2014), *Independence of the Scottish Mind* (2014) and *The People's Flag and Union Jack: An Alternative History of Britain and the Labour Party* (2019). His latest co-edited book is *A Better Nation: The Challenges of Scottish Independence* (2022). His writing, commentary and research can be found at www.gerryhassan.com.

James Henderson is an independent researcher concerned with participatory and action research and policy and practice development. He has worked with and within the community sector to build understanding of the community economy and its potential to deliver both practical action and social change, and within the third, university and public sectors, particularly in relation to public service reform.

Lynn Henderson is a senior national officer of the Public and Commercial Service Union, the largest civil service union. She heads up the union's teams covering Organising, Campaigning and Learning. She is convenor of the Jimmy Reid Foundation Project Board and chairs Politics for the Many, the trade union campaign for electoral reform. She served as STUC President in 2018–2019.

Michael Keating is Professor Emeritus of Politics at the University of Aberdeen and has been writing about Scottish politics for almost 50 years. His latest book is *State and Nation in the United Kingdom: The Fractured Union* (2021).

George Kerevan is an economist and former SNP MP for East Lothian. At Westminster, he served on the Treasury Select Committee and was Chair of the All-Party Parliamentary Group on Fair Business. He writes regularly for the media in Scotland.

Dr Eleanor Kirk is a Research Associate in the School of Law at the University of Glasgow. She was previously the Ailsa McKay Post-Doctoral Fellow at Glasgow Caledonian University. Her recent work has focused on employment tribunals, precarious work and contesting 'bogus' self-employment, and has been published in journals such as *Work, Employment and Society*, *Economic and Industrial Democracy* and *Capital and Class*.

Alex Law is Professor of Sociology at Abertay University. His research interests include class, civic nationalism and the state-formation process in Scotland. He is currently working on a study of the civilising process in Scotland.

Dr Ruth Lightbody is a Lecturer in Politics at Glasgow Caledonian University. Her research focuses on deliberative democracy and democratic innovations, particularly exploring how they can be used to implement policy changes which tackle social inequalities and environmental issues.

Kenny MacAskill is Alba Party MP for East Lothian and was Scottish Justice Secretary (2007–2014) while serving in the Scottish Parliament from 1999 to 2016. A columnist with *The Scotsman* and *Scots Magazine*, he is the author of several books on radical Scottish history: *Jimmy Reid* (2017), *Glasgow 1919* (2019) and *Radical Scotland* (2020).

Henry Maitles is Emeritus Professor of Education at University of the West of Scotland. He researches and teaches on values, citizenship and teaching the Holocaust in schools. His most recent book is the co-authored *Understanding and Teaching Holocaust Education* (2016).

Robin McAlpine is Head of Strategic Development at the Common Weal.

Gerry McCartney is Professor of Wellbeing Economy at the University of Glasgow. He was formerly a GP in Paisley before he trained in Public Health. He led the Public Health Observatory for Scotland in 2010–2021. His research has focused on the causes and appropriate responses to the stalled mortality trends since 2012, excess mortality known as the 'Scottish/Glasgow Effect' and health inequalities.

Janis McDonald was the Chief Officer of deafscotland, a membership organisation which worked to ensure deaf people have equal access, rights and citizenship. deafscotland merged with the ALLIANCE, where she is now Associate Director (Sensory). She has worked on a number of projects for legislative reform to ensure the provision of Inclusive Communication is delivered in specific services such as social security and in the management of the COVID-19 response.

Robert McMaster is a Professor of Political Economy at the University of Glasgow. He has published in a range of journals, including the *Cambridge Journal of Economics*, *Journal of Business Ethics*, *Journal of Institutional Economics* and *Review of Radical Political Economics*. He co-authored *Health Care Economics* (2017).

Niamh McNulty is a Politics graduate from the University of Edinburgh, where she focused upon Sustainable Development. She is a co-founder of Climate Camp Scotland, a grassroots direct action group taking aim at the fossil fuel industry to promote climate justice and a just transition.

Dr Gerry Mooney is Professor of Scottish Society and Social Welfare at the Open University in Scotland. He has published extensively on social justice and welfare policy, Scottish devolution, criminology and class.

Dr Carlo Morelli is a Senior Lecturer in Economics at the University of Dundee. His research interests are in inequality and poverty with a focus upon social policy and devolution, with publications on free school meals, funeral poverty and inequality, and devolution. His research interests also explore economic history in the late twentieth century, including the decline of Dundee's jute industry.

Jenny Morrison has been a socialist activist in Glasgow for the past 15 years. She currently works as a researcher at the University of Glasgow, where she focuses on the relationship between feminism and the radical left and social reproduction theory.

Dr Gareth Mulvey is a Lecturer in Sociology at the University of Glasgow. He primarily researches and teaches around issues of migration, migration policy and the impact of policy on diverse migrant communities. His other interests are concerned with social policy, particularly poverty, and about the relationship between central and devolved government in Britain and the impacts upon social policy.

Emma Saunders is a geographer who has been part of the housing movement in Scotland in the last five years and works around supporting tenants in Scotland to campaign for better rights.

Eurig Scandrett is a Senior Lecturer in Public Sociology at Queen Margaret University and researcher on environmental justice movements. He jointly edited *Bhopal Survivors Speak: Emergent Voices from a People's Movement* (2009) and *Environmental Justice, Popular Struggle and Community Development* (2019). A union activist, he represents the University and College Union Scotland on the Just Transition Partnership.

Rory Scothorne is completing a PhD at the University of Edinburgh titled 'The Radical Left and the Scottish Nation: Print-cultures of Left-wing Nationalism, 1967–1983'. He writes regularly on Scottish and labour politics for the *New Statesman*, the *Guardian*, the *London Review of Books* and *Le Monde Diplomatique*.

Mary Senior is the Scotland official for the University and College Union. She served as President of the Scottish Trades Union Congress in 2020–2021, and was a member of the Institute for

Public Policy Research's Commission on Economic Justice, which published its *Prosperity and Justice* report in 2018.

Dr Regina Serpa is a housing researcher and a chartered planner based in Scotland. She is currently a Primary Investigator on a University of Stirling-based comparative three-country study of migrant homelessness. Previously, she practised for several years as a consultant at a private research firm in Scotland in addition to teaching at the University of Stirling, and has provided homelessness services at a Scottish local authority and practised in planning at community development corporations in Boston and Chicago.

Linda Somerville is Deputy General Secretary at the Scottish Trade Union Congress. Before joining the STUC, she was the Director of the National Union of Students in Scotland, leading policy and campaigning work on further and higher education. Linda was invited to join the Royal Society of Arts in 2015 in recognition of her work to increase the participation of women in science, engineering and technology in her role as Director of Equate Scotland. She is currently a member of the Time for Inclusive Education Board and the Jimmy Reid Foundation Project Board.

David Spaven has spent his working life in and around the rail industry, primarily in freight marketing management and consultancy. In his spare time, he has campaigned for sustainable transport since his teens. He was the first Chair of Transform Scotland, the sustainable transport alliance (1997–2006) and a member of the Rail Passengers Committee Scotland (1998–2005) and the Climate Challenge Fund Panel (2008–2011). He is also an established railway author, with nine books published, including *Mapping the Railways* (2013) and *Highland Survivor: The Story of the Far North Line* (2016). He writes in this volume in a personal capacity.

Francis Stuart is a Policy Officer with the Scottish Trades Union Congress. He is the author of its reports *Broken Promises and*

Offshored Jobs (2019) and *Scotland's Renewables Jobs Crisis & Covid 19* (2020), which analysed offshoring of jobs in the renewables industry. He also co-authored the STUC's *The People's Recovery: A Different Track for Scotland's Economy* (2020). He previously worked for Oxfam Scotland, where he led participatory research on 'Decent Work for Scotland's Low-paid Workers'. Before Oxfam, he worked for the Scottish Council for Voluntary Organisations and Friends of the Earth Scotland. He is a workplace rep and President of the GMB Apex Branch.

Willie Sullivan is a campaigner and works for the Electoral Reform Society as its Senior Director. He is particularly interested in the question of power: who has it, what do they do with it, and how do we create or change the institutions of society to share power most fairly?

Dave Watson is a policy consultant. He was previously the Head of Policy and Campaigns at UNISON Scotland. He is a member of the Jimmy Reid Foundation Project Board and Secretary of the Socialist Health Association Scotland. He blogs at http://unisondave.blogspot.com/.

Dr Sean Whittaker is a Lecturer in Law at the University of Dundee. His research interests include environmental law, public law and information law, with a focus on the operation and implementation of the Aarhus Convention. He is also Executive Director of the Centre for Freedom of Information, a research centre which conducts academic analysis on information law and the associated principles of transparency and accountability.

Geoff Whittam is a Professor at the Glasgow School for Business and Society, Glasgow Caledonian University. He has contributed several articles to *Scottish Left Review* and worked with a number of unions, including UNISON and the STUC. He is also a community activist, being on the Board of Sunny Govan Community Radio and the Scottish Community Development Centre.

Index

Alba party 40, 46
anti-Catholicism 195
Avoid-Shift-Improve (ASI) 222

Barnett formula 137, 138, 139
basic income 5, 129–30, 132, 155
BBC Scotland 241, 271
Brexit 8, 45, 49, 59, 80, 117, 164,
    171, 202, 243, 244, 252, 294,
    302–3, 304, 307

capitalism 3, 4, 5–6, 11, 12, 15,
    17–18, 24–5, 31–2, 35, 38, 44,
    52, 55, 77–8, 106, 123, 143, 186,
    219, 250, 258, 260, 261, 268
China 36, 41, 45
citizens' assembly 106, 277, 284
    290, 292, 299
civic nationalism 196, 204, 259
class 1, 4, 8, 11, 15, 16, 19, 26, 36,
    27, 38, 46, 58, 91, 98, 99, 130,
    136, 143, 144, 155, 156, 157,
    252, 253, 256, 258–9, 262–7
climate change 6, 14, 23–6, 28–9,
    30, 31, 86, 209, 220, 278, 290
collective bargaining 32, 48, 49,
    56, 57, 58, 123–4, 162, 163, 164,
    167, 168, 169, 186
colonialism 24, 25, 30, 31, 32, 143,
    144, 199, 200, 210, 248, 249
Common Weal 235

community ownership 216
community wealth building 131,
    155, 251, 308
competitive nationalism 259, 268
Communist Party 250
commuters 219
co-ordinated market economy
    (CME) 5–6
constitutional matters 28, 47,
    48, 55–6, 132, 133, 137, 158,
    165, 169, 171, 195, 217, 255,
    294–304, 307
Corbynism 3, 8, 40, 45, 131
Creative Scotland 240, 241

decolonisation 119, 238, 248
deindustrialisation 18, 36, 37, 48,
    97, 250, 262, 264
democratic participation 47, 50,
    68
deprivation 1, 98, 110, 115, 178,
    210
devolution 2, 19–20, 32–3, 66, 300
Devo-max 295, 296, 303, 304
Dunkirk 224

East India Company 199
economic democracy 47–57, 61–2
Economic Democracy Index 49,
    51–2
eco-socialism 32

education 1, 2, 5, 6, 18, 33, 63, 94, 98, 103, 109–19, 155, 192, 210, 203, 237, 238, 242, 243, 244, 260, 262, 267, 275, 299, 305, 306
Edinburgh 39–40, 220, 227, 288
employer power 74, 75–6, 78–9
energy 27, 29, 33, 44, 66, 67, 122, 155, 220, 250, 251 (see also natural resources)
environmental costs 87, 222
environmental justice 6, 25–6, 28, 50, 173, 176–8
environmental sustainability 132
equality 16–19, 99
European Union (EU) 40, 42, 44, 45, 49, 164, 178, 252, 297, 298, 299, 302, 303

Fair Work 164–5, 168
federalism 298–300
feminist economics 187
feudalism 35
financial services sector 5, 37, 51
football 75
freight 227

Gaelic 249
Gender 4, 26, 161, 166–7, 183–92, 236, 238, 239, 242, 270
Glasgow 1, 38, 87, 97, 161, 198, 200, 220, 227, 238, 259, 265, 285, 286, 309
Glasgow effect 97
global financial crisis 5, 85
Governance 19–20, 38, 57, 103, 104, 106, 114–15, 148–9, 154–5

Government Expenditure and Revenue Scotland (GERS) 137, 138

Health 11, 17, 18, 87, 91, 94, 97–106, 111, 116, 130, 152, 157, 163, 173, 174, 175, 210, 236, 237, 290, 299
Highlands 67, 87, 209, 249
homophobia 274
housing 18, 29, 33, 40, 85–95, 97, 99, 103, 104, 121, 128, 130, 180, 201, 203, 221, 301, 305
Human Rights Act 171

imperialism 38, 203, 249
independence 3, 19–20, 28, 32–3, 56, 61–2, 69, 144
inequality 1, 11, 25–7, 28, 30, 31, 32, 73, 121–2, 128, 131, 207, 254
Irish migration 195

Just Transition 25–7, 28, 30, 31, 32, 128, 131, 207, 254

Keynesianism 14–15, 60

labour 15–16, 18, 42, 57, 58, 73, 101, 124, 129, 163, 183, 184, 186–7, 198, 235, 236
labour markets 55, 57, 121, 123, 125–6, 130, 186–7, 189, 239, 243, 251, 301
Labour Party 2, 3, 4, 5, 38, 40, 41, 45, 46, 60, 63, 81, 100, 151, 162, 179, 212, 246, 250, 256, 258,

259, 260, 261, 262, 264, 266, 273, 274, 279, 297, 300
labour share 124
land ownership 67, 94, 141, 207–8, 210, 211, 251
land reform 214
land value tax 217
Leith 198, 219, 288, 289
levelling up 4, 5, 302
liberal market economy (LME) 5–6, 55
local democracy 68, 149, 154, 287, 289, 290–1

Marxism 15–16
Monopoly 13, 35, 61, 62–3, 66, 67, 69, 123, 250
municipal socialism 309
Muslim 200

National Care Service 101–2 (see also social care)
National Culture Strategy 236
Nationalisation 4, 20, 37, 60–8, 101, 145, 261 (see also public ownership)
natural resources 27, 56, 141, 249
neo-liberalism xiv, 2, 3, 8, 35–47, 61, 62, 80, 85, 88–91, 97, 106, 123, 133, 151, 152, 186, 193, 198, 240, 259, 265–6
non-governmental organisations (NGOs) 151, 177, 254, 259
Nordic countries 48, 52, 55, 127, 128, 129, 210
nudges 6, 28, 305

oligopoly 61, 62, 64, 69, 207, 210–11, 215

pandemic 94, 98, 109–10, 160, 213, 228, 244, 290
participatory budgeting 50, 290, 292
participatory democracy 47–8, 152, 155, 287
participatory economics 310
patriarchy 24, 25, 30
political classes (see also class) 271–3, 283
political democracy 47–8
political participation 276–8
populism 47, 284
pre-distribution 4–5, 6, 132
privatisation 61, 65, 66, 97, 100, 101, 109, 151, 224, 225, 268
productivity 43, 44–5, 61, 72, 76, 77, 78, 81, 82, 128
professional-managerial class (PMC) (see also class) xii, 1, 150, 151, 152, 259, 263, 284, 306
public goods 33, 63–4, 119, 198
public ownership 58, 60–9, 216, 225, 306 (see also nationalisation)
public transport 222

racism 30, 186, 195–6, 197, 200–1, 306
Regional Transport Partnerships (RTPs) 222

Scottish cultural identity 197

Scottish Government 2, 20, 27, 28, 29, 30, 32, 40, 43, 67, 70, 86, 88, 89, 91, 92, 93, 94, 95, 98, 101, 105, 110, 113, 116, 119, 132, 133, 138, 140–1, 161, 164, 165, 167, 168, 180, 189, 190, 191, 192, 196, 198, 201, 202, 203, 215, 217, 219, 221, 222, 225, 226, 227, 229, 236, 251, 254, 259, 275, 277, 284, 287, 290, 295, 303

Scottish National Party (SNP) 2, 3, 28, 36, 38, 40, 41, 42, 43, 44, 45, 46, 133, 189, 203, 246, 248, 250, 251, 253, 259, 260, 264, 265, 274, 279, 284, 295, 300

Scottish nationalism 38, 248, 259, 260, 262

Scottish Parliament 30, 32, 45, 66, 109, 133, 156, 166, 171, 173, 176, 178, 180, 185, 188, 212, 244, 247, 260, 264, 270–81, 294, 301

Scottish Socialist Party 185

Scottish Trades Union Congress (STUC) 131, 165, 166, 185, 242, 243, 250, 255, 266, 285

Singapore 49

small and medium enterprises (SMEs) 45

social care 33, 99, 102–6, 160, 164, 169, 181, 275

social democracy 3, 4–6, 8, 14, 56, 70, 150, 258–61, 264, 265, 267, 268, 274, 279

social justice 2, 3, 25–7

social liberalism 3, 261

social security 14, 98, 105, 122, 126–7, 128, 132, 180, 189, 201, 202, 301

social work 102–3

socialism 4, 8, 70, 198, 204, 261

strikes 32, 60, 124–5, 162, 286

sustainability 26, 33, 80, 131–2, 208, 212, 214, 216, 220, 221–3, 228, 251

Thatcherism 109, 261, 264, 279

transport 29, 33, 63, 65, 68, 104, 122, 219–29, 239, 305

transport pollution 220

unions 18, 19, 27, 28, 29, 36, 44, 48, 49, 58, 68, 74, 77–8, 89, 105, 115, 118, 123–4, 132, 162–3, 166, 168, 185, 230, 243, 248, 250, 262, 264, 282, 284–7, 295

Westminster government 297

worker ownership 74, 76, 78, 79, 81

workers' rights 49, 80, 162, 164–8

zero-hour contracts (ZHCs) 161

Thanks to our Patreon subscriber:

Ciaran Kane

Who has shown generosity and
comradeship in support of our publishing.

The Pluto Press Newsletter

Hello friend of Pluto!

Want to stay on top of the best radical books
we publish?

Then sign up to be the first to hear about our
new books, as well as special events,
podcasts and videos.

You'll also get 50% off your first order with us
when you sign up.

Come and join us!

Go to bit.ly/PlutoNewsletter